ETHICAL DECISION-MAKING FROM A CONSEQUENTIALIST PERSPECTIVE

A Study in Philosophical Ethics

ETHICAL DECISION-MAKING FROM A CONSEQUENTIALIST PERSPECTIVE

A Study in Philosophical Ethics

Robert E. French

With a Foreword by
David McGraw

The Edwin Mellen Press
Lewiston•Queenston•Lampeter

Library of Congress Cataloging-in-Publication Data

French, Robert E., 1952-
Ethical decision-making from a consequentialist perspective : a study in philosophical ethics / Robert E. French ; with a foreword by David McGraw.
p. cm. -- (Hors serie)
Includes bibliographical references and index.
ISBN-13: 978-0-7734-4879-7
ISBN-10: 0-7734-4879-9
1. Consequentialism (Ethics) 2. Justice. I. Title.
BJ1500.C63F74 2009
171'.5--dc22

2009005210

hors série.

A CIP catalog record for this book is available from the British Library.

Author photo courtesy of Fox Portrait Studios, Troy, Michigan

The Edwin Mellen Press
Box 450
Lewiston, New York
USA 14092-0450

The Edwin Mellen Press
Box 67
Queenston, Ontario
CANADA L0S 1L0

The Edwin Mellen Press, Ltd.
Lampeter, Ceredigion, Wales
UNITED KINGDOM SA48 8LT

Printed in the United States of America

Table of Contents

Foreword

There are various ways to develop the theoretical foundations of ethics. For example, one could work through the question shared among Plato, Aristotle, Kant, and Sartre, of how (or even whether) ethical law exists and applies. In the present work, this question is involved indirectly insofar as the importance of deliberating and deciding from what is commonly called the moral point of view is strongly developed. However, the author's chief emphasis in this work is on the question over free choice of the will. French is concerned to deny what is commonly called libertarian free will (which he calls absolute freedom). There is a somewhat summary defense of this denial. From there, he goes on to argue why the process of deliberating and deciding is not a mere sham given this denial, as well as what is the right ethical basis for such deliberate decisions.

French's basis is consequentialism. This is taken here to be like utilitarianism, but with various differences. Perhaps the most serious of these differences is the prior constraint of fairness, whereby exploiting another is foreclosed and excluded, regardless of what consequences might follow. On the other hand, this concern for fairness looks solely to the future, apart from any reference to desert or merit for what people have already done (whether good or bad). Even so, this prior constraint eliminates much of the standard basis for objection.

One of the obvious applications of the disregard for merit and desert is the repudiation of retributive punishment. In fact, the opposition to retributive punishment is one of the author's chief concerns in this book. Criminal penalties are considered to be warranted solely in order to deter someone who is ill disposed before the fact and to reform or incapacitate the malefactor after the fact. The misery imposed on the criminal after the fact is defended as called for by established rules, which in turn are justified on the author's basic ground of consequentialism within the prior constraint of fairness. Exemplary punishment to deter others is condemned for using the criminal as a means, contrary to the requirement of fairness.

One who is more Kantian (such as the present reviewer) will consider that many challenges remain. Yet, the book is good for what it is supposed to be. Specifically, this work is a serious answer to the author's basic concern of how deliberate decision is to be reconciled with the denial of absolute freedom, so that moral choice may be possible.

David McGraw
Philosophy Dept.
Univ. of Detroit Mercy

INTRODUCTION

In this book I will present an account of ethical decision-making from a consequentialist perspective both as it relates to personal decisions and to the law. In particular, I will argue that both individual actions and legal systems should be chosen so as to have the best overall consequences within a constraint of being fair to all parties involved. I will use the term 'consequentialism' to refer to ethical systems that determine the morality of decision-making in terms of properties of the causal consequences of the decisions and thus independently of such causal factors behind the decisions as motives or intentions. Properties of consequences will be construed in a broad sense so as to include causally-relational properties among the consequences.

I should note that the term 'consequentialism' is not used consistently in the literature, and in fact is sometimes used interchangeably with 'utilitarianism.' For example, Samuel Scheffler (1994, p. 1), in his influential *The Rejection of Consequentialism*, defines the term as "ranking overall states of affairs from best to worst from an impersonal point of view." This introduces a teleological element with the concept of ranking. Armatya Sen and Bernard Williams (1982, p. 4) credit Elizabeth Anscombe (1958) with coining the term. Anscombe is a bit vague as far as a definition goes, but uses 'consequentialism' to refer to Henry Sidgwick's (1907/1981) position which judges the rightness and wrongness of actions in terms of their expected consequences and denies any moral significance to the difference between foreseen and intended consequences. Sen and Williams (1982, pp. 3, 4) use the term to refer to positions which claim that "actions are to be chosen on the basis of states of affairs which are their consequences." Similarly, R. G. Frey (1984, p. 4) has defined it as "the view that acts are right or wrong solely in virtue of their consequences." Being conceptually minimal, I find Sen and Williams' and Frey's definitions to be more natural than those including teleological and impersonal elements in the definition. Thus, I find them to be more useful for the purpose of building up structure.

An added terminological point that needs to be addressed here stems from the 'impersonal' character of utilitarianism. Here, obligations to any other people count equally with obligations to oneself or to others bearing what W. D. Ross (1930/1988, p. 22) in *The Right and the Good* has termed 'special relations': e. g. family members or parties to promises etc. In order to adequately deal with this subject I believe that it is necessary to separate the issue of judging the rightness or wrongness of actions or social policies in terms of their consequences from the issue of how these consequences are to be described for purposes of ascertaining that rightness or wrongness. In particular, I hold that these descriptions need not just be in terms of the intrinsic properties per se of the consequences, as classical utilitarianism does in terms of the pleasures and pain involved. Instead, I will also allow the descriptions to also make reference to at least some relational properties, such as ones of causal dependency among consequences themselves. This will be crucial in the analysis of what I take to be the essential moral insight of what Immanuel Kant (1785/1959, p. 27) sometimes terms the 'Practical Imperative,' holding that people should always be treated as an end and never just as a means. To cover this terminologically (and I realize that this goes against Anscombe's and Scheffler's usages) I will use 'consequentialism' to refer to the position that judges the ethical rightness and wrongness of actions or social policies in terms of descriptions of those consequences in a broad sense that includes reference to causal relations with other consequences along with intrinsic properties of the consequences.

The major theme of the book is the contention, which I take to be analytically true, that we ought always to pursue both our best fair individual courses of action and that social policies should also be chosen in this manner. In other words, I will argue that we should always choose the best possible course of action from the possible fair alternative courses of action or social policies that we are faced with. I should emphasize that like Ross (1930/1988) I am distinguishing here between the objective rightness and wrongness of actions and social policies (which I will be arguing is determined only by their consequences) and the moral worth of the actions and policies, where I agree with Ross that motivations behind the actions and policies are relevant.

Structurally the book is divided into Two Parts. In Part One I am concerned both with a series of preliminary analyses of concepts and setting the stage for later arguments. These preliminary chapters include analyses of 'should,' 'fairness,' and 'best,' and are followed by a discussion of the free will problem, critiques of the classical theories of moral responsibility and retributive punishment, and finally the development of an alternative 'causal' theory of responsibility. In Part Two I develop a series of practical applications of these discussions as they apply to the judicial and post-judicial systems. It should be emphasized that what I say here is not comprehensive, both in the sense that not all aspects of these systems are covered, and also in that foundational issues concerning what would justify any changes in underlying governmental institutions in order to institute suggested changes are not addressed. I might also note that I believe that other applications of Part One are possible in such fields as discussions of ideal medical ethics, business ethics, and environmental ethics, but I will not develop these in this book either.

A few word usage and punctuation points should also be noted here. With respect to the use - mention distinction, I will use single quotes around words or phrases for mentioning the meaning of the word, the grouping of letters per se, or the grouping together with the meaning. The context should make it be clear as to which of these is occurring. I also use the pronouns 'they' and 'them' in the third person singular when a person's sex is not relevant. I find this usage to be less awkward than the repeated usage of 'he or she' and I think that there is much to be said for non-sexual pronouns when a person's sex is not an issue.

I should also note that my usage of 'action' diverges from the standard usage in action theory, in that I use a minimal concept of just referring to bodily motions per se. I then build up additional structure by speaking of tokens or types of these motions, and of their causes (e. g., motives and intentions) and causal consequences by so specifying. In justifying this usage I would point out that I find it to be particularly useful in referring to possible actions which may be required, allowed or prohibited, since it is only the bodily motions per se which are referred to here. I find that philosophers who include mental states, such as intentionality, in the meaning typically are thinking more of tokens of actual actions and of issues of evaluating these actions for purposes of ascribing responsibility, rather than the process of choosing actions, which is the focus of this book. Also, I find that ordinary English is quite loose when it comes to talk of 'actions' on several different dimensions; e. g., causally both with respect to causes and effects of the actions, on the distinction between possible and actual actions, and also on the temporal duration. I prefer to capture each of these dimensions by specifying it with my language, and keeping the actual term 'action' to a bare minimum.

Chapter One
An Analysis of 'Should'

In this chapter I will analyze the meanings of two key words used in both ethical and rational decision-making in general. These words, which are usually used in at least a roughly-synonymous manner in ordinary English, are 'should' and 'ought.' I will also show a logical connection between the meaning of these words and two other key concepts in these fields, those of 'what is fair' and 'what is best.' In spite of these logical connections though, I will argue that a fundamental grammatical difference exists between 'should' and 'ought' and the phrases 'what is fair' and 'what is best' in terms of what J. L. Austin (1962a) has termed their 'illocutionary force.'

'Should' and 'ought' are difficult words to analyze. This is not so much because they possess any radical ambiguities, but rather both because their standard usage has evolved over time, and because, like the word 'knowledge' (I take it that at least a partial conceptual analysis of 'knowledge' can be made in terms of justified true belief) they possess a primitive compound character. The trick is to break them down correctly when analyzing them. I will begin my analysis by making some comments on the etymologies of both 'should' and 'ought' (which, for the purposes of this book, will be used pretty-much interchangeably) since this will be helpful in showing how historically the meanings of the words have grown so as to at least come close to merging, and I will then move on to give an analysis of what I take to be the modern concepts.

Section One The Etymology of 'Should' and 'Ought'

The following remarks on the etymologies of 'should' and 'ought' are due largely, although not exclusively, to the work of Alasdair MacIntyre (1978,

Essays 15, 16). I will begin by tracing the etymology of 'ought' and will then turn to the etymology of 'should.' It is striking how the words were initially used with quite disparate meanings and how, over time, these usages evolved so as to become close to being synonymous. However, it should be noted in this last regard that even in the modern usage 'ought' is at least typically used to express a somewhat stronger sense of obligation than 'should.'

'Ought' was originally the past tense of 'owe,' and thus signified an obligation to repay a debt. MacIntyre traces the evolution of the word from the Middle Age 'ahte,' translating the Latin 'debebat,' whereby it was used in the literal sense of owing for a debt or services. It then evolved into being an auxiliary verb for use in giving advice, and finally reached its modern unconditional secular use by means of an intermediary religious use whereby it referred to commands of God. Looking ahead, I might note that a similar connection between the determination of what we ought to do and 'what is owed' will later play a role in my analysis of the retributive theory of punishment; it being claimed that punishments are owed lawbreakers as paying them back for their past misdeeds.

'Should,' in turn, was originally grammatically the past tense of 'shall,' which raises an interesting connection with the classical free will problem. In particular, it can be noted, that to the extent that 'shall' is a synonym for 'will,' there is an implication of determinism (that, given the existence of past situations, future situations can only exist in one particular manner), and possibly even fatalism (that the existence of certain situations is inevitable no matter what we do) here towards an action. That is, it is implied that the action both will definitely occur in the future, and 'come what may' for the fatalistic connotation. One difference between the usage of 'will' and 'shall' that possibly is of relevance here is that 'shall' is typically used to refer to the consequences of human action, whereas this at least need not be the case with 'will.' It might also be noted that such phrases as "thou shalt" convey a very strong tone of obligation which is not present with the modern usage". MacIntyre traces the modern word from the

Icelandic '*skyldr*' which signified unquestioned obligations from within the framework of a given society.

Thus, originally the connotation of 'ought' was somewhat narrower in scope than that of 'should,' since, even though it is the case that if one owes a debt, at least all other things being equal, one ought to repay it, there may be many actions which one is also obligated to perform where nothing is, in at least the literal sense, 'owed.' Also, in the modern sense of 'ought,' the sense of obligation is not, at least always, nearly so strong as it was here. It would seem then that 'should' and 'ought,' which initially been words with quite different meanings, have evolved in meaning over time so as to converge together in the modern sense; 'should' becoming much narrower in scope than the original deterministic or even fatalistic notion, while 'ought' has broadened in scope from the original sense of a 'legal-like' debt or obligation.

Another way of stating this last point is that (using terminology developed by Austin, 1962a) the illocutionary (performative) force of the modern terms corresponds most closely with the original meaning of 'should,' and the locutionary (descriptive) forces of the modern terms corresponds most closely with the original meaning of 'ought.' It should be noted that actually Austin makes a three-way distinction between the locutionary, illocutionary and perlocutionary forces of speech acts. The locutionary force is the descriptive content of what actually is said; the illocutionary force is what is performed by saying something; and finally the perlocutionary force is the effect on the listener. I believe that Austin has a point in distinguishing the perlocutionary force from the illocutionary force since we do not always succeed in getting a listener to do what we want them to by verbal means. Nevertheless, this last distinction will not be a germane one for my analysis since I will just be concerned with analyzing the nature of the performative aspects of various terms from the vocabulary of ethics and the law regardless of whether these aspects apply to what the speaker is attempting to accomplish or to the effects on the listener. Thus, I will use the term 'illocutionary force' in a broad sense so as to include both Austin's 'illocutionary force' and his 'perlocutionary force.'

Not only is the distinction between locutionary and illocutionary meaning a key distinction for my analyses of 'should' and 'ought' in this chapter, but it also plays a key role in my subsequent analyses of various value terms; including 'fairness' in Chapter Two, and 'good' and 'bad' in Chapter Three. This completes my analyses of the etymologies of 'ought' and 'should.' I will thus now turn to my analyses of the meanings of the modern words, which, as I have just pointed out, are at least close to being synonymous.

As just noted, in my analyses of the modern usages of 'should' and 'ought,' my central contention will be that both words are fundamentally compound, containing both prescriptive and descriptive components. In Austin's language which was just noted, this corresponds to the illocutionary (performative) and locutionary (descriptive) forces of the words—the illocutionary force corresponding to the prescriptive, or obligatoriness component, and the locutionary force corresponding to the descriptive component. I will later argue that this descriptive component is itself compound, corresponding with our best fair potential courses of action. I should also point out that Richard Hare (1952/1964, p. 18) makes some similar points when he uses the terms 'phrastic' and 'neustic' to refer respectively to the descriptive and prescriptive aspects of 'ought' statements, but in this book I will use Austin's terminology here. Since the concept of a course of action will play a key role in both my analyses of the prescriptive and descriptive components of 'should' and 'ought,' a digression is necessary into my use of that concept before I present my analyses of these components.

Section Two The Nature of Actions

In this section I will provide a partial analysis of the nature of human actions for the purposes of this book. I will use a very broad concept of 'action' here, which goes against most of the philosophical literature on action theory, to refer to tokens of bodily motions in general. To justify this usage, I should note that this book is concerned with the subject of ethically choosing from among possible actions. Actions, in this sense, are best construed as bodily motions inasmuch as the issue of which of which of these bodily motions ought to be objectively chosen to be performed is a separate issue from that of the moral evaluation of the resulting motion. Clearly the nature of the intentions and motives is relevant for this moral evaluation, but this can be done in terms of further characterization of the motions in terms of their causes. As I noted with my discussion of my usage of the term 'consequentialism' I prefer to keep the content of key terms to a minimum, and then to build up structure. Any more restrictive usage will unnecessarily hamper this process.

I also wish to emphasize at the outset of my discussion that I will not take a stand on many of the more controversial issues of action theory here—such as what are the criteria for actions to be identical, when they are identical under different descriptions, and the role of various internal mental states as their causes. In fact, these issues will be pretty much moot as far as at least my purposes go in Part One of the book, inasmuch as since I am defending consequentialism here, it follows that a course of action can be characterized as being 'right' or 'wrong' independently of either its description or the mental state of the agent performing it. Instead, its 'rightness' or 'wrongness' will be determined solely in terms of its causal consequences, and not in terms of the ways in which those consequences are described or such mental states as the intentions, motives, or emotional states of the agent performing the action.

Looking ahead though to some of the issues to be discussed in Part Two, I should note that questions concerning how an action is to be described, along with the subject matter of the intentions, motives, and emotional states of agents will often constitute key issues with respect to the subject of how an agent, who has performed a courses of action with untoward consequences, ought to be dealt with. For example, the nature of the intentions of an agent who has performed an act that results in another person's death may constitute a key issue with respect to the question as to whether to classify the act as 'murder' or instead as some lesser crime, such as 'manslaughter' or 'negligent homicide.'

In any event, for the purposes of this book, I will simply define a series of terms connected with actions which will be crucial for my analysis of 'should' and 'ought' in this chapter, along with my discussions of the concept of ‘fairness’ in Chapter Two, of the concept of our ‘best potential course of action’ in Chapter Three, and the free will problem in Chapter Four. I should emphasize again that not everything which I will say concerning these terms will be in accordance either with our ordinary English talk about 'actions' or the usages made in the modern philosophical literature on action theory. I might note though that I do not find either of these usages to be consistent on such issues as the type - token distinction or the issue of what causal antecedents and consequences are to be included within the concept of an 'action' per se. For example, sometimes the ordinary English usage of 'action' involves a broad sense which includes at least some of the consequences of bodily movements, such as when we speak of an 'act of murder,' but it can also be noted that we sometimes use 'actions' in ordinary English in a narrower sense, such as when we speak of an act of raising one's hand. Again, I will not even try to either capture all of our ordinary language intuitions concerning 'actions' with my terminology, and I am fully aware that my usage is not consistent with the philosophical literature of action theory, which, as far as I can see, always uses a more expansive sense of 'action' than that of bodily movements. Instead, I openly admit that I am rationally reconstructing my terms in such a manner as will be useful later on in my treatment of ethical decision-making.

With the preceding remarks in mind, I will now introduce a series of action-related terms which will be useful in both formulating key points and also in making key distinctions in the remainder of the book. The first term which I wish to define in this regard is that of an 'action.' By an 'action' I wish to refer to tokens (as opposed to types) of bodily movements in a narrow sense, whereby only the actual bodily movements per se are included. As a matter of emphasis, I will sometimes refer to these action tokens as 'actual actions' as well. In any event, no reference is made to either the causal antecedents or the causal consequences of these bodily movements. Inasmuch as action tokens and not action types are being referred to, my usage here is like that of Donald Davidson (1980) and Alvin Goldman (1973), but unlike that of Roderick Chisholm (1976, Ch. 6), who uses 'actions' to refer to action types.

It can be noted that my usage of 'action' is both in a sense broader and in a sense narrower in scope than much of the usage in the philosophical literature of action theory. It is broader in the sense that in the literature typically the usage of 'actions' is confined to intentional bodily movements, and a distinction is thus drawn between bodily movements which are internally caused, which 'we do,' and ones which are externally caused, which 'are done to us.' My usage of 'action' is also narrower than much of the literature in the sense that I include within the conception of an 'action' neither any of its causal consequences (as Davidson does but Goldman does not), nor any of its causal antecedents, such as intentions or motives. Still my conception of an action is somewhat similar to the conceptions of Arthur Danto (1973, Ch. 2) and of A. I. Melden (1961, Ch. 13) although not identical with either one. Danto, for example, introduces the concept of a 'basic action,' which is defined as the direct pairing of a bodily movement with its intentional causation. The concept is neutral on issues concerning how these bodily movements are to be described. Melden, in turn, identifies 'actions' with bodily movements which can be interpreted in the vocabulary of our ordinary 'action' language.

While my conception of an 'action is like Danto's conception of a 'basic action' with respect to the issue of being neutral regarding different descriptions, it differs in that it does not include any of the causal ancestry of the bodily movements. It also differs from Melden's conception in that it need not be subject to interpretations using another vocabulary. Thus, instead of including any of the causal history (in either direction), or other interpretations of bodily movements within my conception of an 'action' per se, as I previously noted I prefer to build up structure here by confining the term 'action' to a conceptual minimum. I will then build up structure by referring to voluntary bodily movements as 'voluntary actions' (which I will be analyzing in Chapter Four) and by referring to intentional bodily movements as 'intentional actions (which I will be analyzing in Chapter Six). Analogously, I will refer to the causal consequences of bodily movements as the 'consequences of actions.' Before analyzing the concept of the 'consequences of actions' in more detail, it is necessary to first introduce a pair of terms, 'possible actions' and 'potential actions,' which, in contrast with my usage of 'action,' I will use to refer to action types and not action tokens.

I will use 'possible action' to refer to various action types which an agent is faced with on a particular occasion (I will sometimes refer to action types specifically as 'action types' as well. The only constraint which I wish to place on the definition of 'possible actions' is the logical coherency of the actual performance by an agent of an action token of the action type constituted by a possible action. Thus, it need not be the case that the agent will either be physically capable of the action in question or even have the environmental opportunity to perform it. Still, the concept of a 'possible action' will play a key role in my treatment of both the free will problem and the judicial system; e. g., in discussing whether "we are free to perform a given possible action" and raising questions about which action types should either be required or forbidden by the law.

I will now turn to my analysis of a 'potential action.' As with the case of 'possible action,' I will be using 'potential action' to refer to action types. In fact, potential actions will constitute a subclass of possible actions. They can be defined in terms of the types of actions which a given agent has both the ability and opportunity to perform. In other words, they involve the types of actions which a given agent would succeed in performing should they attempt to perform them. I might note in this regard that in Chapter Four I will be analyzing a closely related concept to that of a 'potential action,' that of 'physical freedom' along much the same lines. In particular, an agent will be characterized as being 'physically free' to do something if they would succeed in doing it if they were to try, and where they have both the ability and the opportunity to act in the given way. It can also be noted that the concept of a 'potential action' is narrower in scope than the concept of a 'possible action,' since there will typically be many logically possible action types which we either do not have the ability or do not have the opportunity to perform. Looking ahead, I might also note that the concept of a 'potential action' will be a key concept both in setting forth the system of consequentialist decision-making which I am espousing in this book, and also with respect to the free will problem.

I will now introduce some terms which are key for defining the concept of the 'consequences of an action.' The first term which I wish to introduce in this regard is that of a 'situation.' I use the term 'situation' in a broad sense so as to both refer to the existence of tokens of both various standing conditions and also the occurrence of transitory events. I will predicate both of these sorts of situations as 'existing.' When I wish to refer merely to a type of situation, with no commitment being made to the existence of a corresponding token, I will specify this by speaking of the 'situation type.' To simplify language, in places where I speak merely of there 'being a situation' this will be interpreted as referring to the existence of a token of the relevant situation type. I will use 'world state' to refer to whole sets of situations which have evolved at a given point of time.

I will now turn to my analysis of the concept of the 'consequences of an action.' I will both analyze an active sense of the 'consequences' which we actively cause to have happen and a passive sense of what we passively allow to have happen. It is true that some consequentialists, such as John Stuart Mill in *On Liberty* (1859/1975, p. 12), have questioned whether the active - passive distinction can be coherently drawn under a completely consequentialist framework, since it may appear that the consequences will be the same in both cases. For example, somebody ends up being dead regardless of whether we actively take their life or passively allow for them to die. Nevertheless, I believe that it is possible to draw the active - passive distinction in this context. Looking ahead, I might also note that the distinction will play a key role in both my analysis of negative rights in Chapter Two and in a distinction between active and passive sense of 'causal responsibility' which I will draw in Chapter Six.

Since, in both my analyses of the active and the passive sense of the 'consequences of an act,' a key concept involves 'lack of action' (which I will term a 'null act'), a few preliminary remarks are needed on that concept. A 'null act' can be defined in terms of the complete lack of any bodily motions except for normal breathing and other life-supporting motions. It might be thought that complications arise here concerning such responses to a null act as agents raising questions as to why no actions are being performed—e. g., asking "Why aren't you talking?" However, since the point of introducing the concept of a 'null act' is to serve as a benchmark for comparing the results of either actual or potential actions, any such hypothetical reactions by others to the hypothetical null act are to be ignored. The active - passive distinction concerning consequences of actions can now be defined as follows.

I will define the active sense of the 'consequences of an act' in terms of the differences between two possible 'world states'—the one resulting when the proposed potential action is undertaken and the one resulting from a null action. In other words, an agent's actively causing consequences involving the existence of a situation *X*, is to be analyzed in terms of the agent performing an action whose world state includes *X* in cases where *X* would not have occurred if the agent performed a null act. In contrast, an agent's passively allowing a situation *X*, is to be analyzed in terms of the fact that there was at least one potential action open to the agent where the resulting world state would not include *X*, and where *X* would have been included in the world state if the null act was performed.

I wish to now take note of an alternative analysis of 'consequences of actions,' which was originally developed by John Mackie (1974, p. 62), and which was subsequently simplified by Jonathan Bennett (1988, Sec. 18). Bennett's analysis here involves analyzing the active sense of the 'consequences of an action' in terms of the types of situations for whose existence the action constitutes a necessary part of a sufficient condition. Mackie's analysis is more complicated, being in terms of 'INUS' conditions where the action constitutes an insufficient but necessary part of an unnecessary but sufficient condition for the consequences. Using Bennett's analysis, the passive sense of the 'consequences of an action' will then involve the claim that there was a potential action such that, if it was performed, it would have been a necessary part of a sufficient condition that the effect not occur. It should be noted that the sense of 'necessary' and 'sufficient' which are being used in the foregoing analyses are those of physical necessity and physical sufficiency. The meanings of these concepts can in turn be fleshed out in terms of what is respectively physically allowed or physically necessitated by a set of physical initial conditions together with the laws of physics (as these laws actually are and not necessarily as they are given by modern physics).

I will now show that, when an implicit assumption is added, the foregoing analyses of the active and passive consequences of an action are equivalent with the analyses in terms of world state types. First, it can be noted that, by the definition of a 'necessary condition,' a situation of a given type would not have existed if a necessary condition for its existence was missing. Thus, if one refers to the complete set of situation types for the existence of which an action constitutes a necessary condition, none of these would have been created in the action's absence. This leaves open the question though as to what would happen in these situations' stead if the necessary condition was absent. I take it that an implicit assumption being made here is that situations would then correspond in type to the world state types which would have been causally determined by the various other causally antecedent conditions. Once this implicit assumption has been made explicit, as far as I can see the two analyses are in fact equivalent.

An added point here is that in Chapter Three in my analysis of Kant's Practical Imperative, I will enlarge on the foregoing analysis of 'causal consequences of courses of action.' In particular, I will include reference to certain relationships between one consequence of a course of action, as just defined, and another one. One type of case here is a case of common cause and involves courses of action with two, or possibly more, causally-independent consequences. When there are two consequences here where one is desired and the other undesired this is sometimes called 'double effect.' A second type of case involves referring to causal relationships between two consequences as just defined, usually from an undesired consequence to a desired one.

There is one final concept which I wish to introduce before leaving this topic, that of a 'course of action.' By a 'course of action' I will refer to a series of bodily movements performed in order to accomplish some goal. Sub-goals (goals which must be met in order to accomplish other goals; i. e., means to an end) will also be reached by means of 'courses of action.' This concept of a 'course of action' has the merit of clearly delineating among different sets of actions since no matter how individual actions are delineated, sets of those actions will still be clearly marked out in terms of those being used to accomplish particular goal states. It also will turn out to be a key concept in resolving a series of paradoxes which have been alleged to afflict act utilitarianism. I will discuss these paradoxes in some detail when I investigate the descriptive components of 'should' and 'ought,' but first I will turn to my examination of the prescriptive components.

Section Three The Prescriptive Aspect of 'Should' and 'Ought'

In this section I will present an analysis of the prescriptive aspects or components of 'should' and ought.' First, it can be recalled that before I entered into my digression into the nature of actions and courses of action, I noted that when it is claimed that some individual potential course of action should be performed, the pursuit of that potential course of action is in some sense recommended. I will now turn to an analysis of the nature of this recommendation. The prescriptive component of 'ought' which constitutes a recommendation that a potential course of action be pursued has evolved over time, as previously sketched, from a societal or even a legal obligation, to a divine command, to finally a secular suggestion or recommendation. However, a case can be made that the modern sense of 'ought' here is still the most primitive sense since it at least makes sense to ask whether or not we ought to obey local social customs, the law, or even God's commandments. This last question is related to Plato's question in the *Euthyphro* as to whether an act is good because it is commanded by God or whether instead God commands it because it is good.

As Charles Stevenson (1944) has pointed out in the context of the emotivist ethical theory and Hare (1952/1964) has pointed out in terms of the logic of imperatives, the strength of the illocutionary force constituting the prescriptive component of the modern sense of 'ought' varies according to different circumstances. Sometimes, as with moral obligations, it is very close to being an order—e. g., you ought to save the drowning boy. However, there are other times when it is just used to express a mild suggestion—e. g., you ought to pick the red dress over the blue one. Of course, all the cases in between can also be present. Thus, it does not follow that just because we ought to pursue a potential course of action of a given type that we are morally obligated to do so, even though if we are morally obligated to pursue a potential course of action of a given type it follows that this is what we ought to do.

Some so-called 'critiques of consequentialism,' such as that of Scheffler (1994) would appear to involve a failure to take note of the foregoing point. In particular, Scheffler construes 'ought' statements as being statements about duties, and then argues for the existence of 'agent-centered prerogatives' which allow agents to exercise their individual freedom, perhaps within certain other ethical constraints, to act otherwise. Even here it is noteworthy that Scheffler, in defending a hybrid theory with both consequentialist and deontological elements, fails to find sound motivations for 'agent-centered restrictions' (such as those based off of special relationships or prohibitions on causing harm in order to prevent greater harm), which would prohibit agents from performing best fair possible courses of action. In any event, to make it clear how my system can handle Scheffler's point, some clarification is warranted on how I am using the concept of 'moral obligation' before proceeding further.

'Morally obligatory actions' can be defined as being action types which it is morally forbidden not to perform. Analogously, 'legally obligatory actions' can be defined as being action types which it is legally forbidden to perform. 'Morally forbidden actions' and 'legally forbidden actions' can in turn be defined as action types where the performance of corresponding actions make the agent be liable to some sort of penalty—e. g., some type of censure for breaking a conventional moral rule or follow-through in the post-judicial system in the case of breaking a legal statute, at least if the act is performed without a good excuse. In this regard it can be noted that Bernard Gert in *Morality: Its Nature and Justification* (1998, p. 180) argues with respect to 'moral rules' that "those who unjustifiably violate these rules be liable to punishment." It can be noted that it is more clear-cut as to who is authorized to impose a penalty in the case of the legally forbidden acts (where the authorized agent is the state) than in the just morally-forbidden case. Even in the latter case though, other authority figures can sometimes be pointed to, as in the case of parents possessing the authority to punish their children.

It is useful to introduce some terminology at this point for referring to morally or legally forbidden acts. Inasmuch as 'untoward' possesses the connotation of not being favorable, and hence implies that there is a better action which ought to be performed, I will refer to action types which are either morally or legally forbidden as being 'untoward acts.' I will then refer to the consequences of actual courses of action of these types as 'untoward consequences' and the corresponding situations as 'untoward situations.' I will also speak of 'untoward characters' to refer to dispositions of agents to perform untoward acts.

I should note that I will be elaborating both on the nature of apropos penalties when either moral rules or legal statutes are broken and on the concept of an excuse in Part Two. For present purposes though, I just wish to make two points on these subjects. The first point involves the application of the principle (that I will be arguing for in Chapter Three), that in general the minimization of harms should take precedence over the maximization of goods. I am using 'goods' and 'harms' here to refer to situations that possess at least a preponderance respectively of good and bad properties as these are analyzed in Section Two of Chapter Three. Inasmuch as penalties inherently involve harms, it follows that the imposition of penalties is only justifiable for the purposes of the mitigation of harms, and not for the production of goods. The second point is that, for a variety of reasons, I will hold that a rule prohibiting the activity in question must already be in place before the imposition of a penalty is justifiable. Otherwise, the situation would be akin to that of *ex post facto* legislation, which I will be arguing in Chapter Seven is inherently 'unfair,' in a sense to be analyzed in Chapter Two, to the person being penalized.

It can be noted that it follows from the foregoing definitions that when a course of action is neither morally nor legally obligatory, even though it is what we should do (as in the example just given of picking the red dress), failure to perform the course of action should not result in liability to a penalty. Still, I wish to hold that the decision-making process here is an instance of 'moral decision-making,' as I am using the term, inasmuch as the agent is doing what they ought to do, using the 'moral ought,' as I have previously defined that term. Also, it should be emphasized again that the strength of the illocutionary force of the 'moral ought' here may vary significantly; ranging from a very weak suggestion or recommendation, to constructive criticism, and then all the way to strong exhortations and verbal reprimands of varying degree. In none of these cases though is the person being addressed liable to a penalty if they decide to act otherwise.

Cases of non-morally-obligatory 'shoulds' can now be classified in several distinct categories. The first category involves 'supererogatory acts,' which are courses of action that, while being morally praiseworthy, are not morally obligatory. Using J. O. Urmson's (1958) language, these would include acts of 'heroism' (where an agent, in spite of personal danger, goes beyond his duty so as to prevent a harm from occurring) and 'saintliness' (which Urmson uses in a non-religious sense to refer to cases where an agent goes beyond their duty and, in spite of personal temptations to the contrary although no personal dangers need be involved, either causes good or prevents harm from occurring). A second category of cases here involves situations where there is not all that much at stake with respect to how one decides an issue and where the illocutionary force of the 'should' statement is merely that of constituting a mild recommendation with no moral obligation being implied whatsoever. An example here would be the case discussed earlier where a woman is trying to decide which color dress to buy; while there may be an objectively best fair decision, clearly no moral issues need arise here.

It is important to again stress the fact that 'should' can be used both with respect to obligations or duties, and to other instance of moral decision-making. In fact I believe that this point holds the key for getting around a common criticism of act utilitarianism; namely that it is too stringent in determining our moral obligations. While act utilitarianism may home in on one particular potential course of action as being the one which we should pursue, as just shown it does not also follow that there is any moral obligation to pursue a course of action of the given type. This completes my discussion of the prescriptive aspects of 'should' and 'ought,' and I will thus now turn to my discussion of the descriptive aspects of the words.

Section Four The Descriptive Aspect of 'Should' and 'Ought'

With regard to the subject of the descriptive components of the meanings of 'should' and 'ought,' I wish to defend the strong claim that we ought always to choose our 'best fair potential course of action' is analytically true. That is, I wish to claim that it is part of the very meanings of 'should' and of 'ought' that the potential course of action which ought to be performed in any given situation can be identified by means of discovering which is the best of the possible fair ones. It can be noted that the parallel with 'best' here may have even been in place for earlier senses of 'ought' and 'should' whereby a much stronger senses of obligation was present than with the modern usage. Consider in this regard such phrases as "you had better do it" or "it is best that you do it," where the implication is that one is under an obligation, possibly even from a divine source.

It can be noted now that my claim concerning the connection between what we ought to do and our best fair potential course of action is stronger than one made by Fred Feldman (1986, p. 207). Feldman claims that the foregoing connection with the concept of 'best' (Feldman does not discuss the connection with the concept of 'fairness'), rather than being an 'empty tautology,' instead involves a stipulative definition. However, while I hold that the claim is a tautology, I do not see why it need be 'empty.' Just because the connections expressed by tautologies are true by definition, it does not follow that the connections are in any sense 'arbitrary.' In fact, I find many tautologies to be extremely elucidating concerning deep semantic connections between concepts. I should also note that a number of philosophers have also taken note of this connection between the concepts of 'best' and 'should' including, but not limited to Aristotle

(*Nicomachean Ethics*, Book 3), Moore, (1903/1971, pp. 25, 206, 250), Max Black (1964) and Kurt Baier, (1965, Ch. 2).

In any event, while I will be returning at the end of this chapter to the subject of whether or not there are any analytic connections between what we should do and what our best fair courses of action are, I wish to now take note of a logical connection in the opposite direction to the one just noted. This is that if some fair potential course of action is also our best fair potential course of action, it follows that we ought to perform it. It thus follows that what we ought to do and our best fair potential course of action are logically equivalent—i. e., that their denotations are the same here. It should also be noted in this regard that a parallel reverse entailment does not hold from a potential course of action just being fair to it being the case that we ought to pursue it. This is because, as I will argue shortly, typically there will be several distinct potential courses of action to choose from all of which are equally fair.

It is important to note that the potential course of action which should be chosen is not merely being labeled by calling it the 'best fair potential course of action,' as it would be if it was merely called the 'right' or the 'correct' thing to do. Instead, I will argue that 'best' possesses a descriptive content in virtue of its being the superlative form of comparison of 'good,' and that 'fairness' also possesses a descriptive content. I will be making a number of remarks with respect to the subject of the nature of these descriptive contents of 'fairness' and of 'best' both later in this section and in Chapter Two and Three, but first I wish to take note of the logical relationships between the denotations of the terms.

Since 'best' is the superlative form of comparison of 'good,' a utilitarian (in the broad sense of teleological consequentialism) analysis of the descriptive content of 'should' would seem to be quite straight-forward. However, the issue arises as to how well such an analysis squares with what I take to be an equally-primitive claim, that we should always act fairly.

To begin my discussion of the foregoing point, I wish to raise the issue as to whether the concept of 'fairness' is like the concept of 'goodness' in admitting of degree, or whether instead it is 'all or nothing.' Certainly it is the case that we can speak of degrees of 'unfairness,' such as by claiming that one potential course of action is more or less unfair than another potential one. However, the positive concept of 'fairness' per se does seem to be all or nothing, and in this respect differs from 'goodness.' This is also borne out by such expressions as "at least be fair" or "that would only be fair" which point toward the concept as only ruling out various unfair potential courses of action, but not 'homing in' on one particular course. At least typically then many different potential courses of action will be equally fair. However, except in the case of ties in overall value content in the preponderance of good consequences over bad consequences, only one potential course of action will be the best possible. Thus, the denotation of 'fair potential courses of action' in a given circumstance will typically be much broader than that of the 'best fair potential course of action.'

Even though, as I just noted, a central contention of this book is that it is analytically true that we should choose our best fair potential course of action, it can be pointed out that Feldman's claim that we should always pick our best potential courses of action independently of questions of fairness does not at least necessarily follow from this contention. In fact, it is not always at least obvious that the best (at least in the act utilitarian sense which I will be developing in Chapter Three) potential course of action will also be a fair one. In particular, cases can be cited where the overall utility (I am using 'utility' here as a general measure of value, and will be elaborating on the concept in more detail in Chapter Three) is maximized at the expense of the interests of an individual or a small group of individuals. Examples here would include sacrificing a Christian to the lions for the delight of a coliseum full of Romans, or forcing somebody to sacrifice organs to save other lives. Ultimately, I believe these examples show that a morally-adequate version of consequentialism needs to be concerned with the nature of means and not just with ends. However, considerations can also be raised which either mitigate or constitute evidence for denying altogether the contention that the best potential courses of action will not always be fair.

Several considerations are sometimes raised which may mitigate the claim that best courses of action are not always fair, a number of which are discussed by Anthony Quinton (1989). One consideration here is the law of diminishing marginal utility, which holds that a great increase in goods to those well off need not possess a greater utility than a small improvement with respect to those not nearly so well off. For example, the utility of an extra dollar to a poor person may be considerably greater than the corresponding utility to a rich person. However, it might seem that it is still possible to construct cases, such as with either the just-given organ transplant case or certain cases involving medical research, where, even taking the principle of diminishing marginal utility into account, overall utility is still maximized at somebody's expense. For example, the increase in overall utility associated with the future cures which would come about through information gained in the process of a medical experiment, might more than compensate for the resulting loss associated with what happens to the 'victims' of the experiment. Thus, while appealing to the principle of marginal utility may at least partially alleviate the foregoing problem, it would seem that it does not completely resolve it.

Other considerations can also be raised for denying altogether that our best courses of action will not always turn out to fair. In particular, it could be held that the very unfairness of cases, such as those just mentioned of interests of minorities being sacrificed in order to at least superficially maximize overall utility, causes them not to be our best alternatives. In further support of this claim, it could even be argued that the constraint to always act fairly is built right into the concept of 'the best.' In particular, it can be noted that it sounds odd to say that we ought to perform a course of action even though it is not fair, in much the same manner as it sounds odd to say that we ought to perform a course of action even though there is a better alternative. Assuming that there is a single course of action which we ought to perform in both of these cases, it would follow then that the best course of action is also a fair one.

In any event, it is not necessary for me to resolve the issue as to whether best potential courses of action are always fair. This is because my claim is merely that we should always choose our best fair potential course of action, and not our best potential course of action independently of issues of fairness. Thus, I am claiming that only fair potential courses of action should be compared in deciding which course of action should be chosen. The potential course of action which we should pursue on any particular occasion will then be the best fair potential course. In effect then, I am claiming that utilitarianism needs to be tempered by a fairness constraint, and the foregoing approach would seem to be a straight-forward method to accomplish this purpose. Because I am using the concept of 'fairness' as a constraint on what sorts of potential courses of action are to even be considered in picking out the best potential course of action, I will present my analysis of the connection between 'should' and 'fairness' before presenting my analysis of the connection between 'should' and 'best.' I will thus now turn to that analysis.

To begin my analysis of the connection between 'should' and 'fairness,' I wish to state by stipulation that the concept of 'fairness,' as I am using it, is consequence-oriented; i. e., that what makes a situation be fair or not depends solely on the consequences of a course of action rather than on the motives. In this regard, I might note that in Chapter Two I will be analyzing the concept in terms of the nature of the distribution of goods and harms among the members of a population. In particular, while I will be examining several different possible criteria for fairness which have been historically given there, I will argue that the most fundamental criterion involves whether the distribution of goods and harms is impartial. However, I will not pursue the nature of these details further here, and will leave the detailed working out of the theory for Chapter Two.

It can be noted that to some extent my claim that the concept of 'fairness' is exclusively consequence-based goes against ordinary usage to the extent that under that usage aspects of a decision-making process are deemed to be relevant in determining whether a potential course of action is fair or not. For example, the issues of whether an agent was truly deciding in a 'disinterested' manner, and whether a decision which was to be made 'arbitrarily' was truly made at random or not, would ordinarily be deemed as being relevant for determining the fairness of a resultant course of action. However, in defense of my usage, it can be noted that the concept of a 'disinterested decision' can be analyzed in terms of the nature of the results of the decision in distributing goods and harms, and that even when a distribution cannot be made evenly here (as in cases where certain goods and harms, including lives lost, cannot be evenly divided up), and where there are no relevant differences in terms of needs or abilities, the key issue is still whether the uneven distribution is objectively random. It can also be noted that John Rawls, in defending his position of 'justice as fairness' in his *A Theory of Justice* (1971, p. 30) states "All ethical doctrines worth our attention take consequences into account in judging rightness. One which did not would simply be irrational, crazy."

A second issue regarding the nature of 'fairness' concerns the breadth of the reference frame with respect to which potential courses of action are to be deemed to be fair or not. It would seem that at least two people need to be involved in order for the issue to arise, since such phrases as "being unfair to oneself" are used to refer to sacrificing one's own interest for that of others. Examples of quite narrow points of view are obvious though, as in cases raising issues of fairness in dealing with just one's own immediate family or friends. What is deemed fair from these narrow points of view may not be deemed fair from a wider point of view; i. e., it may involve infringing on somebody else's basic rights. For example, if I give a job to somebody because they are the best qualified from among an inner circle of friends or family members, this decision need not also be considered to be fair from a wider point of view. Other examples of intermediate points of view (points of view more limited in scope than the unlimited moral point of view which I will shortly define) here would include just looking out for what is fair from the viewpoint of an organization (possibly a business, but also possibly a crime syndicate), a town, a state, or a nation. It can be noted that so long as the reference frame for an 'ought' statement is the same as that of the people being considered in the decision-making process here though, it will remain the case that the statement "I ought to do what is fair" will be true. I will shortly be making an analogous point for the statement "I ought to perform my best fair potential course of action."

It should be emphasized that the scopes of each of the foregoing 'oughts' and judgments concerning what was fair was restricted, in the sense that they only considered the fairness of a course of action with respect to a limited group of individuals—my family or organization, my town, or my nation. They thus did not take into account everybody and everything that relevantly could have been taken into account. In contrast, I wish to define the 'moral ought,' and the resultant moral judgment of what is fair, to possess unlimited scopes, and thus to take into consideration the consequences of potential courses of action on absolutely everybody in any way affected. What I wish to call 'the moral point of view' can also be defined now as the limiting case of raising issues of what is fair and what is best from wider and wider points of view; the net result corresponding to the complete lack of prejudice or 'provincialism' (taking the point of view of some narrower class of individuals) in making decisions. I might note that questions can be raised about whether other animal species, or possibly the unborn, should be included in the moral point of view, but I will not deal with these issues in this book.

In view of the foregoing considerations, it follows that typically we will be faced with a number of equally fair (from the broadest possible viewpoint) alternative potential courses of action to decide from. Obviously, then, just appealing to what is fair will not be enough to make a decision concerning which potential course of action ought to be pursued. Here though we can also appeal to the principle that we should also pick the best potential course of action, the net effect being that we should pick our best fair potential course of action. In other words, at least for practical purposes in reaching decisions, fairness can be used as an initial constraint in determining what our permissible potential courses of action are, and then the criterion of picking our best potential course of action can be appealed to for actually making a decision from among these fair alternatives. Thus, I will now turn to my analysis of the connection between what we should do and what is best.

To begin my discussion of the connection between 'should' and 'best,' I wish to show how making the claim that we should always pursue our 'best fair potential course of action' rather than just the 'best fair potential action' resolves the group of paradoxes previously-mentioned which have been alleged to afflict many versions of act utilitarianism. Probably the most important of the alleged paradoxes to afflict act utilitarianism here is one, first pointed out by Hector Castaneda (1968), that when we are required to perform two or more potential actions, if the criterion for a potential action being required is that it is the best potential action (Castaneda does not consider the issue of fairness here), then each of these potential actions will have to be both better and worse than each of the others. They will each have to be better than any of the others since, by definition, they each must be the best potential action. They will also each have to be worse than the best potential action, since each of the other potential actions must also be the best potential action. Another, at least structurally similar, paradox involves cases where one potential action, which by itself will not lead to the best potential consequences, is nevertheless an integral part of a series of potential actions that together will lead to the best potential consequences. Does it follow then that we should not pursue such a potential action?

Both of the foregoing purported paradoxes can be avoided by noting that under the version of act consequentialism which I am defending, it is a 'potential course of action,' and not necessarily individual potential actions per se, which must be looked at in determining what would be the best fair potential choice. It can be seen then that Castaneda's paradox will not follow since just because one is obligated to perform a potential action (no matter how these 'potential actions' are individuated) constituting a portion of such a potential course of action, it does not follow that one is not obligated to perform the potential actions constituting the remaining portions of the course as well. Each portion contributes towards the consequences of the whole potential course of action being the best fair potential course of action, even though the individual potential actions which constitute its portions, when they are just considered by themselves, may not lead to the best fair potential consequences.

Thus, when it is claimed that some particular potential course of action should be performed, the effect is to also claim that the pursuit of the individual potential actions constituting the portions of that particular potential course of action is both the best fair means from the options open to us for achieving some particular goal, and also that the goal itself constitutes at least a sub-goal towards the achievement of some best fair potential state. However, the question arises at this point as to what the relevant reference frame should be for this 'best fair potential state' to be with regard to.

As I pointed out with my discussion of the connection between 'ought' and 'fairness,' the contexts or reference frames of both 'ought' statements and statements concerning the issue of what the best fair potential course of action is can vary. So long as the same context or reference frame is being used for both, it is true that we ought to perform our best fair potential course of action. It can also be recalled that the moral point of view involves using these concepts from an unlimited context, taking into account everybody and everything that could possibly have relevance to the case under consideration. I will now illustrate these points by means of discussing a number of related examples.

My first example involves playing a game of chess. This is a situation which at least can be completely devoid of any moral implications (in the sense of involving any moral obligations, as I previously analyzed that concept). Assuming that an agent is trying to win the game, then the move that the agent ought to make at any time during the game will coincide with the best possible move from among the legitimate moves with which the agent is faced (I take it that the issue of fairness does not arise here) for the purpose of winning the game. This analysis can also be expanded on in terms of the pursuit of a nested series of sub-goals (such as a sub-strategy involving capturing the opponent's queen), whose successive fulfillment will lead to the accomplishment of the objective. The rationale for pursuing a series of sub-goals here will exactly parallel that for pursuing overall goals, and an analogous point holds if the sub-goals are in turn broken down into smaller units. I might note also that there may be a perfectly objective algorithm, possibly discoverable by a computer program, for identifying what this best possible move is from within the context of any particular goal system. I should note that I will be making use of the chess example again in Chapter Four. However, for my present purposes, I would like to move on now to discuss a group of examples where the reference frames for determining what is best steadily increase in size until, for the unbounded case, the moral point of view is reached.

If I am just looking out for my own well being (the point of view of egoism) then it follows, to pursue the chess analogy, that the 'move' that I ought to make in the 'game of life' (I will be pursuing the analogy between life and a game in more detail in Chapter Four as well), will coincide with my best potential fair 'move' or 'course of action' from within the same egotistical reference frame. Similarly, if I have a somewhat wider point of view, such as the various ones which I mentioned in my preceding discussion of different possible scopes for judgments of fairness, then once again the potential course of action which I ought to pursue in this context will be the same as my best fair potential course of action from within the same context. Again, it can be noted that the moral point of view here will not be restricted in scope. Thus, under that viewpoint the potential course of action which I should pursue will be the best fair one taking into account the effects of the course of action on everybody. Looking ahead, I should also note that I will be making much of these points concerning different reference frames for 'ought' and 'best fair' statements in Part Two in Chapters Seven and Eight respectively on the Judicial and the Post-Judicial systems.

I have noted that the illocutionary force behind 'ought' statements varies in strength according to different circumstances. In order to make some further points concerning the connection between 'ought' and best,' it will be helpful to contrast the logical relationships between 'ought' statement and those stating moral obligations. First, it should be emphasized again that we are not always morally obligated to follow potential courses of action that we should pursue. This should be obvious both from cases of supererogatory actions, which are morally praiseworthy but not morally obligatory, and also from examples such as the one which I gave earlier where it was claimed that somebody should pick a red dress over a blue one. It nevertheless is the case that the fact that a potential course of action is morally obligatory logically entails that we should perform it, and it will thus also coincide with our best fair potential course of action.

My next point is that an 'ought' statement is logically weaker than an 'obligation' statement. This is because, while the fact that a potential course of action is morally obligatory entails that we should do it, the converse at least does not necessarily hold. Similarly, an 'ought not' statement is logically weaker than an 'impermissible' statement, in that, while it is the case that if a potential course of action is morally impermissible it logically follows that it should not be done, once again the converse entailment at least need not always hold. Thus, there is a wide range of potential courses of action, the merely morally permissible, which lie in between the classes of the morally obligatory and the morally impermissible. But the question arises as to where the logically weaker 'ought' and 'ought not' statements fit in here. Is there a corresponding set of potential courses of action of which it can be said neither that we ought to pursue them nor that we ought not to pursue them? Or, at least with the exception of ties among the relative values of two or more potential courses of action, is it instead true that if it is not the case that we ought to pursue a potential course of action, this then entails that we ought not to pursue it? I wish to defend the latter claim here.

As far as I can see, in any given situation it at least makes sense to raise the question as to what an agent ought to do. While there may be times when there is no practical way to answer this question—i. e., to discover what the best fair potential course of action is—the question itself is always at least intelligible. As I noted, a complication which may arise involves cases where there is a tie for best among several different potential courses of action; i. e., where two or more choices are equally good or equally bad. Here, by the 'best fair choice' criterion of action, an agent should choose from among the members of the group that is tied for being the best fair potential course of action, but the criterion does not pick out the particular member which ought to be chosen. I might note in this regard though that it will be extremely rare for the consequences of two or more potential courses of action to be equally good or equally bad to the exact same extent. Still, there may be a practical problem in that we may not be able to 'weigh' the consequences of competing alternative fair potential courses of action with sufficient precision so as to be able to determine which one is in fact the best fair alternative. In any event, it seems to be clear that when a best fair choice does exist, an agent should pursue the corresponding potential course of action. Also, to simply my subsequent discussion I will speak as if the best fair course of action homes in on just one course, with the implicit assumption that in the case of ties, the moral choice is to be made from among these tied courses.

Having analyzed the connections between the concept of 'should' and the respective concepts of 'fairness' and 'what is best,' I would like to now close the chapter by making some comments on David Hume's claim that it is not possible to derive an 'ought' statement from an 'is' statement.

Section Five The Is - Ought Gap

In his *Treatise on Human Nature*, Hume made the following argument that it is not possible to derive an 'ought' statement from a statement just concerning matters of fact—i. e., an 'is' statement.

> In every system of morality, which I have hitherto met with, I have always remarked that the author proceeds for some time in the ordinary way of reasoning, and establishes the being of a God, or makes observations concerning human affairs; when of a sudden I am surprised to find that, instead of the usual copulations of propositions, is, and is not, I meet with no proposition that is not connected with an ought, or an ought not. This change is imperceptible; but is, however, of the last consequence. For as this ought or ought not expresses some new relation or affirmation, it is necessary that it should be observed and explained; and at the same time that a reason should be given for what seems altogether inconceivable, how this new relation can be a deduction from others, which are entirely different from it. (Hume, 1739/1975, p. 469)

Hume's basic point here then is that there is always a logical gap between purely factual statements and value judgments concerning what potential courses of action 'ought' to be pursued. It may also be noted that Hume's basic argument was later paralleled by A. J. Ayer who in his *Language, Truth and Logic*, (1936/1952, Ch. 6), argues for emotivism by posing essentially the same dilemma. If ethical claims are synthetic, as Hume's argument would seem to show, then, barring the existence of the synthetic a priori as held by Kant, they are only knowable through experience. However, at least according to Ayer, it is manifestly not the case that ethical values per se are ever experienced. Thus, Ayer argued that statements in ethics are strictly speaking 'nonsense' and that their status involves nothing more than the expression of various subjective emotions towards various states of affairs.

Coming to terms with these basic gaps has played a key role in the work of a number of twentieth-century ethical philosophers. For example, Hare (1952/1964, Ch. 3) argued that an imperative statement can never be deduced from an indicative statement. As I pointed out though, it is questionable whether 'ought' statements are always best construed as imperatives. Instead they appear to have a wide range of illocutionary forces. Still questions could be raised about how these forces can be derived from purely factual content.

There has also been a debate though concerning how to interpret the claim that Hume is making in the passage, Some, notably Ayer, have claimed that Hume is arguing that the is - ought gap is unbridgeable, since one of the statements at least cannot be deduced from the other, and since Hume disparaged inductive reasoning. Others, notably MacIntyre (1978, Essay 13), have claimed that Hume was merely critiquing previous systems of ethics, and thought that essentially utilitarian justifications could be given for bridging the gap. Still others, notably John Searle (1964) although not in the context of interpreting Hume, have argued that the gap which Hume pointed to is in fact deductively bridgeable. However, it is noteworthy that Searle's purported counterexample to Hume involves instances of stating a promise, where the prescriptive force of the utterance would appear to derive its force from the existence of certain social customs involving promise keeping. In fairness to Searle, it should be noted that he holds that the existence of these social customs, in effect, is built into language itself. Still, questions could be raised concerning the justifiability of a language's own built-in assumptions. That is, one could question the justification of the linkage between the descriptive and prescriptive components of the phrase 'I promise' which are ordinarily taken to commit one to following the social mores binding a person who utters the phrase 'I promise' to the subsequent fulfillment of what is promised.

Regardless of the merits of what MacIntyre says as a proper exegesis of Hume, I would agree with him in his claim that, while there is a gap between purely factual statements and value judgments concerning those statements, there may still be legitimate ways for bridging the gap. The question arises though as to what reasons could possibly be given for bridging the gap without having the same problem which gave rise to the gap in first place recur within the line of justification given by the reason. That is, the justification here must contain a value judgment (such as that promises ought always to be kept) itself, and the question thus arises as to how this latter claim is to be justified.

My response to the foregoing challenge is to note that what I, in effect, have been doing in this chapter is to offer what Robert Nozick (1974, p. 18), following Adam Smith (1776/1952, p. 194), has termed an 'invisible hand' argument. Such an argument involves showing that it is possible to build on a series of non-controversial premises by means of a series of non-controversial moves to a surprising (at least concerning the amount of structure involved) conclusion. In particular, I wish to claim that the moral connections between 'should,' 'best,' and 'fair' supervene on non-moral connections by means of deductive carryovers brought on by the changes of context and viewpoint which occur with the transition to the moral point of view. The non-controversial premises which I have in mind for being built on involve the connections which I previously took note of between 'should,' 'best,' and 'fairness' in non-moral contexts. I will first make some points concerning the connection between 'should' and 'best,' and then concerning the connection between 'should' and 'fairness.'

As I have been arguing earlier in this chapter, I take it that the claim that the connection between 'should' and 'best' which occurs in non-moral contexts is analytic, is non-controversial. In fact, as Black (1964) has pointed out with respect to such contexts as that of an agent picking out their next move in a game of chess, not only is it the case that the connection between the terms is clearly an analytic one, but also clearly objective criteria can be given for determining what the agent's best possible move (or 'course of action' for the more general standpoint of the 'game' of life) is. The question then can be raised as to when, as reference frames are gradually expanded in the transition to the moral point of view, the connection between 'should' and 'best' would either cease to be analytic, or where the determination of what is best would lose its objectivity. In order to make this transition two distinct moves are requisite. Since I either have developed or will be developing both of these moves in some detail elsewhere, I will merely briefly state the main points here.

The first move concerns the reference frame from which an agent is making their decision. As I noted earlier, the shift to the moral point of view involves enlarging the reference frame of an agent from a self-centered egotistical one to progressively wider ones until the unlimited moral point of view is reached. So long as the same reference frame is used for both, I can see there is no reason for thinking that the connection between 'should' and 'best' should cease to be analytic because of this shift.

The second move, which I will be developing in more detail in Chapter Three, involves the shift that is made here from a non-cooperative standpoint to a cooperative standpoint. In other words, this involves a switch from individual agents choosing their courses of action as if no other agents are going to assist them in attaining their goals, to choosing courses of action in accordance with the best roles (where these roles are possibly assigned by others) of the individual agents in a cooperative effort to attain a goal. As with the case of the shift in reference frames, there is no obviously-apparent reason for thinking that a loss of analyticity should result from this shift either. In fact, looking ahead, it can be noted that in Chapter Three I will be arguing that the rules for cooperation are objective in nature.

The situation with respect to the concept of 'fairness' is more subtle, since as was previously noted, in at least cases dealing with the distribution of goods that go beyond the necessities of life, several distinct criteria for 'fair' distribution have historically been given. The question thus arises as to which, if any, of these criteria are relevant for the analysis here. It can still be noted though that issues of fairness can be raised from the perspective of different reference frames. For example, a fair distribution from a narrow reference frame of just members of one's immediate family may not be fair when considered from the broader reference frame of a community as a whole. Thus, a transition can be made here from a narrow point of view to the unlimited moral point of view. As with the case of the concept of 'best' there is no reason for thinking that a loss of analyticity should result from this shift.

One criticism that could still be made here involves the fact, which I pointed out earlier, that the very concept of 'should' is compound, containing both prescriptive and descriptive (in the sense of stating what is both best and fair) elements to it. It could be questioned then as to why the illocutionary content of 'should' has to coincide with the locutionary content since it could be held that the fact that they do coincide in ordinary English just shows that the ordinary English word is theory-laden. In other words, it could be argued, as Hare (1981, Ch. 11) does, that in the process of analyzing moral language all that we are really doing is discovering the presuppositions made by the language. Thus, it could be claimed that by showing that ordinary English implicitly assumes that we should always do what is best in no way actually justifies the claim that we should do so. In order to develop my reply to this objection, it is necessary to enter into a short digression on the concept of 'supervenience.'

The concept of 'supervenience' was first developed, although with a different terminology, by Moore (1922, Ch. 8). It was further developed explicitly by Hare (1952/1964, Ch. 5). The basic idea behind the concept is the claim that one concept (possibly corresponding to an unobservable property, such as a value concept) can apply to a situation in virtue of the possession by the situation of another property, such as an observable property. In such a case the first concept is said to 'supervene' on the second property; it being a higher-order concept which applies to the situation in virtue of the situation's possession of the lower-level property. It can be noted that the concept of 'supervenience,' as thus elucidated, essentially coincides with the concept of 'being a criterion.' This is because the existence of one situation is stated to be a criterion for the existence of a second one when the second one exists in virtue of the existence of the first.

In the case of value terms (e. g., 'fairness' or 'unfairness,' or 'goodness' or 'badness'), I will argue that the illocutionary aspects of the terms will constitute the supervening properties. The locutionary aspects of the terms will then constitute the lower-level properties which are being supervened on. Since I will be arguing that multiple criteria exist for these lower-level properties it may be useful to enter into a short digression on what is meant by multiple criteria, before illustrating the supervening process with a few examples of value terms.

To begin my discussion of the meaning of 'multiple criteria,' it can be noted that there may be more than one criterion (multiple criteria) for the existence of the same situation in cases of what are sometimes known as 'cluster concepts.' A good example here, which was discussed by Ludwig Wittgenstein (1953/1967, Remarks 66, 67), is that of being a game. As Wittgenstein notes, the multiple criteria for being a game include being done for amusement, having sides, winning and losing, and being rule-governed. However, some games are not done for amusement (e. g., professional sports), some games do not have sides (e. g., solitaire), and some games may neither have winners and losers or be rule governed (e. g., children's games which are made up as they go along). It can be noted then that while an activity may lack any of the given individual multiple criteria for being a game and still be a game, it would still be the case that if it were to lack all of the criteria, it would be contradictory to call it a 'game.'

I will now make use of some of the foregoing points in order to illustrate the supervening process of illocutionary aspects of value terms on the locutionary aspects for which multiple criteria exist. For example, in my analysis of 'unfairness' in Chapter Three, I will argue that the illocutionary aspect of the term involves a complaint on the part of the agent who is asserting that the situation is unfair. I will also argue that this illocutionary aspect supervenes on any of a number of distinct multiple criteria which can be given for the locutionary aspect of the claim that a situation is unfair. Examples here will include situations where a person is used just as a means, and situations where not everyone comes out ahead as the result of the way in which goods and harms are distributed among the members of a population. Similarly, in Chapter Four I will argue that the illocutionary aspects of 'goodness' and 'badness' (which will respectively be approval and disapproval on the part of the person making the value judgment) will supervene on any of a number of distinct multiple criteria which can be given for the locutionary aspects of the claims that a situation is either good or bad. For example, among the distinct multiple criteria which I will cite for the existence of a situation to be good are included being pleasant, being an object of desire, and being an object of interest.

As with the situation with games, it should be emphasized that in all of the cases of the predication of a value term to a situation, people would not be contradicting themselves if they were to claim that value term applied to the situation in spite of the fact that the situation was lacking one of the multiple defining criteria for the value term in question. However, people would be contradicting themselves if they were to deny that a situation possessed each of the multiple criteria for a value term while still holding that the value term applied to the situation.

The question can also be raised at this point as to the type of linkage which exists between supervening properties and the properties being supervened on. Is it an analytic link, like the linkage between an integer being a prime number and the fact that the integer is only evenly-divisible by itself and one? Does the linkage involve some other type of necessity, such as physical necessity (e.g., with the linkage between being a carbon atom and the possession of the various chemical properties of carbon) or psychological necessity? Instead, the position which I will be defending in this book is that the linkage between the illocutionary and locutionary aspects of value terms is justificatory in character. That is, I hold that the fact that a situation meets at least one of the multiple criteria for the locutionary content of a value term will constitute justification, in the sense of being a good reason, for holding the attitudes expressed by the illocutionary content of the value term.

The concept of 'being a good reason' can in turn be fleshed out objectively in terms of either constituting evidence for the existence of ultimate ends or in terms of constituting effect means for the fulfillment of these ends. The ends and means referred to here may in turn be construed either with respect to the point of view of the person making the value judgement or instead with respect to a wider point of view such as either the moral point of view or that of other people who are cared about. I will be developing the details of how the fulfillment of either ends or means to them is possible from different points of view in my discussion of the concept of 'best' in Chapter Three. Some of the points which I will be developing in Chapter Two concerning the concept of a 'fairness constraint' on utilitarianism will also be relevant here.

It is also possible to make use of these last points in order to explicate the connection between the locutionary and illocutionary aspects of 'should' and 'ought.' As with the case of value terms, I believe that the linkage between these aspects is justificatory in character. In other words, I hold that the justification for recommending the pursuit of a course of action (the illocutionary aspect of 'should' and 'ought') is the fact that it is the best fair course of action for the agent in question (the locutionary aspect of 'should' and 'ought'). I might note that MacIntyre (1978, Essay 14) at times at least appears to be sympathetic towards this type of linkage between ‘is’ and ‘ought’ terms. This completes my discussion of supervenience and I will now turn to my discussion of fairness.

Chapter Two
An Analysis of Fairness

In the last chapter I argued that it is analytically true that we should always do what is fair. I also argued that it is analytically true that, given this constraint of choosing from fair potential courses of action, that we should always choose our best potential course of action. Here, both the concept of 'fairness' and that of 'what is best' were taken to be completely consequentialist in character, in the broad sense of 'consequentialist' given in the introduction which includes causal and other relationships among the consequences of courses of actions in their descriptions for purposes of evaluation. I also argued that the moral 'should' coincides with our best fair potential course of action from within the widest possible context; i. e., with regard to everyone being affected by the decision.

In this chapter I will analyze the concept of 'fairness' in some detail, and will then present my analysis of the concept of a 'best fair potential course of action' in Chapter Three. Thus, in this chapter, I will offer a consequentialist (in the broad sense of the term) justification of a subject which purely teleological consequentialist theories (i. e., the various forms of utilitarianism) do not seem to be capable of providing an adequate account of, namely rights. Since issues of fairness can be raised both on an individual and a societal level, I will both give accounts of why agents should possess certain rights, and why the set of social policies which are adopted for a society should be 'fair' in character. To lead into these topics, I will begin the chapter by presenting a list of at least often-purported 'rights' and 'freedoms.' I will then make a few remarks on the logical structure of claims to these 'rights and freedoms.'

Section One Rights and Freedoms

Lists of purported basic 'rights' (sometimes also called 'freedoms') vary significantly both in terms of length and apparent primitiveness. For example, consider the following lists of 'rights' which have been historically asserted:

(1) John Locke's list of the 'natural rights' of life, liberty, and property.

(2) Thomas Jefferson's list in the Declaration of Independence of the 'inalienable rights' of life, liberty, and the pursuit of happiness.

(3) The list in the Bill of Rights constituting the first ten amendments of the United States Constitution, including the 'freedoms of' religion, speech, and the press; the 'rights to' assemble, petition for redress of grievances, bear arms, due process, and a speedy trial by jury; and finally the 'rights against' unreasonable searches and cruel and unusual punishment.

(4) The French declaration of the 'Rights of Man and of the Citizen' including the 'rights to' private property, the inviolability of the person, and resistance to oppression; and guarantees of all citizens to be considered equal before the law, to have the right to participate directly or indirectly in legislation, and not to be arrested without judicial order.

(5) Franklin Roosevelt's 'four freedoms' of the 'freedoms of ' speech and religion, and the 'freedoms from' want and fear.

(6) The United Nations' Universal Declaration of Human Rights including the 'rights to' equality before the law, protection against arbitrary arrest, fair trial, own property, work, choose one's work freely, equal pay for equal work, form and join trade unions, rest and leisure, an adequate standard of living, education; and 'freedoms of' thought conscience, religion, opinion and expression, and of peaceful assembly and association.

(7) Rawls's list of 'basic liberties,' including political liberty (the right to vote and to be eligible for public office, together with the freedoms of speech and

assembly), liberty of conscience and freedom of thought, the right to personal property, and freedom from arbitrary arrest and seizure.

Clearly, the 'rights' and 'freedoms' included in the foregoing extensive and, to some extent, both overlapping and motley lists vary significantly both in terms of their intuitiveness and primitiveness; i. e., dependencies on other 'rights' and 'freedoms.' Also, creators of these lists of 'rights' and 'freedoms' have in general just stipulated which 'rights' and 'freedoms' are to be included on the lists without offering theories to justify the inclusions. Thus, almost without exception, no objective mechanisms have been given by creators of the lists of 'rights' and 'freedoms' for determining which, if any, of the 'rights' and 'freedoms' which they cite are truly basic, or which ones are to supersede others when they come into conflict. In fact, some such as MacIntyre (1981, p. 67), have expressed skepticism concerning whether an objective basis can be given to rights at all. I believe that several points can be developed towards giving some objectivity to this subject though. I might note that some of what I say here has been influenced by Judith Thomson's (1990) *The Realm of Rights*, and by various readings in Frey (1984).

First, I wish to draw attention to a few points concerning both the vocabulary and the grammar by way of which the different 'rights' and 'freedoms' on the lists are stated. It can be noted that some member of the lists are labeled as 'rights' while others are labeled as 'freedoms.' Also, some of the 'rights' are stated in terms of the 'right to' the existence of situations of a certain type while others are stated in terms of the 'right from' the existence of situations of a certain type. I should note that the distinction in terms of whether a right is stated as being a 'right to' or a 'right against' the existence of a certain type of situation is not all that fundamental, since the two forms of speech are mutually translatable. For example, an agent's 'right to' the existence of a given type of situation is logically equivalent to their 'right against' having the existence of that given type of situation being denied them. Similarly, freedoms 'to' or 'of' the existence of various situations, are equivalent to freedoms 'from' interference with the pursuit of those situations.

Looking ahead, I might further note that I will be making similar points to those just made concerning the logical equivalency of certain 'to' and 'against' expressions later on in Chapters Four and Seven. In particular, in Chapter Four I will argue for the logical equivalency between claims to be 'free to' perform given possible courses of action and claims to be 'free not to' perform other possible courses of action. Similarly, in Chapter Seven I will argue for the logical equivalency between laws requiring certain possible courses of action and laws prohibiting certain other possible courses of action.

Concerning the distinction between a 'freedom' and a 'right,' I first wish to point out that the locutions in terms of 'freedoms' can be translated into locutions in terms of 'rights.' For example, the 'freedom of speech' becomes the 'right to free speech,' and 'freedom from want' becomes the 'right to be free of want.' However, it is noteworthy that the converse is not always the case, since such purported rights as rights to education or to health care cannot be construed as freedoms. Thus, it is necessary to distinguish between two distinct categories of rights; negative rights and positive rights. I will now proceed to elaborate on both of these in some detail.

Roughly, negative rights consist in the permission to perform various types of action without the interference of others. Two variants of these rights exist. The first variant (which I will develop in detail in Chapter Four and term 'liberty') roughly translates into the lack of external coercion. These negative rights do not create obligations on other parties except in the passive sense of 'action' (analyzed in Chapter One) of not interfering with the exercise of the right.

The second variant of negative rights, sometimes called 'claim rights,' and which I will term 'negative claim rights' to distinguish them from 'positive claim rights,' do create obligations on others (e. g., the government) to protect the exercise of the rights. To the extent that civil liberties are construed as claims whose exercise is protected by other parties, they are best construed as claim rights. An ambiguity can now be noted in the phrase "you had no right to act that way" between the claim that the act was forbidden (the denial of the first variant) and the claim that the act was not protected by others (the denial of the second variant). Examples of negative claim rights include the rights to free speech, to assemble, and to privacy. The right to privacy (which interestingly is never explicitly stated in the U. S. Bill of Rights), for example, roughly translates as the freedom of either an individual or a group to live their life as they wish so long as others are not causally affected.

The second category of rights, positive rights, involve claims to benefits. These 'rights' (but not 'freedoms') consist in claims to the existence of various types of situations which the agents themselves do not have complete control over. Thus, unlike negative rights, they create positive obligations on the parts of others to create these situations. These are sometimes called 'positive rights,' 'positive claim rights,' or 'entitlements.' Examples of positive rights would include such often-alleged rights as those to education, to shelter, to medical care, to a job, and to police protection.

My next point involves noting that many purported positive rights (e. g., the right to life, and several often-claimed purported rights which were not on any of the previous lists such as those to shelter, nutriment, breathable air, and at least rudimentary medical care) involve what may be termed the 'necessities' of life, as opposed to matters of mere desire. I will argue, citing a 'doctrine of necessity,' that rights to these necessities of life should take precedence over other rights. Since it may be doubted as to whether an entirely sharp distinction can be drawn between necessities and matters of mere desire (sometimes also known as 'matters of mere preference,' 'wants,' or 'luxuries'), a brief digression into the distinction may be useful at this point.

To begin my discussion of the distinction between necessities and matters of mere desire, it can be noted that if 'necessities' are defined as commodities which we literally cannot live without, then even such commodities as shelter outside the dead of winter, or any foods constituting more than is required for an absolutely minimal sustenance would be classified as 'matters of mere desire.' However, if the concept of needs is enlarged to take care of these sorts of cases it may be feared, in the other direction, that the meaning of the concept will continue to be expanded to such an extent that, as Herbert Marcuse (1964) fears, the labeling of matters of mere desire as 'needs' will be used by governments in power to maintain the status quo. For example, these governments may try to keep the masses in line by encouraging people to work hard to accumulate so-called 'necessities' that they have no time left over to question inequities in the political system, and thus possibly revolt.

To help resolve matters with respect to the foregoing issue of so-called 'needs' having a tendency to multiply, I wish to take note of an analysis of 'needs' given by David Braybrooke (1987). Braybrooke analyzes what he terms 'course of life needs' in terms of what is requisite to prevent 'functional disrangement' of a person from either a purely physical, a psychological, or even a social perspective. While noting that there is a tendency to expand lists of 'needs' even under this analysis, Braybrooke points out that, when challenged, the list can be retracted so as to just include a relatively-short 'basic' list, which Braybrooke gives in terms of both physical functioning and social functioning needs. It will be this relatively-narrow 'basic' sense of a 'need' which I will be using from here on. This completes my digression into the distinction between 'needs' and 'objects of mere desire.' Before I make use of these analyses in analyzing what it means to act in a 'fair' manner, I wish to make a few remarks on the issue of whether rights and duties are best construed as being absolute or whether they instead just apply *prima facie*, and thus may have exceptions in extenuating circumstances.

If a right is held to never possess exceptions, it is deemed to be 'indefeasible,' 'irrevocable,' or 'absolute.' In contrast, if a right can be overridden (e. g., if it is in conflict with another more stringent right), then the right can be labeled '*prima facie*,' in analogy with Ross's (1930/1988, p. 19) conception of 'prima facie duties.' If a *prima facie* right must also be conferred by another party (e. g., the state), it is often termed a 'privilege.' A good example of a privilege is that of possessing a driver's license, since such a license is both conferred and can also be revoked by the state. An example of conflicts between purported '*prima facie*' rights here would include the conflict, pointed out by Oliver Wendell Holmes, between the right to free speech and the right to life when 'fire' is yelled in a crowded theater. Another example would be the conflict between the respective rights of a free press and to a fair trial when there is a log of pretrial publicity concerning an upcoming criminal case. The issue arises then concerning which *prima facie* right should win out in these cases. I will be addressing this subject in subsequent sections.

A related concept to that of an 'absolute right' is that of an 'inalienable right.' As used by Jefferson, an 'alienable right' refers to a right which cannot be transferred to another agent. Inalienable rights are sometimes termed 'natural rights' (which Locke in his *Second Treatise on Government* (1690/1960, Ch. 2) discusses as being derived from 'Laws of Nature'), in the sense that they are held to be inherent in the human condition, and not derived by prior agreements, as in the case of legal rights. Obvious questions can be raised as to how so-called 'natural rights' are to be justified. However, since I am just introducing terminology here, I will not make a stand on this issue. I also will not take a stand here on the issue as to whether an inalienable right can ever be overridden or not; i. e., whether or not it is merely *prima facie* in character.

It should be clear form the foregoing considerations that one key issue to be dealt with in this chapter is whether it is possible to justify the existence of any rights in the strong sense of being exceptionless and hence irrevocable, or whether instead all rights are merely *prima facie* in character, albeit with different degrees of stringency. Also, it should be emphasized that both senses of 'rights' here need to be distinguished from 'duties' since there is no moral or legal obligation for people to exercise their rights but they are obligated, at least all things being equal, to act in accordance with their duties.

Section Two Tensions between Rights-based Theories and Utilitarianism

The existence of the rights and freedoms listed in the previous section (no matter which list is taken to be most primitive) is often deemed to be paradoxical for teleological consequentialist theories like utilitarianism. This is because what is being maximized according to utilitarianism is the general overall utility of all the people in a society, and since 'rights,' by definition, apply to individual agents. Hence, there is a built-in tension between utilitarianism and the ascription of at least absolute rights to individuals. For instance, the fallacy of division would obviously be involved if it was concluded from the fact that some type of situation was the best possible for an overall society, that it was also the best possible with regards to the interests of each individual agent in the society.

It can also be noted that 'best' solutions will often involve compromises from among the conflicting interests of different individuals, while the whole concept of compromise is anathema to the concept of decision-making by principles—be they purported 'rights,' principles of etiquette, or even particular moral rules or legal statutes—whenever it is claimed that these principles do not possess any exceptions. In short, it would seem that the maximization of overall utility will at least sometimes involve the unfair distribution of either benefits or harms with a society; i. e., distributing benefits or costs to one group in a society at the expense of some other group. Thus, the 'rights' of the latter group would be violated, at least according to some of the lists of 'rights.'

I will now illustrate the foregoing points by means of citing a few examples.

(1) A case where it is extremely expensive to provide a certain group (say, the severely handicapped, senile, or mentally retarded) with even the minimal

conditions for a productive life and where these same resources could be used elsewhere to greatly increase the standard of living for some other class of people in the society who were still, even initially, at least somewhat better off than the former group.

(2) Situations in medical research where, in developing a cure for some dread disease, some people's 'rights' are violated, such as if they are not told that they are part of the 'control' group and thus not receiving the most effective treatment for what ails them.

(3) A healthy person is deliberately sacrificed so that their organs can be used to provide transplants to several people desperately needing these organs.

(4) An enemy city is bombed to stop a war sooner.

(5) A drug offender is given an extremely long prison sentence so as to make an example to other potential drug dealers.

It would seem that in each of these cases partiality is being shown towards the interest of a whole society at the expense of the rights of a few of its members. Thus, in each of these cases fairness is not being shown towards these individual members or groups. An added issue concerning utilitarianism here stems from its 'impersonal' character. Here, obligations to any other people are held to count equally with obligations either to oneself or to others bearing Ross's (1930/1988, p. 22) 'special relations'— e. g., family members or parties to promises etc.

The question arises at this point as to how this tension between utilitarianism and theories which ascribe irrevocable 'rights' ought best to be resolved. In accordance with the fairness constraint previously sketched, I hold that rights that are truly irrevocable, and thus are not merely *prima facie* in character, will take precedence over utilitarian considerations. Since in this book I am grounding these irrevocable rights in the concept of fairness, I will now turn to that analysis.

Section Three The Nature of Fairness

In this section I will give a consequentialist account of 'fairness.' In order to adequately deal with this subject, I believe that it is necessary to separate the issue of judging the rightness or wrongness of actions or social policies in terms of their consequences from the issues of how these consequences are to be described for the purposes of ascertaining that rightness or wrongness. In particular, as I noted in the Introduction, I hold that these descriptions need not just be in terms of the intrinsic properties of the consequences, and will allow the descriptions to also make reference to causally relational properties among other consequences. This will be crucial in the analysis of what I take to be the essential moral insight of Kant's (1785/1959, p. 27) Practical Imperative holding that people should always be treated as an end and never just as a means. I also hold that, to use a phrase of Austin (1962b, p. 70), the negative usage, 'unfairness' 'wears the trousers,' in the sense that the positive usage is defined in terms of the absence of the negative usage. Thus, I will begin my treatment by analyzing the illocutionary aspect of the negative concept of 'unfairness,' and will then move on to analyze the locutionary aspect of the concept.

The illocutionary aspect of the meaning of 'unfairness' is the expression of a complaint on the part of either a single individual several individuals in a group against other members of the group or possibly the whole group in the collective sense. A second point concerning this illocutionary aspect involves the feature of supervenience, which it can be recalled I analyzed in Chapter One in terms of the holding of one (typically non-observable) property in virtue of the possession of other (typically observable) properties. Thus, instead of holding that the illocutionary aspect of 'unfairness' is an observable property (such as color) of situations per se, it rather either supervenes on the situations in virtue of relations of these situations to conscious agents, or supervenes on the relations per se between the situations and the conscious agents. For the purposes my discussion in this chapter, it will not matter which of the foregoing interpretations of the supervening relationship is taken. In other words, I am holding that given the existence of certain observable relations between a particular situation and various conscious agents, it will follow that either the illocutionary aspect of 'unfairness' applies to the situation or it does not; it possessing the property of 'unfairness' in virtue of the supervenience on these observable relations.

The issue can now be raised concerning the nature of the linkage between the illocutionary and the locutionary aspects of 'unfairness.' As I noted in Chapter One, my claim here is that the linkage is justificatory in character. That is, I hold that the negative attitude associated with the claim that a situation is unfair is justified by observable facts concerning whether or not it possesses any of the multiple criteria for unfairness. In particular, I will be claiming that if an agent is treated in an unfair manner then they would be justified in complaining against this fact inasmuch as what I will term their 'moral interests' are at least to some extent being sacrificed for the ulterior purposes of either other individual agents or an overall group. If none of the multiple criteria for unfairness are present then the situation can be judged as being fair. Of course, the preceding claims are compatible with the claim that asserters may be mistaken in that their complaints of unfairness may not actually be justified by the empirical facts to which they appeal. I will now turn to my analysis of the locutionary aspect of 'unfairness.'

Since the concepts of an 'interest' a 'moral interest' and an 'immoral interest' play key roles in my analysis of the locutionary aspect of 'unfairness' I will begin with a digression into the meanings of those concepts. Looking ahead, I might note that the concept of an 'interest' will also play a key role in my analyses of 'goodness' and 'badness' in Chapter Three. To begin my analysis of 'interest' it can be noted that when it is said that an agent has an 'interest' (or a 'stake') in a dispute it is being claimed that they stand to gain or lose something of value (i. e., either an item that is needed or an item that is merely desired, which I will term a 'want') depending on the outcome of the dispute. It can be noted that both needs and wants, inasmuch as they are possible situations, have the same ontological status as the consequences of possible courses of action or of social policies. In both cases the existence of tokens of the situations in question is contingent upon the occurrence of other events; e. g., the actual performance of the actions or the actual enactment of the social policies in question. It can also be noted that 'interest' is ambiguous between referring to a property of an agent (e. g., having a need or a desire), and the item which is needed or desired. In my usage I will use 'interest' in the first sense to refer to the fact that an agent has a need or a desire, and will use 'item of interest' to refer to the corresponding items which are either needed or desired.

Of course the fact that an agent has an interest in a dispute does not entail that other considerations cannot override the interest. That is, only a *prima facie* stake is being claimed here, not an absolute one. In order to avoid cases of sacrificing the moral interests of one party in order to advance the interests of others with these overrides, it is necessary to put a restriction on the nature of these overriding considerations that they only pertain to agents themselves and not to others. A distinction can now be drawn between 'moral interests' and 'immoral interests.' Inasmuch as I am introducing the concept of a 'moral interest' in order to explicate a theory of rights, it would be circular to analyze 'moral interests' as just those interests whose fulfillments do not conflict with the rights of others. Thus, instead I will present my analysis in terms of the needs and mere desires of different parties. Since I will be analyzing 'moral interests' in terms of those interests that are not 'immoral' (i. e., to use Austin's phrase again, I am claiming that 'immoral interest' wears the pants in the analysis), I will analyze 'immoral interests' first.

I will now present a stipulative, but non-arbitrary, definition of an 'immoral interest.' It should be emphasized at the beginning of my discussion, that in speaking of 'immoral interests' here I do not wish to imply that there is anything immoral about having the needs or desires in question. Instead, the claim is that it is immoral to act in such a way as to fulfill the needs or desires in question. I wish to define the 'immoral interests' of an agent so as to consist of two distinct components. The first component will be comprised of those needs of the person whose fulfillment conflicts with either needs of other agents which these others have a stronger claim to and which, if taken by the first party would seriously endanger the second party, particularly in a non-reversible manner. The second component will be comprised of those mere desires or wants whose fulfillment conflicts with either needs (including those whose occurrence can only be foreseen probabilistically) of others or with items of mere desire of others which have been established by stronger claims of these other agents. Again it should be emphasized that needs and wants per se are not being labeled as being 'immoral' here, but instead that actions taken in order to bring about their fulfillment are. The 'moral interests' of an individual can now be defined so as to include all of the individual's basic needs together with those items of mere desire which it would not be immoral for the individual to pursue.

As far as the issue of whether a distribution of items of needs and wants is fair or unfair to either an agent or a group of agents, it would appear that only the moral interests of the agents involved count in the determination. For example, I may desire some of the possessions of another person, but it does not follow that a social system is unfair when it does not provide me with them. As I will be elaborating on later, a stronger claim than one to wants can be made to the items of necessity constituting basic needs, even if they are not in a person's possession. This ends my digression into the concepts of an 'interest' and a 'moral interest,' and thus I will now turn to my actual analysis of the locutionary aspect of 'unfairness.'

To begin, I wish to take note of what I take to be an analytic linkage between the concepts of 'unfairness' and 'partiality.' If the existence of a situation does not possess any of the criteria for creating partiality towards the interests of an agent, then it can be characterized as being 'impartial' or 'fair.' It might be thought that acting in an 'impartial' manner just means taking the moral point of view, inasmuch as it is identified with a complete lack of provincialism, or being 'partial' to just the interests of a small part of a society. Thus, it may seem that acting impartially is consonant with what is permissible under utilitarianism, even if this does involve taking advantage of a few people for the overall societal welfare. However, I believe that it is possible to distinguish between 'strong' and 'weak' senses of 'impartiality' here. The weak sense will just coincide with the moral point of view, and thus does not allow decisions to be 'partial' just to the interests of any part of a society, as with institutionalized forms of racism or sexism. Thus, it forbids actions or policies which favor the interests of subgroups, such as ones of the same race or sex, at the expense of the moral interests of individual members of the overall society who are not also members of the subgroup.

The strong sense of 'impartiality' concerns decisions which are justified under the moral point of view, but where the moral interests of either an individual or a small group of individuals are sacrificed for the greater good of the overall society of which these individuals are members. Thus, under the strong sense of 'impartiality,' a decision made under the moral point of view may still be considered to be 'partial' to the interests of the majority of the members of an overall society and not to be 'impartial' to the moral interests of the minority groups making up the overall society. It can be noted that lack of 'impartiality,' in this strong sense, corresponds to what Mill (1859/1975, p. 6) called the "tyranny of the majority," inasmuch as Mill also was concerned with protecting the moral interests of minority groups from being sacrificed for the greater good of the majority. As my criteria for ascribing either 'fairness' or 'unfairness' to a situation, I will be using the respective strong senses of 'impartiality' and 'partiality.'

The locutionary aspect of what it means to act in an unfair manner can now be analyzed in terms of the showing of partiality by infringing upon the moral interests of others for the sake of either furthering the interests (whether moral or otherwise) of an individual or a whole group. It should be emphasized that this does not imply that it need be unfair to an individual when their moral interests are infringed on for that person's own sake. For example, I am not being unfair to a person if I deliberately cause pain to them, or even cause bodily harm, if this also saves their life. In this context, it should be emphasized that, under my analysis of an 'interest,' in stating that a person has an interest in a situation, only a *prima facie* stake is being asserted with respect to a situation. This *prima facie* stake can then be overridden by other considerations, so long as they pertain to the interests of the same person.

There are two distinct, although to some extent conceptually inter-connected, strains to the concept of 'fairness' which I will analyze separately in my next section; (1) a distributive justice strain concerning the manner in which various good and harms are distributed among the members of a population where nobody is actually adversely affected in the process, and (2) a strain which is best referred to negatively, whereby violations of a 'fairness constraint' (which I will be elaborately on in my next section) in the sense of the strain, involve situations where either an individual or a group of individuals is helped at the expense of another individual or a group. These violations are thus prohibited by Kant's Practical Imperative that people should always be treated as an end and never just as a means. In my next section, where I will give an account of distributive justice based on purely consequentialist principles, I will first develop some preliminary points that are relevant to both of these strains, and will then move on to develop consequential accounts of both strains separately.

Section Four An Account of Distributive Justice

I will now elaborate on the subject of a consequentialist account of the distributive justice strain of 'fairness;' i. e., what a fair distribution of goods and harms will involve when the issue of effects of the actions or policies on other people is not being raised. I will then move on to discuss the strain of 'fairness' which prohibits people from being used just as a means.

To begin my discussion of distributive justice, I wish to take note of three different possible bases which have been historically advocated for distributing goods and harms among the members of a population; those where they are distributed equally among all of the different members (as espoused by egalitarian theorists, and by Thomas More (1516/1964) in his *Utopia*); those where they are distributed on a basis of need (as espoused by Marxist theories); and those where they are distributed on a basis of merit (as under meritocracies, as advocated by some 'libertarians'). The question arises at this point as to which of foregoing possible methods of distributing goods and harms among the members of a population is also fair. In attempting to answer this question, I believe that much depends upon both what sorts of goods and harms are being distributed, and also upon the particular situations of the members of the population among whom the proposed distribution is to be made. For one point, it can be noted that it is only meaningful to speak of a distribution in accordance with need when what is being distributed involves basic necessities; i. e., anything from Braybrooke's list of 'basic needs'. Inasmuch as I have analyzed 'moral interests' as including basic needs, it follows then that when such basic necessities are involved a distribution in terms of first taking care of these basic needs is the only fair one, at least when there is a sufficient supply of the basic necessities to go around. In other words, the doctrine of necessity which I previously mentioned in my section on rights previously using a rights-based vocabulary, and reaffirming a principle which I stated earlier in the chapter, rights to at least the basic necessities of life take precedence over other purported rights.

It can be noted now that, even if we grant (as I just have) Marx's claim that at least basic necessities should be allocated in terms of need, the question still arises as to what constitute fair criteria for the determination of goods which go beyond basic necessities (i. e., matters of mere desire), since the 'need criterion' no longer applies here. One point that can be made regarding these cases is that the system for allocation should be consistent; i. e., that relevantly similar types of cases should be treated in the same manner. Beyond this principle though, the situation does not appear to be entirely clear-cut. For example, some (e. g., egalitarians) would advocate allocations which are distributed evenly. Others would try to base allocations on individual merit, at least in situations, such as in hiring and firing decisions where the concept applies. Interestingly, there are divisions among this latter group between those who would base merit in terms of personal desert (in which case the distinction between retributive and distributive justice would break down), and those who would base it in terms of personal abilities, as measured in any number of possible ways. I should note in this regard that Joel Feinberg (1970) has done an excellent job of distinguishing among these various different criteria and at pointing out that they really are not identical.

Thus, it would seem that just analyzing the concept of 'fairness' will not tell us which of the foregoing analyses should be picked as the relevant sense for determining principles of distributive justice, so long as the usage is consistent throughout. In other words, in being fair we cannot show partiality towards the interests of any individual or small group of individuals which is not in accordance with the individual's or group of individuals' particular merits under one of these conceptions of 'fairness.' It is not clear though, at least given what has been said so far, as to which sense is the most primitive. However, besides the foregoing negative points, I also think that within the context of consequentialism it is possible to make some positive remarks regarding the subject of which senses of 'merit' are relevant for determining principles of distributive justice.

Since I am confining my discussion to consequentialist systems, it can first be pointed out that any senses of 'merit' which are based solely in terms of desert per se will not be relevant to my discussion, inasmuch as I hold that desert is a past-oriented concept and not a future-oriented one. I might mention that Feldman (1997, p. 185) disagrees with this last claim, to which he gives a purported counterexample of the Make-a-Wish Foundation giving benefits to children with terminal illnesses as opposed to randomly-chosen children saying "since the children are quite innocent, and are going to suffer terrible harms, they deserve extraordinary benefits." I do not find this example convincing though since it can be as plausibly construed that because the terminally-ill children did not deserve death due to any actions in the past, they do not deserve death now, and that the present benefits to some extent even things out for these facts about the past.

From the preceding considerations it follow that senses of 'merit' which are based in terms of either past contributions or past effort, will only be relevant to the extent that these past contributions constitute evidence for future performance. That is, they are irrelevant to the extent that they constitute evidence for desert in virtue solely of what occurred in the past. It can also be noted in this regard that, in view of the future orientation of consequentialism, the sense of 'merit' which is most relevant (at least for situations where it applies, such as in hiring procedures) for this position is the one in terms of abilities, since that sense is the only one that is exclusively future-oriented. In fact, it would seem that, inasmuch as the only way in which any of the senses of 'merit' contribute to a consequentialist system is as evidence of future abilities, the 'ability' sense of 'merit' is the most primitive one from a consequentialist perspective, and that the others would be reducible to it. In summary, the only relevant senses of 'merit' that I need to be concerned with here are future-oriented ones, and it would seem that the most fundamental sense here is the sense of 'ability.'

As far as the issue of a fair distribution of needs and mere wants is concerned, it would appear that only moral interests count. For example, I may desire some of the possessions of another person, but it does not follow that a social system is unfair when it does not provide me with them. As I have argued though, a stronger claim than the one to mere wants can be made to the items of necessity constituting basic needs, even if they are not in a person's possession. Thus, these needs will be considered to be moral interests. Examples here, taken from Braybrooke's list of basic needs, would include claims to food, shelter, and basic medical care even when a person cannot afford to legitimately obtain these on their own. The doctrine of necessity, which I previously mentioned, can be invoked to justify this claim to basic needs. In a nutshell, this doctrine states that taking care of basic needs should always take precedence over taking care of mere desires, even when different agents are involved. In other words here it is claimed that one party has a positive right to the item fulfilling the need and that this positive right overrides other rights (e. g., property rights) to the same item by other parties. I take this doctrine to be somewhat controversial, since it might be held that it would be merely supererogatory (which it can be recalled from Chapter One means to be praiseworthy but not a duty) for the person with the prior claim to relinquish their claim here. However, I believe that the moral primitiveness of the doctrine of necessity can be justified, and I will now present a justification of the doctrine by using a variant on an argument given by Rawls.

In his account of distributive justice in *A Theory of Justice*, Rawls (1971) presents a variant on a social contract theory in defending an account of justice as fairness. As I pointed out in Chapter One, it is noteworthy that Rawls clearly emphasizes the role of consequences into account in judging fairness. Rawls places agents in a hypothetical 'original position,' behind a 'veil of ignorance' concerning their actual standing in their society, determine the rules of distributive justice for that society. I have a partial disagreement with Rawls's account of decision-making in the original position, which he claims will involve the maximin decision procedure of maximizing the minimum. In particular, Rawls makes the claim that people in the original position will use this decision procedure in order to motivate his difference principle holding that economic inequalities are only permissible when the least-well-off members of a society are helped in the process. My partial disagreement with Rawls can be motivated by taking note of a dispute between Rawls and John Harsanyi (1976, Ch. 4) on which decision-making procedure participants in the original position will use.

In contrast to Rawls's use of the maximin decision-making strategy with the difference principle, some utilitarians, notably Harsanyi, have argued for a 'Bayesian' approach for decision-making in the original position, whereby the criterion for making decisions there is in terms of maximizing the overall 'expected utility' (calculated by multiplying the probability of a potential course of action having a particular consequence by the utility of that consequence, and then summing up the results for the different possible consequences) of the different potential options. The claim then is that the participants in the original position should pick that option which maximizes this quantity regardless of whether it also maximizes the welfare of the least advantaged. I believe that the dispute between Rawls and Harsanyi can be best resolved as follows.

I find that it makes the most amount of sense to use the maximin decision-making procedure when we are dealing with things which we cannot afford to lose; i. e., the necessities or basic needs of life. It would appear then to be most rational to 'cover our losses' (the concept of 'failsafe' can also be brought in here) with respect to these basic needs, such as those on Braybrooke's list, by using the maximin strategy. However when we go beyond these 'basic needs' to matters of mere desire (such as deciding who gets to eat gourmet meals at fancy restaurants, who gets to live in a mansion, or who gets to have cosmetic surgery), then it is rational to take more risks and thus to use another decision-making procedure such as that of maximizing average utility or even maximax (going for broke or maximizing the maximum when things go our way) in these cases.

It follows from the foregoing considerations concerning the moral primitiveness of the doctrine of necessity that, all things otherwise being equal (e. g., with property right claims), conflicts between parties where what is a mere want on the part of one party and an item of necessity for the other party should be won by the party where the item is one of necessity. It also follows that societal policies should be steered towards taking care of the basic necessities of individuals prior to providing for mere wants. Examples here would include using taxes to fund basic universal healthcare, foodstamp programs, or public housing. If there is a concern that some will take advantage of such a system and not lead productive lives, one solution might be some version of workfare, as opposed to welfare, for those at least capable of being productive. If such a social safety net is in place, then the role of an individual agent in need will be to make use of the system. I will now discuss the second strain of 'fairness,' which involves using people just as a means.

Violations of the second strain of 'fairness,' involve issues where there is a violation of Kant's Practical Imperative holding that people should always be treated as an end and never just as a means. In elucidating the meaning of this imperative, I will first make some points concerning its role in Kant's system, and will then make some conceptual points on the meaning of the imperative per se. Kant (1785/1959, p. 39) asserts in his *Foundations of the Metaphysics of Morals* that the two versions of the Categorical Imperative are equivalent; the first version, which is akin to the Golden Rule, being that agents should act only in accordance with those maxims which they can will at the same time to be universal laws. In his *Critique of Practical Reason* (1788/1956, p.73) Kant again claims this equivalency and also (p. 90) attempts to derive the Practical Imperative from considerations involving respect for the autonomy of the wills of other agents. I find these claims to equivalency of the two imperatives quite dubious however.

In particular, it can be noted that, unlike Kant's first version of the Categorical Imperative which is purely formalistic (i. e., claims that the rightness or wrongness of a potential course of action can be determined solely in terms of whether or not it can pass a formalistic test for being 'universalizable'), the Practical Imperative can be interpreted as being completely consequentialist in character. This is because the key issue for determining the morality of an action under the Practical Imperative is whether the consequences of the action involve using anyone solely as a means. Thus, I take the Practical Imperative to be immune from the various counterexamples to the first version of the Categorical

Imperative deriving from its purely formal character. For example, a person may be willing to universalize various unsavory practices if they do not personally mind that they be inflicted on themselves, such as in the case of a sado-masochist universalizing the infliction of pain. In fairness to Kant though I should note that philosophers such as Marcus Singer (1961) have shown that it is possible to reformulate the first version of the Categorical Imperative so as to get around at least most of these counterexamples. It must also be admitted that I am giving the Practical Imperative a quite different justification from the one which Kant gave to it, which was in terms of the principles being synthetic *a priori* in character (being held to be universally valid for all rational agents), and where the moral worth of actions was held to be completely independent of the consequences of the actions.

Still, one aspect of Kant's justification for the Practical Imperative involves a point in common with my theory; that being that since humans possess an intrinsic value, they deserve a certain amount of respect in virtue of possessing this value. However, in contrast to Kant, who grounds the intrinsic value of human lives in the alleged fact that we are autonomous (self-determining, in the sense of possessing 'absolute freedom,' which is a concept which I will be developing in Chapter Four), I should note that I will be arguing against the existence of such an autonomy in Chapter Four. Instead, I will ground the intrinsic value of humans on the fact that we possess consciousness; which, again, is a point which I will be developing in more detail in Chapter Three. Under either account of what makes humans possess an intrinsic value though, it can be noted that when we are just using someone as a means, we are in effect just treating them as possessing instrumental value (in terms of what can be accomplished elsewhere by so treating the person), and may not also be respecting their intrinsic value as a person. What, in effect, is being asserted here then by the Practical Imperative is that it would be 'unfair' (in the sense of being partial against the person's moral interests) to the individual people so treated to treat some people just as a means and not also as an end. Thus, it would seem that to use people just as a means would involve not according a proper respect towards their right to have a say in the determination of their own futures. That is, one would not then be respecting either their autonomy (under Kant's justification), or the fact that they possess consciousness under my justification.

It can be noted next that, as with a teleological end, the manner in which a person is used as a means will itself be the consequence of an action or a social policy. Thus, Kant's imperative can be at least partially fleshed out in meaning as prohibiting possible courses of action or social policies which have consequences on one party which are causally dependent on the consequences of how another party is treated (the party used just as a means) but not vice versa. Only 'adverse consequences' (which is a concept which I will be analyzing in my discussion of positive and negative utility in Chapter Three) on the second party are meant to be prohibited here since otherwise the second party would not be used just as a means. Some further qualifications are required here as well. For one point, clearly it is only with respect to their moral interests that Kant wishes to prohibit a party from being used just as a means. For example, at least typically one is not using another party merely as a means if one prevents them from committing a crime.

A few distinct cases of means - end relationships should be distinguished here. In one type of case (as I noted earlier, sometimes called 'double effect') a course of action serves as a common cause for two events, only one of which is desired; e. g., unwanted collateral damage from some act which also has a good consequence. In the other type of case there is a causal relationship between two consequences (typically from the unwanted consequence to the desired one), only one of which is desired. A good example here is a medical experiment which results in useful knowledge for curing a dread disease but where the person being experimented on does not benefit. Both of these types of cases would be morally dubious since someone is both being used just as a means and is being harmed in the process.

Before making a few points of both comparison and contrast between the approaches to distributive justice of Rawls and Kant, I wish to take note of a few points concerning how the two approaches can be used to resolve conflicts with other ethical principles. To begin I will discuss the subject of conflicts in the fulfillment of needs; i. e., how disputes are to be settled when more than one party has a claim to an item of necessity. It can first be noted here that often, and perhaps even typically, what is a need for one person will not also be a need for another person. Hence, in these cases, all other factors (such as prior claims) being equal, the person with the need would have the stronger claim here. A complication arises though in cases where the item that would fulfill the need of one person is not itself of an item of necessity for a second person, but where the second person also has a prior claim to the item; e. g., by a property right. Examples here include the well-known cases of a hunter lost in the woods who breaks into a well-stocked hunting cabin belonging to somebody else; the case of stealing a car in order to escape an armed and threatening pursuer; and the case of stealing food or medicine in either a situation involving a severe shortage or because of poverty.

The just-mentioned cases tend to be more controversial than the previously-discussed case of claims to necessities that do not conflict with claims by others. This is because these cases involve violations of property rights and hence raise questions about the fairness to the parties whose property rights would be violated. However, as I noted in my discussion of Rawls, it can be argued that property rights need not be seen as being completely ethically inviolable and that claims to necessities are ethically more primitive due to the doctrine of necessity. Kant's Practical Imperative still applies to these cases though and thus the second parties in the cases (e. g., the respective owners of the cabin, the car, or the food) should not be used just as a means. In these examples then, the hunter should compensate the cabin owner for the property if (and when) he is able to do so at a later time. Similarly, the car thief should return the car to the owner when they are able to do so and the stealer of the food should repay the owner when and if they are able to do so. It can also be noted that, under my analysis, the doctrine of necessity applies whether another party is just unaware of a situation (as in the previously-cited cases) or even if they explicitly deny access to the item needed by the first agent. Thus in both of these cases the doctrine of necessity would supercede the claims of the other parties.

I will now turn to a discussion of cases where providing for the needs of one party is at the expense of the needs of the other party. In these cases, under my analysis the needs in question will be among the moral interests of both parties. Still, something has to give in cases where both sets of needs cannot be met. To resolve these sorts of cases where one party has a prior claim to a need (as in the organ transplant case, the party being sacrificed has with respect to their physical body), it can be noted that the person with the prior claim is being used just as a means. This is because they do not personally also benefit by what takes place. Thus, in the organ transplant case, since the party being sacrificed has a more primitive claim (based if nothing else on an inalienable property right, which interestingly Locke (1690/1960, p. 287) also claims, but which I will not justify further in this book) to their own body, it would be unfair to that party for the other parties (the parties needing the organs) to take the organs even if this maximized overall utility. Similar remarks would apply to the medical experiment case and the case of bombing an enemy city. In cases where no prior claims are involved by either party, and their needs are equivalent, then an impartial means must be brought in for arbitrarily deciding whose needs will be fulfilled; e. g. by random means such as a lottery.

I will now make a few points of comparison and contrast between the approaches of Rawls and Kant which will lead into a discussion of a 'fairness constraint' to be placed on utilitarianism which can handle the just-mentioned cases within a consequentialist, albeit not a completely teleological, framework. The approaches of Rawls and Kant can be seen to both have some features in common and also to have significant differences. One feature that is held in common (and which contrasts with all variants of utilitarian theories which I will be distinguishing in Chapter Three), is that they both include a prohibition on allowing considerations of maximizing overall utility to be at the expense of any individuals adversely affected in the process. Also, again unlike utilitarianism, according to both Rawls and Kant, maximizing utility within their constraints would be merely permitted and not mandated. However, they differ on the terms in which this prohibition is put into place. In particular, Rawls insists that people actually be helped in the process, at least if they are members of the least-advantaged group of a society. Kant in turn allows the overall utility to be maximized only in cases where no one is adversely affected in the process; i. e., where some people are used just as a means to an overall end. It should also be emphasized in this regard that Rawls, with his difference principle, is primarily concerned with the consequences of possible social policies, where the role of the individual would be confined to any assigned roles in carrying out these policies. In contrast, with his Practical Imperative, Kant is primarily concerned with stating a restriction on possible individual actions.

To the extent that there is a disagreement between the approaches of Rawls and Kant on the issue of distributive justice, my approach would be to create a synthesis of the approaches in terms of points previously developed in this chapter concerning the importance of respecting the moral interests of everyone affected by a decision. In particular, note can be made of the modification which I suggested in discussing Rawls's theory, that the maximin decision-making procedure only be used regarding the necessities of life and not elements (e. g., mere wants) that go beyond it. Thus, a compound distributive justice principle can now be stated combining these features of Rawls and Kant. This principle holds that consequences of decisions are not allowed to harm people (from Kant), and that people must also play any assigned cooperative social roles for purposes of helping to provide for the basic needs of those whose basic needs are not already being taken care of (from my modification of Rawls). In cases of conflict between the two parts of this principle (e. g., in cases where the only way to protect the moral interests of some people is to interfere with the moral interests of other people), then, as I noted in my analysis of 'fairness,' the qualified doctrine of necessity can be invoked which prohibits possible courses of action where another party either is put at risk for or actually receives any non-reversible harms in the process of fulfilling the needs of the first party.

A point of contrast can now be stated between the consequentialist system which I am advocating in this book and the systems of Rawls and Kant with respect to the issue of maximizing overall utility in a fair manner. It should be emphasized again that both Rawls and Kant merely allow considerations of maximizing overall utility to be invoked within the confines of the foregoing fairness constraint, and do not mandate it; i. e., make it a duty. In contrast, in my consequentialist system I will, at least sometimes, construe it as a duty to maximize overall utililty within the confines of these constraints. In other words, I both hold that a distributive justice (or fairness) constraint, as just given, needs to be put on the utilitarian theories which I will be discussing in Chapter Three, and also agree with these theories that there sometimes are duties to maximize overall utility, but only within these confines.

In summary, I am proposing that a 'fairness constraint' be placed on utilitarian ethical theories so as to avoid ethically problematic cases where overall societal utility is maximized at either the expense of an individual agent or a group of agents. I have argued that the concept of 'fairness' used in this constraint can itself be analyzed solely in terms of features of the consequences of actions or of social policies. I have also argued that two distinct consequentialist strains of 'fairness' can be analyzed in this regard; one in terms of distributive justice where claims to needs are given precedence over claims to wants, and one based on

Kant's Practical Imperative prohibiting either individuals or groups from being used merely as a means. I will now turn to my discussion of teleological (i. e., utilitarian) systems of ethics, which I am holding may be imposed within the confines of the fairness constraint just discussed.

Chapter Three
An Analysis of 'Best'

In the last chapter I argued that we should only pursue fair potential courses of action and social policies, and in this chapter I will present a criterion for picking particular potential courses of action which should be chosen from the set of fair potential courses. To ease the discussion I will use 'course of action' to refer to both individual courses of action and to the choosing of social policies. It can be recalled that in Chapter One I argued that we should pursue our best fair potential course of action. I will attempt to show here that there is enough content in this concept so that it can actually be used as a criterion for choosing a particular potential course of action. At times this criterion of choosing our best fair potential course of action will be used to determine whether different fair potential courses of action are morally acceptable or not. Even when no moral issues are involved it will still show us what we 'should' (in a non-morally-binding sense) do.

As I noted at the end of Chapter One, the relative merits of different fair potential courses of action here are to be judged solely in terms of their consequences. Since the concept of 'best' is teleological, the type of decision-making theory which will result here will have aspects in common with utilitarianism, although within the confines of a fairness constraint. I am using 'utilitarianism' in a broad sense here to refer to the class of consequentialist theories which are both teleological and use the moral point of view, without being confined to any particular account of what ought to be maximized under the theory; e. g., pleasure, happiness, or something else. I will begin my discussion by distinguishing among various senses of utilitarianism which have been historically advocated.

Section One Different Types of Utilitarianism

To begin my discussion of different variations on utilitarianism, it can be noted that, by the very definition of the position, all versions of utilitarianism make the claim that decisions should be based in some way as a function of the relative 'utilities' of the consequences of the different potential courses of action and social policies being considered. As I noted in Chapter One, I am using 'utility' in a broad sense to refer to the sum of the good consequences of a course of action minus the harmful consequences. Specific versions of the theory though will still possess both quite different specific conceptions of the nature of 'utility' and of algorithmic methods for determining the 'sum' of these utilities. In particular, some instances of more narrow conceptions of 'utility' would include Jeremy Bentham's (1781/1988) 'hedonistic' conception of the preponderance of pleasure over pain; Mill's (1861/1969) conception of 'happiness' which would include 'higher-order' pleasures such as intellectual ones; Hume's (1751/1948) conception of 'usefulness'; and R. B. Perry's (1926) conception of being a 'matter of interest.' It can also be noted that an ordinal conception of utility, which is hinted at by Mill when he discusses preferences, has been emphasized in the twentieth century by economists. Before proceeding further, some key distinctions among different versions of utilitarianism should be introduced.

First, note can be taken of a distinction which is often made between 'act' and 'rule' utilitarianism. This distinction was originally made by Rawls (1955), with the actual terms having been coined by Richard Brandt (1959). Act utilitarians hold the position that the overall utility of individual potential courses of action should be maximized. They also hold that while it may be useful to appeal to 'rules of thumb' in this regard to help reach decisions faster, whenever it is clear-cut that overall utility can be maximized by breaking one of these rules of thumb, we are justified in doing so.

In contrast, rule utilitarians hold that whole rule systems should be chosen in such a manner that, when the rules are generally followed by members of a populace (or, for some versions the rules are internalized by the members; see Brad Hooker (2000)), overall utility is maximized. However, unlike act utilitarians, rule utilitarians hold that these rules do not have exceptions, and thus that we must act in accordance with them even in individual situations where we would maximize overall utility by breaking the rules. I do not find this distinction between act and rule utilitarianism to be as fundamental as some, such as Hooker, do. This is because I find the distinction to break down as rules become more and more complex; i. e., as exceptions, based on act utilitarian considerations, are built into the rules themselves. In the limit, each rule here would just pertain to one highly-specific type of situation (there being a different rule for each slightly-different type of situation), and thus the position would then coincide with act utilitarianism. It can be noted that there is a tradeoff here though between the complexity of a rule and both its ease of application and the range of the cases to which it can be applied. I should also note that I will be later using a comparable distinction, in a broader sense than the strictly-utilitarian one just given, when I speak of 'act' and 'rule' forms of 'consequentialism.'

A second distinction concerning different types of utilitarianism, which in some respects I find to be more fruitful than the preceding one, is the distinction between positive and negative utilitarianism. Positive utilitarians hold that overall utility should be maximized even when this means that harmful consequences themselves will not be minimized; e. g., when another alternative potential course of action would produce significantly greater good consequences than the one that actually minimizes harms. Negative utilitarians, on the other hand, hold that we merely have an actual duty to minimize harms, and that the production of goods is merely supererogatory. They thus claim that the minimization of harms (both in the passive sense of not causing their occurrence and also in the active sense of preventing harms which would have occurred if not for the occurrence of the course of action in question) should always take precedence over the production of goods. I might note that the term 'negative utilitarianism' appears to have been coined by Ninian Smart (1958) in criticism of a version of the theory apparently advocated by Karl Popper in *The Open Society and its Enemies* (1945/1950, Ch. 5, n. 6). I should emphasize that Smart's criticism of Popper there (that in some realistic scenarios the doctrine would call for painlessly destroying the human race) do not apply to the system I am advocating since it includes death itself as a harm to be minimized.

I will now try to give a partial motivation to the position of negative utilitarianism, if this is construed as the claim that we only have a moral obligation to minimize harms and that we have no such obligation to maximize goods. To begin my argument here it can be recalled that in Chapter One I defined the concept of 'moral obligation' in terms of an agent being liable to the imposition of a penalty if they do not act in accordance with an obligation. It can be further noted that the imposition of a penalty inherently constitutes a harm; e. g., either loss of freedom, or the suffering of pain, or even death. It would obviously be circular to claim that because of the foregoing definition of 'moral obligation' negative utilitarianism must be true, since to do so would simply be to assume that minimizing harms should always take precedence over maximizing goods.

Still, I believe that some points which I will be developing later in this chapter concerning the linkage between value terms and personal preferences can be used to at least partially motivate the position of negative utilitarianism. In particular, later in this chapter I will be fleshing out the concept of 'best' in terms of a situation type being better than any other potential ones. I will also be fleshing out the concept of 'better' along lines suggested by Mill (1861/1969, pp. 38, 39) in terms of people's preferences. To the extent that people possess preferences, given the choice, for fewer personal harms instead of more goods (which sounds quite plausible when the harms are at all severe), then the position of negative utilitarianism will be to that extent motivated. It should be emphasized though that the subject of this book is broader than that of just specifying our moral obligations, and thus positive utilitarianism may still very well at least be germane to the determination of what we should do when issues of conflicting moral obligations do not arise.

In view of the foregoing points about negative utilitarianism, it can be noted that in decision-making contexts where potential harms are not involved it is morally permissible (in the sense that an agent will not be liable to the imposition of penalties), to use a narrower point of view than the moral point of view in making the decisions; i. e., by using any of the forms of provincialism or even egoism. For example, an individual may have no moral obligation to given to charity, even if doing so is morally praiseworthy. Thus, if they instead use the money to make themselves be happier, say by going to a movie, they are not doing anything which is morally prohibited, even if it is the case that there would have been a still better fair potential course of action.

Another key distinction which can be drawn between different versions of act utilitarianism concerns the issue as to whether they are 'cooperative' or not. By 'non-cooperative act utiltitarianism' I am referring to the position holding that an individual should choose the potential course of action which has the best overall consequences taking the courses of action of other agents as a given. In contrast, by 'cooperative act utilitarianism' I am referring to the position holding that cooperating groups of agents should determine what would be the best potential course of action for the whole group (again taking the actions of non-cooperators as a given), and where each individual agent is then assigned his best role within the group context. A cooperative version of utilitarianism has been worked out in detail by Donald Regan (1989) and Michael Bratman (1999, Part 2) has done a lot of work on analyzing 'cooperative decision-making.' Cooperative versions have the merit that such paradoxes as the prisoner's dilemma (which I will be discussing later) can be avoided.

Thus, according to cooperative utilitarianism, by opting for a cooperative scenario, sometimes decisions made cooperatively by agents together will result in the existence of situations of a significantly better type than those which would have existed if these decisions had been made by individual agents acting exclusively alone. I should note that the version of act consequentialism which I will be defending in this book will be cooperative in character, although there is one key difference with Regan's versions. Regan make the issue of cooperation out to be all or nothing, and I view this as being unrealistic. Often, two parties who are cooperators on one issue are bitter rivals on another. As the saying goes, politics, at times, makes strange bedfellows. Thus as H. A. Prichard (1949, p. 175) has pointed out, cooperation may either involve more than one party working towards a common end by seeing to the attainment of complementary means to that end, or instead involve parties with quite disparate ends sharing in the attainment of common means to those disparate ends.

To enlarge on these points in a bit more detail, it can be noted that in order to cooperate on either ends or means, some communication (even if it does not involve explicit agreements) is necessary among the communicators. This is necessary both for reasons of avoiding duplication of effort and also to ensure at least consistency among approaches. It can also be noted that there can be dangers of either getting ends and means mixed up with each other, or also continuing to pursue means even after ends have shifted. A good example of this last type of situation would be the case where, in spite of a change in career path, a person (perhaps out of habit) still continues to follow courses of action which are not conducive to achieving the new path, but only the old one. Another example here would be the case of a country continuing to spend large sums on an armament program after any threats to its security have disappeared. In view of the foregoing points concerning mixed and complicated cases of cooperative efforts, I will treat the issue of cooperation as being subject both to degree and to context in my subsequent treatments of the topic.

Before continuing to develop a theory of cooperative act consequentialism in more detail, I wish to take note of two distinct issues which may, at least when looked at *prima facie*, lead to someone being skeptical about the feasibility of even the general enterprise of teleological ethical theories, even with a fairness constraint. In the first place, someone may be worried that if we pursue a potential course of action just slightly different from what is the best fair potential course of action, this will make us be liable to moral censure. Secondly, someone may be worried that the way in which different people will judge the relative merits of various goods and harms will vary, and thus that there will be no objective manner for determining which fair potential course of action is really the best potential one. It can be noted that the two issues are logically dependent, in the sense that the first one only arises if, with respect to the second issue, there is always an effective means for determining what the best fair potential course of action is. It is important that these two issues not be conflated though, and thus I will deal with them separately, starting with the first one.

With regard to the first issue, that we have a moral obligation to perform our best fair potential course of action, I wish to re-emphasize a point which I developed in Chapter One. That point is that 'should' and 'ought' are not always used to express moral obligations (in the sense of entailing liability to penalties if we act otherwise), since their 'illocutionary force' is often milder, as in the case of a mild recommendation. Thus, even while I am arguing that what we should do always coincides with what our best fair potential course of action is, it certainly does not follow here that we should be liable to censure of any type if we do something different. It will all depend on the details of the situation in question as to whether any reaction is called for at all, and I will be dealing with this subject in detail in Part Two in Chapters Seven and Eight respectively on the judicial and post-judicial systems.

With regard to the second issue, that the concept of 'the best' is so subjective that one person could arbitrarily contradict another person's claim that one situation is better than another one, I wish to argue that this can be seen not to be the case once the concept of 'the best' is sufficiently well understood. In other words, I will argue that the notion of 'our best fair potential course of action' in fact is both considerably more subtle and possesses more objective content than may appear on the surface, and thus does provide an objective criterion.

To begin my argument here, it can be recalled from my analysis in Chapter One that 'best' is the superlative form of comparison of 'good.' Thus, the claim that a particular fair potential course of action is the best potential course entails that its 'summation' of good and bad consequences must be at least as great as the analogous 'summations' for all other fair potential courses of action. This is, of course, consistent with the consequences of the best fair potential course of action not themselves just being good, to the exclusion of all bad consequences, since they could still involve a significant, albeit minimal, amount of harms. Before moving on to give an analysis of what a 'summation' of goods and harms entails, it is necessary to first make digressions both into the natures of goodness and badness.

Section Two An Analysis of 'Good' and 'Bad'

In this section I will defend the position that the value terms 'good' and 'bad,' like 'should' and 'ought,' possess both illocutionary and locutionary aspects to their meanings. In particular, I will argue that the respective illocutionary aspects of 'good' and 'bad' are commendation or approval, and discommendation or disapproval, on the part of the person making the assertion. I will also argue that it is part of the meanings of "good' and 'bad' that the commendation or discommendation here is not arbitrary, but that instead it is justified by locutionary aspects of the situations which are characterized as being good or bad. Hence, the commendation or discommendation can also be said to supervene on the just-mentioned locutionary properties. I will now elaborate in more detail on both the illocutionary and locutionary aspects of 'good' and 'bad,' beginning with the illocutionary aspects.

The illocutionary aspects of the meanings of 'good' and 'bad' were analyzed in some detail by members of the emotivist school in ethics; notably by Ayer (1936/1952, Ch. 6) and Stevenson (1944). Stevenson's analysis is somewhat more sophisticated than Ayer's, but both analyze value judgments in terms of either the expression of positive or negative emotions on the part of the speaker and the attempt to evoke similar emotions on the part of the listener. I hold that Ayer and Stevenson make an error in thinking that their analyses constitute complete analyses of value judgments, since the analyses ignore the locutionary aspects of the meanings of 'good' and 'bad.' Still, I believe that if the analyses are more narrowly construed as just being of the illocutionary aspects of the meanings, then they are basically on the mark. Before turning to my analyses of the locutionary aspects of 'good' and 'bad' I wish to make a few remarks on the nature of the linkage between the two aspects.

As with my analyses of the illocutionary and locutionary aspects of 'should,' 'ought,' and 'fair,' I will construe the linkage between the supervening illocutionary force and the locutionary force of 'good' and 'bad' as being justificatory in character. That is, I will argue that when the existence of a situation is characterized as being respectively 'good' or 'bad,' then a claim is being made that the respective illocutionary forces of commendation or discommendation on the part of the asserter are justified by empirical facts about the situation in question. I will also argue that there are multiple criteria for the respective locutionary aspects of goodness or badness.

Of course, the preceding claims are compatible with the claim that an asserter may be mistaken in that their commendation or discommendation may not actually be justified by the empirical facts that they appeal to. Still, I am claiming that there is at least some objectivity to the justificatory linkage between the illocutionary and locutionary aspects of value judgments. In particular, I will argue that when a speaker asserts truthfully that a situation is good or bad, then the respective illocutionary aspects of commendation and discommendation are objectively justified by facts concerning whether or not the existence of the situation fulfills the interests of the speaker or other agents the speaker cares about. The fact that the commendation or discommendation is justified in one of these manners will then constitute the locutionary aspect of the assertion that the situation is respectively good or bad. I will now develop the subjects of this locutionary aspect in somewhat more detail.

When the existence of a situation is justified in being good in virtue of properties it possesses per se, it is termed 'intrinsically good.' In contrast, when a situation is justified as being good in virtue of the nature of the existence of other situations which it will causally lead to, it is termed 'instrumentally good.' A plausible list of intrinsic goods would include life itself, political freedom (as distinguished from the concept of 'freedom of the will' which I will be analyzing in Chapter Four), pleasure, and beauty. A good example of an instrumental good would be money, since (with the possible exception of misers) it is not desired for its own sake, but rather in terms of what can be gained from it.

It can be noted that there is a tie-in between the concepts of being an 'intrinsic good' and being an 'end,' and between being an 'instrumental good' and being a means. Intrinsic goods, like ends, are pursued for their own sake, while instrumental goods, like means, are pursued for the sake of something else. Thus, it can be noted that instrumental goods are justified by the intrinsically good situations which they are judged to be at least likely to causally lead to. It should be emphasized though that means need not always be intrinsically good in character (e. g., suffering pain when going to a dentist), and thus the concept of a 'means' is broader than that of an 'intrinsic good.' Ends though will always involve intrinsic goods, since they are always desired for their own sake.

Since instrumental goods are being analyzed in terms of their effective conduciveness towards the achievement of ends, it can be noted that the same situation may be instrumentally good from one perspective and not instrumentally good from another perspective. For example, a thick, boring book may possess instrumental worth as a doorstop even though it does not possess much instrumental worth as judged by its intellectual contents. Similarly, a gun may be judged as being instrumentally good in terms of its ability to accurately propel a bullet at a target, but not in terms of its probable use being conducive towards maintaining a peaceful society. A related point to make here is that the criteria in terms of which a situation is judged as being instrumentally good may not be the same as those which were originally intended by the designer or author. For example, a novel or a movie that was originally intended to be taken as a serious work of art, may possess its greatest instrumental value on quite other lines; e. g., if taken for comic relief.

It should also be noted that the same type of situation may serve both as a means and also as an end. For example, taking a trip may both serve as a means for getting to one's final destination and also be pursued for its own sake, say if the drive is particularly scenic. Another point to make here is that there can often be a hierarchy of ends, whereby the pursuit of one end also constitutes a means for attaining a more ultimate end. A good example here is the pursuit of the various stages of the educational process, where the attainment of each stage (e. g., passing a certain grade) serves as a means for attaining the next stage of the hierarchy. Even attaining what may seem to be the ultimate end of the process here (e. g., getting a degree), may also serve as a means of obtaining a still further end (e. g., getting into a career), which may serve as a means to make more money, and so on.

This completes my discussion of the nature of instrumental goods. Since these goods have been analyzed in terms of causally leading to intrinsically good situations, it would seem that the concept of an 'intrinsic good' is the more primitive concept. Thus, I will now begin my analysis of the locutionary aspect of intrinsic goods by taking note of tie-ins with the concepts of 'interests' and 'desires.' I will then turn to a brief discussion of the nature of badness. Finally, I will conclude the section by making a few remarks on the connection between consciousness and goodness and badness.

The first point which I wish to address concerning the nature of intrinsic goods involves an analogous distinction to the one which I made concerning 'should' and 'ought.' This involves the width of the point of view being used; i. e., whether the well-being of everybody is being taken into account as with the moral point of view, or whether any of the various forms of provincialism are being used instead. The analogous distinction with respect to goodness and badness is the issue of with respect to what group of people a given situation is being characterized as being 'good' or 'bad.' For instance, what constitutes an intrinsic good for one person, may not constitute an intrinsic good for someone else. A good example here is that of tastes in food. Still, I will now argue that a general theory of intrinsic goodness can be developed in terms of the identification of at least relatively-universal common needs and desires. It should be emphasized that, unlike the situation concerning the connection between 'ought' and 'best,' a distributive and not a collective usage of these common needs and desires will be used. That is, even in the case of universal goods, my position is that what makes a situation be a universal good is the fact that it fulfills either the interests or desires of individual agents, for each (or nearly each) of the agents.

I will now address the issue of how the illocutionary aspects of intrinsic goods (i. e., universal approval) can be justified by presenting two criteria for the locutionary aspects of intrinsic goods; universal needs and desires. In particular, I will try to show that there is a justificatory linkage between these illocutionary aspects and general features of human nature. I will argue that the justificatory linkage here both involves universal desires (e. g., for pleasure) and intrinsic needs; e. g., for health. To begin my argument, it can be recalled from Chapter Two, that I am using 'interest' in a sufficiently broad sense so as to refer to both needs and mere desires. Thus, the common needs and desires which constitute general features of human nature will also constitute universal interests. Next, it can be pointed out that if a situation possesses a feature which constitutes a universal characteristic of human nature, it follows that it will apply to each person individually. Thus, from the definition of an 'interest,' the situation will constitute an interest of the individual. It then follows that using either the moral point of view or even just the point of view of narrow self-interest, inasmuch as these are defined as looking out for the interests of the group involved, a reason is being given for the individual to approve of the situation. This, from the preceding analysis of 'goodness,' will then make the situation be good for each of these individuals, and thus be a universal good.

An interesting tie-in can now be noted between the foregoing discussion and the analyses of 'intrinsic goodness' given by Mill and Perry. In particular, it can be noted that Mill (1861/1969) presents an analysis of 'intrinsic goodness' in terms of what people are able to desire. Perry (1926) in turn develops a sense of 'interest' which is sufficiently broad so as to include both needs and matters of mere desire. I will now expand on both of these analyses, beginning with that of Mill.

In his *Utilitarianism*, Mill tried to broaden Bentham's (1781/1988, Ch. 3,4) analysis of what is good and bad solely in terms of bodily pleasures and pains, by means of distinguishing among various pleasures not just in terms of their 'quantity,' but also in terms of their 'quality.' In particular, Mill claimed that intellectual pleasures possess a higher quality (and thus a higher utility) than purely sensual bodily pleasures. Mill further argued that there was a linkage between the respective concepts of 'goodness' and 'badness' and the respective concepts of 'being desirable' and 'being undesirable.' Consider, in this regard, the following famous passage where Mill states that it is better to be Socrates dissatisfied than a pig satisfied.

It is better to be a human being dissatisfied than a pig satisfied; better to be Socrates dissatisfied than a fool satisfied. And if the fool, or the pig, are of a different opinion, it is because they only know their own side of the question. The other party knows both sides. (Mill 1861/1969, p. 39)

While, as I noted, the overt use which Mill makes of this passage is to claim that one can distinguish among pleasures in terms of their qualities and not just their quantities, it can also be noted that Mill's actual criterion for determining greater utilities is in terms of preferences, in this case the preference of Socrates for the intellectual life. It can also be noted that the concept of 'preference' is an ordinal concept (which just establishes an ordering but does not introduce any absolute magnitudes) rather than a cardinal concept, which does establish an absolute magnitude. This is because a preference merely establishes a ranking among various goods and harms without stating by how much.

As I noted earlier in my discussion of negative utilitarianism, the comparative form of comparison of 'good,' 'better,' is also an ordinal concept inasmuch as when it is claimed that one situation is better than another one, no claim is made either about whether the situations themselves are good or not, or about the extent to which one is better than the other. It can be further noted that, by introducing an ordinal sense of' 'utility,' Mill to some extent anticipated the sense of 'utility' in terms of preferences utilized by modern economic theory. It should be emphasized though that, as used in economics, utility is at least typically seen as being maximized from a narrow (e. g., an egotistical) point of view, and not the moral point of view, as with Mill's theory.

Mill also argued that the sole criterion for a situation's being desirable was that it was in fact desired. In an influential critique of Mill contained in his work *Principia Ethica* (1903/1971 Ch. 3), Moore argued that the concept of 'good' is indefinable, and he accused Mill of committing the 'naturalistic fallacy' for 'defining' it in terms of a 'natural property,' namely that of what people actually desire. It is noteworthy here that, as even Moore admits, there is a sense of 'desirable' which is synonymous with being good. But still the question arises then as to whether or not the fact that people actually desire that a given situation exist constitutes evidence that it is 'desirable' in this sense. In the following well-known passage, Moore argues against a claim made by Mill that grammatically the relation of 'desirable' to 'able to be desired' is analogous to the relation between 'visible' and 'able to be seen,' in the sense of meaning the ability to possess the corresponding property:

> The fact is that 'desirable' does not mean 'able to be desired' as 'visible' means 'able to be seen.' The desirable means simply what ought to be desired or deserves to be desired; just as the detestable means not what can be but what ought to be detested and the damnable what deserves to be damned. Mill has, then, smuggled in, under cover of the word 'desirable,' the very notion about what he ought to be quite clear. 'Desirable' does indeed mean 'what it is good to desire'; but when this is understood, it is no longer plausible to say that our only test of that, is what is actually desired. Is it merely a tautology when the Prayer Book talks of god desires? Are not bad desires also desirable? (Moore 1903/1971, p. 67)

Thus, Moore argues that it is not a mere tautology to claim that a situation which is desired is 'desirable' in the sense of being good, since it is at least conceivable for it to be the case that situations of undesirable types may also be objects of desire. In this regard Moore cites the case of a 'bad desire.' Apropos examples of what Moore is referring to would include the case of a child molester who desires to molest young children, or the case of a person desiring a cigarette in spite of the long-term health risks. There is a problem though if we use Moore's analysis of 'desirable' as what ought to be desired in the context of even a partial analysis of the meaning of 'good.' This is because I have previously analyzed 'ought' in terms of a prescription to perform our best fair course of action; i. e., maximizing the preponderance of what is good over what is bad in a fair manner. Thus, the analysis, in effect, would be circular since it is analyzing 'goodness' in terms of other cognate forms of 'goodness.'

I believe that it is possible to take cognizance of the force of Moore's point that it is possible to have 'undesirable' (in the sense of non-good) desires, without being committed to a circular analysis by presenting an alternative minimal analysis of 'desirable' which contains common features of the analyses of both

Mill and Moore. It is valuable at this point to do a bit of ordinary language philosophy, by investigating the issue as to in what circumstances in ordinary life a situation would be claimed not to be good in spite of the fact that it was desired by an agent. As far as I can see in all cases here (e. g., the ones of the child molester or the cigarette smoker) what seems to be really going on is that additional evidence is being invoked beyond the fact that the situation is desired; e. g. the effects on the child in the child molester case and the long-term health risks on the cigarette smoker. The role of the additional evidence then is to take back a claim to goodness which was *prima facie* established by the claim that a situation was desired.

Next, it can be noted that, inasmuch as the cognate form of 'desirable' in all of its senses is 'desire,' there should be at least some linkage between the various senses. Thus, at a minimum it would seem that the fact that a situation is desired is at least positively relevant to establishing its 'desirability,' even in the sense of being good. If this is the case, then it would follow that the burden of proof would fall on another party to show that the situation is not 'desirable,' in the sense of being good, in spite of being desired. In other words, I am claiming that the fact that a situation is desired constitutes at least *prima facie* evidence of its 'desirability' in the sense of being good. To sum up, it seems to me that it is analytic to claim that being 'desirable,' in the sense of being good, entails that if a situation is desired then this fact constitutes *prima facie* evidence for the situation's being good, and that this claim can only be taken back by means of providing positive evidence to the contrary.

One caveat which should be brought in here, and which concerns both the analyses of Mill and Moore, is that philosophers ranging from Plato to Descartes have claimed that we can only desire a situation of a given type if a situation of that type does not currently exist. However, it can be noted that we certainly would wish to characterize certain existent situations as being good, and hence desirable. In order to rectify matters here, it would seem that both Mill's and

Moore's analyses need to be reworked in terms of subjunctive conditionals. Mill's claim would then be expressed as the claim that the existence of a situation of a given type is desirable if and only if, should a situation of that type not currently exist, we would be able to desire that it exist. Analogously, Moore's claim would then be that the existence of a situation of a given type is desirable if and only if, should a situation of that type not currently exist, then we ought to desire that it come into existence. This completes my discussion of Mill's theory of the nature of 'goodness' and thus I will now turn to my discussion of Perry's theory of value.

Perry, in his *General Theory of Value* (1926, Ch. 5), presented an explication of 'goodness' in terms of being an object of interest. Perry uses 'interest' in a broad sense so as to include instincts, desires, feelings, willings, and the associated family of states, acts, and attitudes. As I noted in Chapter Two, one might want to add needs to this list. An act, in turn, is defined (p. 183) as being 'interested' insofar as "its occurrence is due to the agreement between its accompanying expectation and the unfulfilled phases of a governing propensity;" i. e., a disposition. Perry also conceived of interests as being relative to agents, and claimed that our knowledge of individual interests was to be determined empirically. The net result is that a synthetic attempt is being made to construct values out of the interests that agents actually possess. Perry also held that this enterprise could be objective (in the inter-subjective sense), to the extent that the 'general interest' of a group of individuals is empirically discoverable.

Perry's theory was criticized on two counts by Ross (1930/1988, Ch. 4). First, Ross argued that the theory would lead to a relativism of values, inasmuch as the existence of a situation of a type which may be of positive interest to one agent may be of negative interest to another agent. Also, Ross argued that it does not follow from the fact that goodness is not an observable property per se, that it possesses a relational character. Instead it may be a monadic property that is discernable of situations in other ways than by sense perception; e. g. by the intellect or by intuition. In reply to the first criticism, it can be pointed out that the charge of relativism of values can be avoided to the extent that Perry was concerned with general interests, or universal interests, inasmuch as by definition each individual will at least have these interests in common. With respect to the second criticism, questions can both be raised as to the very existence of the moral intuition which Ross points to and certainly also on the issue as to whether, even should such an intuition exist, everyone will share the same moral intuitions. Also, it should be pointed out that on my account criteria for at least the locutionary aspect of goodness are observable.

In closing my discussion of Mill and Perry, two points of contrast with my account should be noted. First, it should be noted that Perry's sense of 'interest' may be somewhat narrower than mine, since, as I pointed out earlier, Perry did not at least explicitly include mere needs in his analysis. It can also be noted that any attempt to analyze 'intrinsic goodness' by just appealing to desires, as Mill does, will fail as a complete analysis, since there may be bodily needs which an individual does not desire, merely due to ignorance. Thus, the analyses of 'goodness' of Mill and Perry can be seen to complement each other. These analyses can also be seen to justify members of the list of intrinsic goods which I gave earlier, since some, such as health and life, seem to involve both interests and desires, while others, such as pleasure and beauty, would seem to just involve desires. In fact, some intrinsic goods, such as those that are necessary for one's continued good health, but which one does not know about, would be a matter of interest but not of desire. This completes my discussion of intrinsic goods, and I will thus now turn to my discussion of badness.

Since the locutionary aspect of 'good' has been analyzed in terms of what fulfills an interest or desire, it would seem logical for the locutionary aspect of the opposite of 'good,' 'badness,' to be analogously analyzable in terms of the opposite of being an interest or desirable; i. e., in terms of going against interests or desires. Once again, a distinction can be made here between types of situations which are bad in themselves and types of situations which are merely likely to lead to the occurrence of intrinsically bad situations (what I have been calling 'harms'). By analogy with the case of intrinsic goods, where it was seen that these were discoverable by investigating what types of situations are normally the object of positive interest, cases of intrinsically bad situations can be discovered empirically by investigating what types of situations are the objects of negative interest; i.e. types of situations which will normally be avoided for their own sake. A plausible list of such types of situations would include, but would not necessarily be limited to the following; pain, death, disability, and lack of political freedom. An example of an instrumentally bad situation would be the performance of a dangerous daredevil stunt. This is because, even though on a particular occasion no intrinsically bad situations may be involved, it is nevertheless at least likely to lead to such intrinsically bad situations as pain, disability, or even death. I will now close this section by briefly investigating the role of consciousness in the distinction between intrinsic and instrumental values.

With respect to the issue of the role of consciousness in the distinction between intrinsic and instrumental values, my main claim is that intrinsically goods and bad situations always involve states of consciousness per se. This can be seen to contrast with Kant's (1786/1959, p. 9) claim that intrinsic value only lies in the motives of an autonomous free will; e. g., the good will which acts out of duty. Looking ahead, I might note that I will be arguing against the existence of this sense of freedom in Chapter Four. The situation is somewhat different with respect to instrumentally good and bad situations though. While, as I previously noted, instrumentally good and bad situations must at least bear relations to conscious states, they obviously need not also include these states as internal parts of themselves. Thus, I wish to argue against a claim made by Moore that a 'garbage world' would be objectively worse than an extremely beautiful world even if, in principle, no one could ever be consciously aware of either world. In *Principia Ethica*, Moore makes the following remarks in comparing the 'garbage world' with the beautiful one:

> The only thing we are not entitled to imagine is that any human being ever has or ever, by any possibility, can, live in either, can ever see and enjoy the beauty of the one or hate the foulness of the other. Well, even so, supposing them quite apart from any possible contemplation by human beings; still, is it irrational to hold that it is better that the beautiful world should exist, than the one which is ugly; would it not be well, in any case, to do what we could to produce it rather than the other? Certainly I cannot help thinking that it would. (Moore 1903/1971, p. 84)

To begin my argument against Moore, I would first note that it is at least evident that intrinsic values do come into play when conscious beings are being dealt with. For example, conscious beings are clearly capable of being aware of pleasures and pains, and I have argued that these at least constitute instances of good and bad situations. I might note though that some of the intrinsically good and bad situations which I have listed—e. g., political freedom, the fulfillment of desires, death, and disability—while they may involve conscious states, cannot be completely explicated in terms of such states. For example, political freedom and disability clearly involve the abilities or inabilities of agents to perform various potential actions in the physical world, and thus clearly cannot be analyzed in terms of conscious states alone.

In contrast to the situation with intrinsic values, it is easy to see how the existence of physical situations by themselves could be instrumentally good or bad. Examples from science and industry are obvious here. For instance, a car may serve as an instrumental good in virtue of its providing a reliable method of transportation, even though obviously no parts of it are conscious. However, I do not see how purely physical states could just in themselves be intrinsically good or bad, since the question can always be raised as to how any one such state, considered as being in any way better or worse than any other state.

Thus, it would seem that intrinsic goodness and badness are supervenient properties on either the existence of situations in virtue of their relations to conscious agents, or on these relations per se. Since we are dealing with rational reconstructions here, I take it to be arbitrary as to which syntactical construal is to be taken. Under either construal though it would follow that a syntactical error must be occurring with Moore's claim that intrinsic values can exist in the absence of consciousness since the first-place argument (the agent argument) in the relation which must be present in order for a value to supervene on a situation is missing. In this regard I might also note that in Chapter Five I will be arguing that an analogous syntactical error concerning the proper subject matter of values, only in reverse to this case, may be inherent in retributive theories of punishment, although I will also argue there that the error may instead be semantic in character. In any event, to me the utter pointlessness of a physical world where no consciousness is ever aware of it, or causally connected to it, is self evident, and I do not know how to make this point any more strongly.

In closing this section, it should again be emphasized that the analysis of goodness and badness given here involves a somewhat broader conception of those concepts than was given by such classic utilitarians as Bentham, who analyzed them solely in terms of quantity of pleasure and pain. For example, Mill distinguished among pleasures in terms of quality as well as quantity (intellectual pleasures being held to be of a higher quality) and, as Moore pointed out, there are other instances of goods besides pleasures. Also, Moore took note of an 'organic' principle in this context, noting, for example, that the existence of an overall situation may be good as a whole even if this is not true of each of the individual parts making it up. A corresponding example from aesthetics would be that of a beautiful painting whose individual parts are not each by themselves very beautiful at all. Moore's point will also have bearing on my upcoming analysis of our 'best fair potential course of action,' since an overall holistic standpoint will be necessary there as well. Thus, I will now move on to discuss possible ways for 'summing up' the good and bad consequences of fair potential courses of action so as to determine which fair potential course is the best fair potential course.

Section Three The Determination of What is Best

Having discussed the nature of goodness and badness at some length, I would like to now turn to a discussion of the key issue for the whole enterprise of consequentialism of how these values can be objectively 'summed up' so as to determine what an agent's best fair potential course of action would be in any given situation. I have noted earlier that 'best' is the superlative form of comparison of 'good,' and thus it would seem that a possible strategy to pursue here would be to analyze 'the best fair potential course of action' in terms of its being the upper limit of a series of comparisons among alternative fair potential courses of action. Another useful concept to bring in here is the comparative form of 'good,' 'better,' since, as I noted earlier in the chapter, 'better' is an ordinal concept. Hence, for a succession of pairs of alternative fair potential courses of action, the question can be repeatedly raised as to which alternative is better. It would seem then that one fair potential course of action could be objectively analyzed as being 'better' than another fair one if the preponderance of its good consequences over its bad consequences was greater. A 'fair potential course of action' could in turn be determined to be the 'best fair alternative' if no other alternative fair potential courses of action would lead to still better consequences, with the implicit assumption here that ties do not exist.

One key issue, which should be addressed right at the beginning of my discussion here, concerns the amount of information with respect to which decisions concerning the determination of the best fair potential course of action are to be made. It is useful in this regard to take note of a three-way distinction which was drawn by C. I. Lewis (1969, Ch. 2) between potential courses of action which are 'absolutely right,' those which are 'objectively right,' and those which are merely 'subjectively right.' By 'absolute rightness,' Lewis referred to the best potential course of action given all of the relevant facts; i. e., as an omniscient agent would see them. 'Objective rightness' is in turn used by Lewis to refer to the best potential course of action relative to an agent's readily available information,' and 'subjective rightness' is used to refer to cases where an agent's motives were praiseworthy. I might note that Sidgwick (1907/1981, p. 207) also distinguishes between objective and subjective rightness.

Since 'subjective rightness' is not consequentialist in character, I need not be further concerned with it at this point. However, the issue does arise as to whether 'absolute rightness' or 'objective rightness' constitutes the germane sense of 'rightness' for the issues being addressed in this book. It is true that the absolute sense of 'rightness' may convey an absolute standard by way of which the rightness of courses of action may be judged in retrospect. Nevertheless, to the extent that a practical guide to decision-making is being offered here, 'objective rightness' would appear to be the relevant sense. This is consonant of course though with the claim that access to relevant information is to be maximized at least with respect to situations where there is very much at stake and where there is sufficient time and opportunity to gather the information. Looking ahead, I might also note that the distinction between absolute and objective rightness will be relevant to my analysis of excuses involving ignorance of fact in Chapter Six.

A second major issue which should also be addressed at the beginning here concerns whether it should be the total preponderance of goodness over badness in the world which should be maximized in making decisions, or whether instead it should just be the average preponderance of goodness over badness with respect to individuals. It might be noted in this regard that Sidgwick (1907/1981, p. 415) advocated just maximizing the average preponderance of goodness over badness, which may appear *prima facie* to possess considerable merit in view of problems of overpopulation. At least it is not clear to me that a world where there are many billions of people holding onto a marginal, but still positively-valued, existence, is a better world than one which is less populated but where people are on the average much happier. However, it is also not clear to me that it is better to have only one person who is very happy rather than a large number of people who are on average just slightly less happy, which would be *prima facie* evidence against Sidgwick's claim. It would seem then that there is a need for a weighted function here which both takes into account the fact that an increase in population per se need not constitute a great good where there is little average happiness, but which also takes due account of the happiness of others in making it be a better world. I will not attempt to derive the character of such a function in this book though. I might also note that Derek Parfit in *Reasons and Persons*, (1984, Ch. 17) refers to this problem in his discussion of the 'repugnant conclusion.'

Since the moral point of view has been used in the preceding analysis, it follows from a principle of indifference that equal consequences on different people should be counted equivalently in the determination of which fair potential course of action constitutes the best fair potential alternative. Thus, in making rational moral decisions, agents should first look at the various potential world states (which it can be recalled I defined in Chapter One as being physically possible states of the universe) which would result from the pursuit of different alternative fair potential courses of action. Again if it is assumed that ties do not exist, they should then choose the particular alternative fair potential course of action from this group which would result in the world state with the greatest preponderance of goodness over badness.

Since, as I just pointed out, the moral point of view involves acting in accordance with what is the best fair alternative for a whole society where the interests of all people count equally, it follows that the determination of what a 'best fair potential world state' would be can be made independently of any particular point of view. Also thus, at least in principle, it should be possible to make this determination objectively; i. e., where all perfectly rational agents with access to all pertinent information will reach the same conclusions. Therefore, I will not be concerned here with developing particular strategies for individual agents to decide what is the best of the fair alternatives just for themselves. Instead, I will just be concerned with developing strategies for deciding what is a best fair type of world state for societies as a whole. The only question for individual members of these societies will then be that of determining where they best 'fit in' fairly within the context of the larger societal framework so as to act cooperatively with other members in contributing to the best fair potential world state.

The foregoing approach has the merit of resolving certain paradoxes which have often been held to afflict variants of act utilitarianism. In particular, these paradoxes note that while decisions should be made on an individual basis, a 'best fair potential world state' can only be achieved when individuals cooperate among themselves, and that it is not in their best interest to do so if other individuals do not do so too. The best known case here is known as the 'prisoner's dilemma.' Here two prisoners can receive the shortest jail sentence if neither one cooperates with a jailer, but if either one cooperates with the jailer, the other prisoner will be better off if they too cooperate than if they do not. It would seem then that, from an individual point of view, each of the prisoners would be better off, not knowing what the other prisoner is going to do, by cooperating with the jailer. This is because then they will be at least avoid the worst possible consequence. However, it would also seem that they would both be even better off if neither one cooperated, and hence the paradox. Another variant of this paradox concerns an argument that there is no point in individuals voting in an election of any size, since one vote almost never turns a large election. Obviously elections can be lost if enough people think this way.

As far as I can see, the best fair solution to all versions of the prisoner's dilemma involve the use of a cooperative decision-making strategy. Before discussing the character of such decision-making in detail, a brief digression into the concept of 'cooperation' is in order. Judging from its roots, 'cooperation' can be construed as meaning 'operating together.' In order to further elucidate the meaning of the concept, both the ends - means distinction, and the concept of 'working together' must be analyzed.

It can be recalled from my discussions of the topic, both in Chapter Two in the context of Kant's ethics, and also earlier in this chapter, that an end is a situation whose existence is pursued for its own sake, whereas a means is a situation whose existence is pursued for the sake of something else; i. e., an end. It can also be recalled that I noted that there can be a hierarchy of ends, whereby one end may also serve as means for the accomplishment of another end further along the hierarchy and so on. The concept of 'working together' can in turn be analyzed in terms of various agents each performing individual actions of types such that the consequences of the actions, when put together, lead to a mutually desired result. Each agent must thus play an appropriate role so that when the roles are combined together they lead to the accomplishment of the task to be performed.

As far as putting together the concept of 'working together' with the ends - means distinction, two distinct cases need to be considered. In the first type of case cooperators share an ultimate end. Here, by means of cooperating, the cooperators will be playing mutually supporting roles in accomplishing the means to the end. It can be noted that according to Regan (1989) this type of case, where cooperators actually share an end, is the only type of cooperation. However, Prichard (1949, p. 175) has pointed out that it may also be the case that cooperators may not share actually ultimate ends, but merely share common means to disparate ends. It can be noted that, even in this latter case, it is still perfectly rational for cooperators to work together in order to accomplish the common means. 'Cooperation' can thus be analyzed in terms of the processes whereby either a group of agents, sharing a common end, each pursue individual means, which when placed together serve as causal components for the attainment of the common end, or where a group of agents possessing diverse ends, pursue common means to those ends. I will now discuss these two sorts of cases separately.

I will first discuss the case where ends are shared among cooperators and not just common means. I am using the concept of 'shared ends' here in the broad sense to not just include cases where agents actually share an end in common, but also to include cases where one agent, who at least is not a competitor with another agent in trying to attain mutually exclusive ends, aids the second agent in obtaining their goal by not going out of their way very much. A good example of this latter type of case would be an instance of a driver giving another person a ride when the driver is going in the same general direction as the person they pick up. The key point to make in all of these cases is that often much more can be accomplished by people working together than can be accomplished just working individually. In particular, in cases where several conditions must be fulfilled in order to cause a shared goal state to come into existence, as I just noted, each individual agent may only be able to fulfill the task of accomplishing one of these conditions at a time. However, as I also noted, if each of these cooperating agents concurrently performs their assigned tasks the overall goal will be obtained.

I will now turn to the case of cooperating agents sharing a common means to diverse ends. Apropos this context various sayings can be cited, both including the one I gave earlier that "politics makes strange bedfellows," and also talk of "pacts with the devil," or "sleeping with the enemy." It can be noted in these contexts that cooperators in one area will also be competitors in other areas, as in the case of joint projects between otherwise competing businesses. Thus, even though as I have just pointed out, cooperators on a task need not share at least their ultimate ends in common, it is still the case that the individual diverse ends can be accomplished only by means of cooperating on common means to those ends.

In the respective examples of the prisoner's dilemma and the issue of whether it is rational to vote, taking the cooperative standpoint would mean respectively for both prisoners not to cooperate with the jailer, and for everyone with an interest in the outcome of an election to vote. It can be noted that this is true both in the case where ultimate ends are shared and also in the case where merely common means are shared to disparate ends. Thus in particular, if each of the individuals faced with a dilemma like the prisoner's dilemma uses such a global cooperative approach, then they will see that the only individual issue in determining what is best and fair is what their best fair role is in the overall scheme of things. While I will not develop the topic in this book, I might note that there is an obvious parallel between an international arms race and a prisoner's dilemma in that lack of cooperation can have disastrous results. The solution there, as in the prisoner's dilemma, is to stress each party's best fair role in a cooperative scenario.

Other important examples of the results of taking a cooperative standpoint here involve such institutions as those of promise-keeping and truth-telling. In particular, it can be noted that, it may not always be in an individual agent's best interest, even from a long-term point of view, to always keep promises or to always tell the truth. However, there is a strong positive value apropos the value of expectations of others if agents act in this manner, at least in the absence of a very strong excuse, such as that of saving a life. For example, if we can trust what other agents tell us at face value then, at least in normal circumstances, we will be able to take as a given what the person said as being true in making predictions about the consequences of different possible courses of action. Similar remarks hold apropos counting on another person to act as they have promised when they have entered into a promise to do something. I might also note that in Chapter Seven I will show why this point holds the key for understanding why punishing the innocent is essentially never justified even from purely-utilitarian considerations. As Rawls (1955) and H. L. A. Hart (1958/1961) point out, with respect to the truly-innocent, the resultant loss of expectations that they will not be liable to punishment and the resulting insecurity will typically more than compensate for any positive value gained in individual cases by punishing them.

There is also an interesting parallel between the preceding points and Plato's analysis of 'justice' (in the distributive rather than the retributive sense) in Book Four of *The Republic*. There, Plato analyzed that concept in terms of everyone doing their own business, or finding their 'right' or 'best' place. Obviously, an agent's 'right place' will depend on what phase of development the agent's society is in. For example, an agent's 'right place' in a purely-agrarian society may be quite different from an agent's 'right place' in a highly-technological society. In order to explore the ramifications of some of these points a bit further, it will be useful to now investigate an analogy which can be made between the nature of a society and that of a machine. It might be noted that many of the same points could also be made if the comparison was instead with a living organism.

The concept of a 'machine' contains a number (although, as will be seen, certainly not all) of the distinctions which are requisite for determining what the best fair potential state of a society would be. For one point, the means - ends distinction can be clearly made from within the machine context. The 'end,' or 'purpose,' of a machine can be taken for present purposes to coincide with whatever function it was originally designed to perform. The movement of the individual parts of the machine can in turn be thought of as just constituting the 'method' or 'means' which is being used to accomplish the end. For example, in a fairly complex machine, such as an automobile engine, the functions of the various parts—be they valves, pistons, sparkplugs, or whatnot—cannot be understood independently of their functional roles in the whole machine; i. e., in this example, contributing to the eventual rotation of the crankshaft. Their individual performances constitute means and not end in themselves, since the parts are only in place due to their role in the accomplishment of something else.

I take it that people, in at least some key respects, are analogous to the parts of a machine in this last example. By this I mean that a society will 'work' best when different people perform different functional roles with the context of the overall society that they constitute 'parts' of. It should be obvious that the best fair type of state for a society will not involve having everybody doing exactly the same thing; everyone cannot be President for obvious reasons. It needs to also be emphasized that people are not homogeneous in either their abilities or in what they want to get out of life; i. e., their ultimate desires. Thus, the trick in making a society 'work' is for each individual member of it to either find for themselves or be helped in finding their 'right (i. e., best fair) role to play within the larger societal context, taking into full account the moral interests of the individual member.

I should note here that this last point concerning different people playing different functional roles in a society also holds the key for resolving a criticism that is sometimes made of utilitarianism, namely that it would lead to people having a positive duty to perform good deeds in faraway places. With the foregoing function points in mind, it can be seen that even if the giving of such aid constituted a duty on the part of a whole society, it still would not follow that each individual member of such a society would be performing their best fair role by means of becoming actively involved in such an effort. Of course, as I also just mentioned, this does not excuse the society as a whole from getting involved. In particular, if it can afford to give such aid and there is no other society in a still better position to do so, this might even be construed as a duty instead of merely a supererogatory course of action. Even in this case though, only those agents in the society actually assigned the functional role of getting involved in such projects would possess any sort of duty.

It is extremely important to point out places where the analogy between a machine and a society breaks down. One key way involves a disanalogy between people and the parts of a machine. The important point to make is that machine parts do not possess desires—i. e., they do not care what function they perform—whereas individual people obviously do. Since the fulfillment of desires is an intrinsic good, it follows, as I noted that Kant pointed out in his Practical Imperative, that people ought not be treated merely as means (as machine parts can be) but also as ends. This means that people's desires should count as at least one major factor in the determination of what their best fair roles would be within a larger societal context. While the principle "live and let live" can be overstated, particularly when potential victims are involved, it can also be understated, especially in situations where no potential victims are involved. Thus, it follows that three separate factors must be considered in determining what an agent's best fair role to play within a society is; the agent's abilities, the needs of the society, and the agent's desires. As I have noted, if people were exactly analogous to the parts of a machine, only the first two factors would come into play.

The first two of the foregoing factors—abilities and needs—are relevant to the determination of what the best fair type of state of a society would be by way of constituting both means towards achieving the existence of a state of that type and also as factors in maintaining its continuing function. That is, they will function as instrumental goods, being in place due to their role in the creation and continued existence of something else. The third factor, desires, though are relevant as an end in themselves. That is, their fulfillment constitutes an intrinsic good.

A key point to make now is that the determination of what the best fair potential world state is should essentially just be made in terms of the comparable summations of intrinsically good and bad situations in different reachable types of fair world states; i. e., in terms of to what extent these types of states both allow for individual desires to be fulfilled and also minimize various intrinsically bad situations. The consideration that various situations are instrumentally good or bad will only come into play here when considering such questions as whether different types of fair world states are in fact obtainable, and what the costs will be both in terms of the allocation of scarce resources to create the state and those involved in its continuing function.

Questions may be raised at this point concerning the justifiability, within the system which I have been defending in this book, of assigning people particular roles to play in life, even if the people's desires in life are taken into account as one factor in this assignment. In particular, it might seem that there is, at least *prima facie*, a violation of Kant's Practical Imperative since it would seem that individual people are being used as a means for a greater societal good. Thus, it may seem that people are being treated 'unfairly' in the strong sense which I distinguished in Chapter Two. It may also seem that there would be a violation of basic political freedoms.

I wish to make two points in reply to the preceding worries. The first point is to emphasize again that the prescriptive force associated with what an individual ought to do from an overall societal perspective typically only constitutes a recommendation with respect to what type of course of action the individual agent pursue and at least typically does not involve a duty; i. e. a demand for action where recriminations are called for if the type of action is not pursued. It must be admitted though that in extreme circumstances there may be exceptions here. For example, if one agent's best fair assignment from an overall societal perspective is to save another agent's life, and if the first agent does not even attempt to fulfill this role, enforcement may be called for, as with so-called 'Bad Samaritan laws.' The second point is that the maintenance of political freedoms (as I previously noted, I will be developing the concept of 'political freedom' in detail in Chapter Four) constitutes a great good, and thus very serious ramifications would be required to override this good. Still, in very serious cases, such as the life-threatening one just mentioned, it would seem that a good case can be made for an override.

It may also be helpful to illustrate these remarks by taking note of a few examples of societies where only some of the preceding factors have been taken account of. First, in many Marxist regimes, as I understand them, while people's abilities and the needs of the society were taken into account in deciding citizens' societal roles, their desires in life were not. In corrupt governments when, for example, relatives of influential people are given important jobs, obviously the placement may have very little to do with ability. This also occurs with family businesses and the hiring of relatives. Finally, in the practices of 'featherbedding' or 'make-work projects' superfluous jobs are created and thus societal needs (apart from the need for jobs) are ignored. In contrast to what is occurring in these instances, I am arguing that a society works best when all three factors are taken into account.

The question arises at this point as to how different values are to be 'weighed' so as to objectively determine the best fair potential world state. I will not go into the subject of specific algorithms for actually computing the relative utilities of different fair potential world states in detail here. However, I do wish to at least show both how the various intrinsically good and bad situations listed earlier in the chapter are amenable to a quantitative analysis and how good and bad situations from quite different categories can be at least ordinally ranked in terms of individual preferences. I will also briefly discuss strategies for integrating together these values occurring in different fair potential world states so as to determine which fair potential world state in fact would be the best one. While my analysis will have something in common with Bentham's (1781/1988, Ch. 4) 'hedonic calculus,' in that numbers will be associated with the various goods and harms, the analysis will also be much broader in scope than was Bentham's, which was confined to the quantification of pleasures and pains. It can be recalled that I have argued that there are other instances of goods and harms besides them—in particular the good and harms of life and its loss, and of political freedom and its lack—and I will show how these are also amenable to a quantitative analysis.

To begin my analysis, it can be noted that even while, as was just pointed out, there are other instances of goods and harms besides pleasures and pains, it is still the case that these pleasures and pains can be quantitatively analyzed in terms of their intensities, temporal durations, and degrees of pleasantness or painfulness. It can also be noted that these values may be either positive or negative depending upon whether a pleasure or pain is involved; i. e., pleasures will possess positive values while pains will possess negative values. In fact, Bentham, in his 'hedonic calculus,' gave an analysis along these same general lines, although with elaborations in such terms as the certainty of occurrence of the pleasure or pain (where the concept of expected utility, where the utility of an outcome is multiplied by its probability of occurrence, could be utilized); their propinquity (remoteness in time); fecundity (chances of being followed by a sensation of the same kind); and purity (chances of not being followed by a sensation of the opposite kind).

The values of political freedom and its lack are also amenable to a quantitative analysis. Here, unlike with the case of pleasures and pains, the numerical values assigned will always be positive. As an example in this regard, consider the loss of political freedom which occurs in a prison setting. This loss can be analyzed quantitatively both in terms of the temporal duration and in terms of the number of degrees of freedom lost. For example, solitary confinement is a harsher punishment than a confinement in a normal cell environment since it involves the loss of more freedoms found in ordinary life. As far as the values of life and its loss go, it can be noted that these values will be all or nothing since there is no 'in between' state. Also, since I have argued earlier in this section that all people possess the same intrinsic worth, it follows that to the extent that just questions of life, and not various instrumental values associated with the nature of people's lives are concerned, all of these lives should be weighed equivalently in a consequentialist algorithm.

I will now turn to the subject of how it is possible to quantitatively compare goods and harms from disparate categories. My general strategy will be to use a 'Bayesian' approach, via which various goods and harms can be ranked ordinally by means of asking a 'typical' agent (i. e., a rational, disinterested person) which types of situations would be either more desirable or less undesirable to gain or lose. It is unclear here that any one type of good or harm will always take precedence over any other given one. For example, even though most of us would take being alive itself to be the greatest good and its loss to be the greatest harm, under some conditions this is less than clear. It can be noted, for instance, that this issue arises in debates over whether euthanasia is ever ethically justified, where some may hold that the relief from extreme pain caused by death may more than compensate for the harm of the loss of life.

As far as strategies for integrating values from different potential world states go, I will first discuss the concept of a balance. It can be pointed out that a 'balance' implies the existence of at least two opposing forces or interests which are to be 'balanced.' That is, in the process of being 'balanced' these forces or interests are made to counteract the influence of each other so as to maximize the magnitude of the mutually common properties and to minimize the extent of any conflicting properties. It can also be noted that a 'balance' implies that the influence of comparable elements from opposite sides should be 'weighted' equivalently. Since I have argued that the intrinsic worth of each individual person is equal, this shows that each person's contribution or consideration towards the balance should count the same.

To push the foregoing analogy a bit further, the concept of a 'balance' can also be introduced in the context of 'balancing' an equation; or, even better, finding maximum and minimum points of differential equations. Here, the different sides, which initially may be in conflict, are 'evened out' by means of 'adjusting' one side or another so as to at least alleviate the conflict. By analogy then, it follows that in searching for the best fair potential world state, different opposing social forces should also be balanced. That is, these forces should be made to counteract the influence of each other so as to maximize the magnitude of mutually common properties and minimize the magnitudes of the conflicting properties. Also, since within the fairness constraint, I am defending the position of negative utilitarianism when issues of moral obligations arise, I take it that in balancing the foregoing equations, the prevention of harms should at least almost always take precedence over the production of goods. Whether or not this precedence should be an absolute precedence—e. g., whether the production of an enormous good may more than compensate for preventing a minor harm—may be a good question, but I see no obvious non-arbitrary other location for drawing a sharp line.

It is also true that it is often asked how one can put a price tag on a human life. The fact is though that, in making decisions concerning the allocation of scare resources, life and death questions are often involved. Examples here would include decisions on where to put the most effort in developing cures in medicine; decisions on whether or not to make expensive safety improvements such as in highway redesign; and decisions on whether or not to go ahead with expensive pollution controls, where the pollutants are known, at least statistically, to cause deaths. If working with numbers, such as in a cost - benefit analysis, helps us to make better decisions, shouldn't we be using the numbers? This completes my discussion of the concept of the 'best.' Thus, I will now turn to my next chapter where I will analyze certain aspects of the classical free will problem which are relevant for the subjects being discussed in this book.

Chapter Four
The Free Will Problem

In this chapter I will investigate certain aspects of the classical free will problem—what it means to have a 'free will' and whether or not the possession of such a will is compatible with determinism—so as to set the stage for later arguments in the book. There I will be specifically concerned with the issues of the justifiability respectively of ascriptions of 'moral responsibility' and of retributive theories of punishment. Thus, as a treatment of the free will problem, what I will have to say in the chapter will be by no means complete. In particular, I will not be concerned with resolving issues concerning fatalism, predestination, or divine foreknowledge of future courses of action. Still, in order to set up my later arguments, I will at least distinguish the various positions which can be held on the issue of whether or not the ascription of a free will is compatible with determinism. Along the way, I will also present analyses of a series of concepts—including those of the sense of 'could' which is relevant to the issue of whether or not 'we could have done otherwise,' 'coercion,' 'compulsion,' 'prediction,' 'deliberation,' and 'rationality'—which will play key roles in at least some facets of these arguments. I will begin the chapter by distinguishing among the various possible positions which can be held on the issue of whether or not universal causal determinism is compatible with ascriptions of human freedom.

Section One Definition of Positions on the Compatibility of Freedom and Determinism

By 'determinism' I refer to the position holding that all events which occur are completely causally necessitated to occur in that particular precise manner by temporally antecedent events. I am assuming that backwards in time causation does not occur. Thus, if determinism is true then it follows that, given a completely detailed description of a set of physical initial conditions (including both a description of the internal state of affairs of an object plus a description of its environment) plus the laws of physics, as they ideally are and not necessarily as we claim to know them, it will be possible to predict indefinitely far into the future what types of physical events will subsequently be occurring. In particular, if determinism is true all of the details of our courses of action will have been causally fixed by events which occurred in the distant past. Note that this claim does not entail that the character of the courses of action was preplanned by some other agent, such as God.

'Indeterminism' can in turn be defined in terms of determinism being false. In other words, if indeterminism is true then at least the manner in which some events occur is not at least completely causally fixed by what happened prior to them. It should be noted that indeterminism is compatible with the events being causally 'constrained' though, in the sense that only certain types of events ('constrained events') are allowed to occur. Still, which type of events from the set of constrained events that actually occur will not be completely causally determined. This is also consistent with a probabilistic 'weighting' of the chances of actual occurrence of the various allowed possible types of events.

With respect to the free will problem, both 'hard' and 'soft' variants of both determinism and indeterminism can be distinguished. Following William James (1884) who first introduced the terminology, I will use 'hard determinism' to refer to the position that determinism is true and that this claim is held to be incompatible with human freedom. James, in turn, defined 'soft determinism' to refer to the position that determinism, again, is true but where this claim is construed as being compatible with ascriptions of human freedom. In fact, it can be noted that this terminology can also be extended beyond the way it was utilized by James, by also distinguishing between 'hard' and 'soft' variants of indeterminism. These variants can be defined along analogous lines to the situation with determinism. In particular 'soft indeterminism' can be used to refer to the position that it is both the case that human freedom exists and that the universe is not deterministic. Similarly, 'hard indeterminism' can be used to refer to the claim that the universe is not deterministic and also denying that this helps the cause of human freedom. It can be noted that the position of soft indeterminism has often been termed 'libertarianism.' However, I wish to define 'libertarianism' solely in terms of holding that a certain type of freedom exists which is presupposed by ascriptions of moral responsibility. I, following Schopenhauer (1861/1960), will term this sense of freedom as 'absolute freedom.' My reason for not defining 'libertarianism' in terms of indeterminism, is that I will be arguing shortly that indeterminism does not give libertarians what they really want, namely the existence of a sense of freedom which can adequately account for these ascriptions of moral responsibility.

I should also note that I find the much-used terminology, at least in the recent literature, of 'compatibilism' (the position that the existence of free will is compatible with determinism) and 'incompatibilism' (the position that the existence of free will is not compatible with determinism) to be extremely misleading for characterizing different positions on the free will problem. This is both because very different positions can be espoused by incompatibilists (i. e., hard determinism or either soft or hard indeterminism), and because the terminology does not take cognizance of the existence of different senses of 'freedom.' In fact, I find that there is a strong tendency for advocates of the different positions on the free will problem to argue past each other due to their using the term 'freedom' in different ways. In particular, some of the usages of 'freedom' are clearly compatible with determinism while at least one usage clearly is not compatible with determinism. Hence, in order to clarify different usages which can be made of 'freedom,' I will now turn to a discussion of our ordinary-language use of the term. This will be followed by a discussion of possible rational reconstructions which can be made of the ordinary-language usage.

The first point which I wish to make concerning different ordinary-language senses of 'freedom' involves a feature which they all have in common. I take it that 'freedom' (in all of the different senses which I will distinguish) deals with a lack of constraint; the different senses being distinguishable in terms of what type of constraint they are dealing with. I might note that I will later contrast ascriptions of voluntariness with ascriptions of freedom on this point. This is because, as Locke in his *Essay Concerning Human Understanding* (1690/1959, Book 2, Ch. 21) has pointed out, a course of action may be voluntary even though it is constrained. There are also at least two issues on which at least superficially ordinary-language ascriptions of 'freedom' vary markedly; these being the issue of what sorts of entities are to be predicated as either being 'free' or 'not free' and the issue of what sorts of constraint are involved when the existence of freedom is denied. I will deal with the issue of what sorts of entities can properly be predicated as being 'free' or 'not free' first, and will then move on to deal with the issue of constraints.

Appeals to ordinary language for resolving the issue of what sorts of matters are proper subjects for predications of freedom or its lack may at least initially be confusing since sometimes actual courses of action are characterized as being 'free' or 'not free,' sometimes an agent is characterized as being 'free' or 'unfree' in what at least superficially appears to be an absolute sense, and sometimes an agent is characterized as being 'free' to perform certain possible courses of action but not others. I will argue that the differences among these different usages of 'free' and 'unfree' are not as fundamental as they may appear to be on the surface though, and will in fact show that the usage of characterizing agents as being 'free' or 'unfree' relative to various possible courses of action is the most primitive sense. In this regard, I will first show that any ascriptions of agents as being 'free' or 'unfree' in an absolute sense are seriously misleading, since at least typically all that is meant by these ascriptions involves various claims about what sorts of possible courses of action the agents are free or unfree to perform. I will then show that predications of actual courses of action as being 'free' or 'unfree' can also be explicated in terms of what possible courses of action an agent is free to perform at the same time.

I will show now that the claim that agents are only 'free' or 'unfree' relative to various possible courses of action is a more primitive characterization than a characterization in terms of the agents as being 'free' or 'unfree' in any absolute sense. To begin, it can be noted that there are certain possible courses of action which no agents are free to perform, and others which essentially everyone is free to perform. For example, nobody is free to travel to Mars in the next five seconds and essentially everyone is free to scratch their nose in a similar time period. Thus, it clearly makes more sense to speak of 'free courses of action' as a primitive rather than ascribing 'freedom' in any absolute monadic sense to agents per se; a 'free' course of action being a possible course of action that we have both the ability and the opportunity to either perform or not to perform.

The just-noted distinction between abilities and opportunities is an important one, as Anthony Kenny (1975, Ch. 7) has emphasized. I am using 'ability' in a broad sense to refer to both physiological (e. g., muscular) capabilties, and also the lacking of any psychological blocks; e. g., phobias. Opportunities can in turn be characterized in terms of environmental states of affairs external to an agent which would enable them to cause, if they so attempt, the existence of situations of the type which they are being characterized as having 'the opportunity to cause.' An agent can then be said to be 'free' to perform a given possible course of action if and only if they have both the ability and the opportunity to perform it. It would seem then that ordinary-language characterizations of agents as being 'free' or 'unfree' in an absolute sense are to be construed in terms of the relative number, or possibly the relative importance, of the possible courses of action which they have both the ability and opportunity to pursue.

In contrast with the situation for possible courses of action, when actual courses of action are predicated as being 'free' or not, a claim is being made concerning the conditions under which they are being performed. To make this distinction clear, it can also be recalled from my discussion of the nature of 'actions' in Chapter One, that possible courses of action are action types whereas actual courses of action consist of action tokens. In spite of the foregoing points of contrast, a linkage can still be noted between ascriptions of 'freedom' to actual courses of action and claims about what possible courses of action we are free to perform. In particular, it can be noted that to characterize an actual course of action as being 'free' means that there was at least one alternative possible course of action that we were also 'free to perform' (in at least one of a series of distinct senses which I will be distinguishing shortly). Having shown a way to link all three of our ordinary-language usages of 'freedom' together, I will now explore the most fundamental of these senses, what it means to be free to perform a given possible action, in somewhat more detail.

I will begin my analysis of what it means to claim that an agent is either 'free' or 'unfree' to perform a given possible course of action by means of contrasting such claims with claims that the performance of a given actual course of action is voluntary. I first wish to take note of a syntactical difference here. As I have earlier shown, the basic grammar of 'freedom' is that of being a relation. In contrast, 'voluntariness' is a monadic predicate as can be shown by noting that it can only be meaningfully predicated of actual courses of action (instead of possible courses of action, as was the case with ascriptions of 'freedom'), and that its ascription is 'all or nothing.' A second difference between ascriptions of freedom and ascriptions of voluntariness is causal in character. In particular, the predication of 'voluntariness' to a course of action is to be analyzed in terms of the nature of the causes of the course of action and not what constraints are present. As Locke (1690/1959, Book 2, Ch. 21), has noted with respect to someone locked in a room, a person's course of action in such a situation may still be voluntary if they wish to remain in the room even if they are not also free to leave. Looking ahead, I might note that this point will later bear on my resolution of a controversy concerning a purported counterexample given by Harry Frankfurt (1969) to the claim that being free entails the ability to do otherwise. I will now turn to my discussion of what different types of constraints may be involved when it is said that agents are 'unfree' to perform given possible courses of action.

As I have noted, different authors use the term 'freedom' in different ways. None that I know of makes distinctions in quite the way I wish to, although Schopenhauer (1841/1960) comes close. In any event, it will be important to show that only certain senses of 'freedom' are compatible with determinism. A class of senses of 'freedom' which are straight-forwardly compatible with determinism involves relationships between possible courses of action and the existence of compulsive and coercive presences. Schopenhauer defines two senses of 'freedom,' 'physical freedom,' and 'moral freedom' (so as not to prejudge the moral issue I will use the term 'liberty' rather than 'moral freedom' in what follows) in terms of the respective absenses of compulsion and coercion. However, I prefer a four-fold distinction here whereby compulsions and coercive factors are also characterized as being 'positive' or 'negative' in character. Thus, a person will be 'physically free' (in the positive sense) to perform a given possible course of action if there is no compulsive presence blocking them from performing a possible course of action of the given type. They will be 'physically free' (in the negative sense) not to perform a given possible course of action if there is no compulsive presence preventing them from doing otherwise. A similar set of distinctions can be made concerning positive and negative senses of 'liberty;' i. e., we may possess 'liberty' to do something in a positive sense if we are not being coerced from performing a possible course of action of a given type or we may possess 'liberty' in a negative sense (i. e., not be at liberty to do something) if we are not being coerced to perform a given possible course of action.

Before proceeding further, separate digressions are necessary at this point explicating the respective concepts of 'compulsion' and 'coercion.' It should be emphasized that I will be rationally reconstructing both of the concepts for purposes of my further analysis. Thus, not everything that I will say will coincide with either ordinary language usage or the reconstructions of other authors. I believe that my usages are generally consistent with ordinary usages though; it just tightens up these meanings in a sharper fashion.

Compulsions can be classified both, as I just noted, in terms of whether they are 'positive' or 'negative,' and also in terms of whether they are internal or external to an agent's body. As I noted, by a 'positive compulsion' I am referring to a physical situation that compels an agent to act in particular manner. Thus, in the face of such a compulsion the agent cannot act otherwise even if they so try. Similarly, with a negative compulsion, an agent is prevented from acting a certain way even if they try to do so. It can be noted that, as with the intertranslatability of 'rights to' and 'rights from' the existence of various types of situation which was noted in Chapter Two, positive and negative compulsions are also intertranslatable. In particular, a positive compulsion to act a certain way (e. g., to remain in jail) can be translated into a negative compulsion to prevent a possible action (e. g., escaping from jail). Similar remarks will hold for the connection between positive and negative coercive factors. It should also be emphasized that both positive and negative compulsions are typically only partial, in the sense that while they require certain classes of possible actions, they do not completely constrain the possible actions. For example, persons in jail, while they are compelled to remain in jail, are fully capable of performing any number of possible actions within these confines.

The distinction between internal and external compulsions involves the issue of whether the location of the compulsive force is interior or exterior to the body of the agent under compulsion. I will now give examples illustrating each of these cases. An example of an external positive compulsion here would be the case of a person being bodily removed from a room, whereby even if they try to remain in the room they will not succeed. A comparable example of an internal positive compulsion would be that of a person who has an uncontrolled hand tremor, where they cannot stop their hand from trembling even if they try to do so. An example of a negative external compulsion would be that of a person confined to a jail cell, whereby they will not succeed in leaving the cell even if they attempt to do so. Of course they can still perform any number of possible courses of action of types compatible with the compulsive situation, such as scratching their nose. An example in turn of a negative internal compulsion would be that of a person who is paralyzed, whereby they cannot move certain limbs if they try to do so.

It should be emphasized that, as Austin (1961/1979, p. 205) has pointed out in "Ifs and Cans," lack of compulsion from performing a given possible course of action does not mean that we will always succeed in performing a course of action of this type when we so try, but merely that if we try a sufficiently large number of times that we will at least sometimes succeed. For example, I may be physically free to sink a given putt on a golf course, even though I only succeed in one out of ten attempts. Thus, as I am using the terms, the difference between 'compulsive' and 'coercive' situations is that an agent can at least sometimes succeed in acting against a coercive situation; whereas, by definition, this is never the case with a compulsive situation. I will now turn to my discussion of the coercive case.

I believe that coercive situations are best construed in terms of conditional statements. In these statements the antecedent clauses refer to possible courses of action on the part of the coerced agent and the consequent clauses refer to various consequences that the coercing agents lets the coerced agent know will be brought about in response. It can also be noted that typically actions performed as a result of the linkage with these consequences will go against the will of the coerced agent, in the sense of their preferences as they would otherwise be. Thus, not all strong reasons are characterized as being 'coercive,' but typically only ones that go against an agent's preferences.

As with the case of compulsions, coercive factors can also be classified both, as I previously noted, on the issue of whether they are 'positive' or 'negative,' and also in terms of whether they are internal or external. I will use the terms of 'positive coercion' and ‘negative coercion' not just to refer to the fact that they are towards or away from the existence of a given situation (where the two would be intertranslatable, as with positive and negative compulsions), but also with respect to the nature of the coercing factors. Ignoring perverse cases, positive coercive factors may either involve telling the coerced person that they will receive something good (e. g., bribing a person with money) if they act a certain way, or telling them that they will receive less of something bad (e. g., bribing a prisoner by promising an early release from jail if they cooperate). Examples of negative coercive factors may either involve telling the person threatened that they will receive something bad (e. g., threatening to discipline a child) unless they act a certain way, or telling them that they will be deprived of something good (e. g., threatening a person with a partial loss of physical freedom through incarceration).

In the compulsive case, the distinction between internal and external coercive factors involves whether the coercing factor is internal or external to the body of the coerced agent. Again, I will illustrate the various possible cases here. Examples of positive internal coercive factors would include such non-compulsive factors as certain addictions or such psychological 'compulsions' as cases of 'compulsive gambling' or 'compulsive handwashing,' where, if an agent tried hard to do otherwise they would succeed. An example of a negative internal coercive factor would be a non-compulsive phobia. External coercive factors involving other agents would include bribes in the positive case and threats in the negative case. External coercive factors not involving other agents would include such factors as the promise of pleasant weather as a positive coercive factor or the threat of inclement weather as a negative coercive factor. I should note that this last usage stretches the ordinary language usage, which confines the terms to the actions of agents.

The linkage between the antecedent and consequent clauses in coercive situations need not be a necessary one, but instead may just involve significantly increasing the probability of a given consequence. For example, with the case of threatening to play Russian roulette, the threat can be construed as that of being an increased chance of death rather than a guaranteed death itself. However, coercive factors will be more effective to the extent that the coercing agent is able to guarantee the linkage with the consequences in question. Otherwise, the situation will correspond to either an 'empty threat' or that of not following through with a promised reward. In both cases there is a resultant loss of credibility on the part of the coercing agent. This can also result in 'power struggles' where the issue is who is in control of a situation; i. e., who it is who is enforcing the connections linking the antecedent and consequent clauses of the conditionals constituting the coercive situations.

It should also be noted that, as I am using the terms, the issue of whether an action is committed under 'coercion' or not is logically independent of the issue of whether or not it is also 'compulsive.' For example, it may be the case that we are at liberty to perform a given possible course of action because there are no laws (or other coercive presences) against acting in that way, but where, because we are physically incapable of so acting, we are not physically free to perform a possible course of action of the type in question. Looking ahead, I might note that I will be exploring some of the ramifications of these usages in more detail in my discussion of excuses in Chapter Six, my discussion of the nature of law in Chapter Seven, and in my discussion of deterrence in Chapter Eight.

It should be emphasized that not all authors use 'compulsion' and 'coercion' the same way that I do. For example, sometimes situations are labeled as being 'compulsive' (as with those 'psychological compulsions' which can be overcome if an agent tries hard to do so) where under my analysis they will be classified as being merely 'coercive.' The converse situation may also occur, as when a situation where one agent is being physically restrained by another agent is labeled as being 'coercive.' An added point concerning ordinary usage is that 'coercion' is used in ordinary language almost exclusively just to refer to situations which are external to an agent and not those which are internal. Under my analysis though, such internal situations as the just-noted class of 'psychological compulsions' and at least some addictions will also count as being coercive since they impede an agent's ability to choose to act against their presences. While it is thus clear that my usage of the terms 'compulsion' and 'coercion' at time goes against ordinary usage, I believe that this usage can still be justified in terms of its usefulness for the further development of my analysis. For example, it will play important roles both in my subsequent analyses of 'liberty' and 'political freedom' in this chapter, and also in my discussion of excuses in Chapter Six. I will now move on to first make a few remarks on different types of possible compulsive and coercive forces and will then discuss liberty and political freedom.

I wish to now take note of a nice tie-in between the distinction just drawn between cases of internal and external coercive and compulsive factors and the distinction which I earlier drew between abilities and opportunities. It can be seen that cases where an agent is characterized as lacking the ability to perform a given possible course of action would correspond to cases of internal coercive and compulsive factors. In contrast, in cases of lack of opportunity, an external coercive or compulsive factor will be involved. I will now turn to a more detailed discussion of sense of 'freedom' involving lack of coercion; i. e., liberty and 'political freedom.

By 'liberty,' as I noted, I will refer to the lack of coercion in both the internal and external senses just distinguished. Since, as I have defined the term, the presence of 'coercion' is compatible with either the presence or the absence of an additional compulsive force, it follows that liberty will be relative to possible courses of action and not potential courses of action. In other words, the way I am using the term, we may be at 'liberty' to do something (because we are not being coerced into doing it) even though we are physically incapable of doing it. The physical incapacity here may either be due to an internal condition, such as in the case of somebody who is partially paralyzed, or due to some external condition, such as environmental factors including the weather. It can also be noted that, as thus used, the possession of 'liberty' is subject to degrees inasmuch as some coercive factors are more powerful than others. I believe that my usage of 'liberty' is justifiable in these contexts, inasmuch as the ordinary usage does possess a connotation of a lack of societal constraints. Also, it can be noted that even while in ordinary language 'liberty' is sometimes used interchangeably with 'freedom,' an adjectival form of the root, comparable to 'free,' is missing.

I will use the term, 'political freedom,' in a more narrow sense than that of 'liberty' (of which it will be a subclass) so as to only refer to cases of lack of governmental coercion, whether these be in terms of legal statutes or implicitly-understood customs. With respect to both the explicit and the implicit cases here the coercive force involved will be in the form of the threatened enforcement of either the legal statute or implicit custom in question. Thus, it can be noted that we would be politically free to a maximum extent in the case of anarchy. It can also be noted that political freedoms will be relative to different possible courses of action, depending on the set of legal statutes being enforced by a government. The concept of a 'legal right' (in effect, a guaranteed political freedom, such as those stated in the United States 'Bill of Rights') can also be defined in this regard as involving a prohibition (possibly a constitutional one) against certain types of laws being enacted by a government. It is also important to emphasize again that since political freedom is a subclass of liberty, we may be politically free to perform a given possible course of action (because there is no law against performing it) in cases where we are physically incapable of acting that way and thus not physically free to so act.

Not all soft determinists make a sharp distinction between compulsion and coercion, but a failure to do so has resulted in a certain amount of confusion in some of the treatments; the work of Walter Stace (1952) can be cited in this regard. Also, it may be difficult at times to classify certain psychological states, such as phobias and addictions, as being coercive or compulsive. Still, the key question to raise in distinguishing between the two is always whether we could have acted otherwise if we had so tried. Still a further point is that the ascriptions of physical freedom and being at liberty are logically independent of each other. To show that the possession of physical freedom is not a logically sufficient condition for liberty it can be noted that an agent may be physically free to perform a given possible course of action yet not be at liberty to do it. For example, in the case of acting at gunpoint, one typically could still disobey the threatening agent if one tried. There may still be a point to be made concerning proper ascriptions of responsibility here though, since if a crime is committed under external coercion, one would at least be more inclined to hold the threatening party at fault than the person actually committing the crime. To show that the possession of physical freedom is not a logically necessary condition for liberty it can be noted that a person can be physically blocked from performing a particular possible course of action, say because of paralysis, but not be coerced from doing it. In this case the person will be at liberty to perform the possible course of action but not be physically free to do so.

It may be noted that with regard to the two senses of 'freedom' discussed so far, while the existence of various constraints on an agent's possible courses of action were deemed to be relevant in determining whether the agent was 'free' or not in the apropos sense, the scope of the constraints has been limited. That is, these senses of 'freedom' did not take into account all of the factors involved in the causal determination of a course of action; especially those involved with an agent's rational decision-making processes, in the determination of whether the agent was 'free' or not. In contrast, I wish to now discuss a third sense of 'freedom,' which following Schopenhauer (1841/1960), I shall term 'absolute freedom.' This sense of 'freedom' is also sometimes termed 'categorical' or 'metaphysical' freedom due to the claim that its existence is not conditioned by something else. It refers to an agent's alleged ability to either will or not will a certain way given absolutely everything in the agent's background. Thus, in this sense, the scope of background constraints is unlimited, and it may be noted that the ability to do otherwise under this unlimited background scope has often been thought to be a precondition for the justifiability of ascriptions of moral responsibility. In particular, it has been thought that in the absence of this unlimited sense of 'freedom' it would be unfair to hold an agent morally responsible for their courses of action. I might also noted that libertarians have historically been concerned with showing at least the possible existence of 'freedom' in this last absolute sense.

As I noted earlier, I am using 'libertarianism' just to refer to the position that 'freedom' in the absolute sense of the term exists, and whereby the term is neutral concerning the issue of whether or not this sort of freedom is compatible with determinism. I should also note that the absolute sense of 'freedom' is the one sense of 'freedom' which I will be arguing that we do not possess. Thus, the position on the free will problem which I will be defending in this and the following chapter is that of 'alibertarianism,' which I wish to construe solely in terms of the denial of the existence of 'freedom' in the absolute sense, and where the issue of determinism is not prejudiced in either direction thereby. Thus, I will be arguing that we are not 'free' in the absolute sense presupposed by ascriptions of moral responsibility; although of course this claim is compatible with the existence of both physical freedom and liberty.

Also, before proceeding further I should note that my position denying the coherence of a sense of 'freedom' compatible with ascriptions of moral responsibility goes against the trend of most modern literature on the free will problem. This literature is almost exclusively concerned with showing how ascriptions of moral responsibility are justifiable in spite of various concerns pointing *prima facie* to the contrary. In particular, while there have been a number of recent books defending either soft determinism or soft indeterminism, I know of very few recent ones defending either harder determinism or the broader position which I am calling 'alibertarianism.' Two exceptions here include Richard Double's *The Non-Reality of Free Will* (1991) and Ted Honderich's *The Consequences of Determinism* (1988).

Double bases much of his argumentation on a moral nihilism which I find to be repulsive, and to which obviously I am trying to given an alternative consequentialist account. Honderich's account, which defends hard determinism is actually fairly close to my own. In particular, he distinguishes between two senses of 'freedom;' 'voluntariness,' or lack of coercion, and that of being an originating cause. He also argues that since there is strong evidence for the truth of determinism, we should give up the set of attitudes (involving claims to desert) which are contingent on determinism being false, and instead settle for attitudes which are consistent with the issues of non-coercion, or voluntariness. Honderich's philosophy of punishment is quite similar to that of Rawls (1971), in that it appeals to the effects on the least advantaged segments of a society, and thus differs significantly from my own upcoming treatment of the subject in Part Two.

Before turning to my actual arguments for my position, I will take note of a few works where arguments are presented for other positions. It is interesting that, by integrating the effects of what I take to be the strongest arguments in each of these works, the net result is an alibertarian one. In particular, a well-argued book defending soft determinism is Daniel Dennett's *Elbow Room* (1984), and books defending soft indeterminism include Peter van Inwagen's *An Essay on Free Will* (1983) and Robert Kane's *Free Will and Values* (1985).

Kane builds up a carefully-developed model of freedom based on random choices among alternative potential rational courses of action, and also raises some interesting issues about the rationality of choosing ends and not just the means to them. However, I will present arguments in Chapter Five that choosing at random does not give us 'moral responsibility' in the relevant sense which I will develop in that chapter of where we are justified in putting moral labels on people. Van Inwagen (1983, Ch. 5) shows, I think quite effectively, that the concept of 'moral responsibility' must presuppose an ability to do otherwise that is incompatible with determinism. However, he also holds, I think misguidedly, that rational deliberation is incompatible with determinism. On the other hand, Dennett shows, I also think quite effectively, that one can account for rational deliberation in completely deterministic terms, and he thus questions what is to be gained by making the indeterministic move. However, Dennett also holds, I think misguidedly, that ascriptions of moral responsibility are compatible with determinism. Thus, if the Van Inwagen's and Dennett's approaches are taken together, it can be seen that it is at least possible to separate the issue of how rational deliberation is possible from that of whether or not we possess a 'free will' in the sense presupposed by ascriptions of moral responsibility. I will be making use of this point in my arguments for alibertarianism in Chapter Five. Obviously, in developing these arguments a great deal is going to depend on being clear about which of the senses of 'freedom' which I previously distinguished is being used on any particular occasion.

In order to both set up a series of distinctions which will be necessary to give an adequate characterization of the nature of absolute freedom, and so as to also set the stage for my arguments for alibertarianism in Chapter Five, it is necessary to now distinguish between the various senses of 'could have done otherwise' in more detail. I will then both present a detailed account of the nature of absolute freedom and also show how human rationality can be accounted for under either deterministic or indeterministic models of the universe. I will thus show that the issue of the existence of moral responsibility is a separate issue from that of the existence of rationality.

Section Two Senses of 'Could'

To begin my discussion of which sense of 'could' is relevant to ascriptions of moral responsibility, I wish to take note of two senses of the term which I will not be developing further in this section; namely those of what we either legally or morally can do. It is sometimes said that we "cannot do something" if it is either against the law, goes against the regulations of an organization, or involves breaking a moral rule. However, since we clearly are held accountable for our courses of action when we do break these rules, these senses are clearly not relevant for identifying the sense of 'could' that is a presupposition for ascriptions of moral responsibility. Thus, I will move on now to identify other senses of the term.

Sometimes the phrase "could have done otherwise" has been construed as an implicit condition, which Moore (1912, p. 20) rendered in terms of what a person would have done if they had so chosen. However, this conditional sense clearly just corresponds to what I have been calling 'physical freedom,' and clearly it does not follow from the fact that a person would have performed a potential course of action of a given type if they had so chosen, that they also could have chosen to perform a potential course of action of that type given absolutely everything in their background. Therefore, the second-order issue of whether we could actually choose to do otherwise is not dealt with by this analysis, and thus I will again move on now to discuss other possible analyses.

In order to develop my analysis of a series of further senses of 'could' which at least on the surface appear to be germane to the absolute sense of 'freedom,' it is useful to first take note of a link between the concept of 'can' and the concept of 'possibility.' In particular, it seems to be clear that we 'can' only perform a course of action of a given type if it is 'possible' for us to do so. However, it must be noted that 'possibility' possesses an analogous set of ambiguities to those possessed by 'can.' First, I wish to take note of a sense of the terms which I will not be making use of, namely that of 'logical possibility.' This clearly is not the sense that is relevant to the subject of human freedom since with respect to any case where the description of a course of action is logically consistent (i. e., where the description does not entail the existence of logically incompatible types of situations) by definition the course of action in question will be logically possible. It can be pointed out then that there are any number of logically contingent courses of action of which we are incapable, if for no other reason than that they violate laws of physics.

The last point, concerning the fact that our potential courses of action are at least constrained by the laws of physics, suggests an alternative sense of 'possibility' which might seem to be more apropos to the question of human freedom though, namely that of the 'physically possible.' Two distinct senses of 'physically possible' need to be distinguished here. The first holds that the existence of a situation of a given type is physically possible when it can physically occur according to the laws of physics, again as they ideally are, given a set of actually existing physical initial conditions; such as those characterizing the state of a person's body and the state of their environment at a given time. The second sense just involves a physically coherent story, which may or may not ever actually occur. That is, no parts of the story may involve any contradictions with any laws of physics. An example of a physically incoherent story would be one involving the claim that someone traveled faster than the speed of light. Inasmuch as the issue of human freedom is being raised with respect to actually existing agents in the physical world, it follows that the only sense of 'physically possible' which could be relevant to the ascription of this freedom to courses of action would be the first one distinguished.

In any event, a complication arises at this point concerning the question of how precisely the background conditions are to be described when it is claimed that the existence of a situation of a given type is 'physically possible.' Roughly speaking, the more loosely the background conditions are described, the greater the number of situations that will be physically possible under these circumstances. Conversely, the more precisely the background conditions are described, the smaller the number will be of situations that will be physically possible. To illustrate this point with an example from Hume (1739/1975, Book 1, Sec. 14), consider the situation of a billiard ball lying on a flat surface, but where no other background conditions are given. Just given this description, an extremely large number of types of physical situations are physically possible provided that appropriate other physical background conditions are introduced. For instance, the ball could be pushed in any direction within its degrees of freedom, or it could even be removed from the table altogether. However, once more and more background conditions are specified, the physically possible options are continuously cut down until eventually, when all of the conditions are specified, assuming the truth of determinism, the existence of only one type of situation is physically possible; that type of situation whose existence is causally determined by those antecedent conditions.

I will now switch to my discussion of a case more germane to the actual free will problem, namely the situation with respect to the human brain. It would seem here also that the more specifically that situations (i. e. brain states) are described the fewer will be our physically possible options. In fact ultimately, if determinism is true, it would seem that we would only have one physically possible option, that which we are causally determined to do given the exact nature of our brains. I might note that analogous points could also be made, *mutatis mutandis*, for non-physical accounts of free will also, as with accounts in terms of so-called 'agent causation.' The question arises then as to in what senses can it still be held that we are 'free' to do otherwise?

In order to answer the foregoing question it is necessary to develop some of the foregoing ideas in somewhat more detail. In particular, a distinction needs to be drawn between what is physically possible for an agent to do provided that appropriate signals emerge from their brain (or possibly just a small portion of it), and what is physically possible given all of the minute details of their brain. It should be pointed out that exactly where in the brain to make the delineation between relevant portions of it can be a controversial matter. For example, to introduce a concept which I will be developing in more detail in my next section, it is sometimes maintained that we cannot perform a course of action of a given type if we possess a 'phobia' against it. I take it that an agent has a 'phobia' against a possible course of action if there are at least no non-coercive or non-compulsive external circumstances in which they will perform it. Presumably, taking the whole brain into account, appropriate signals could, at least in principle, be sent from it and thus produce courses of action prohibited by the phobia, but also presumably for some much smaller portion of the brain this would not be physically possible.

However, regardless of what is going on in the brain in the case of phobias, it would seem that in the case of either dealing with the whole brain, or just a relevant small portion of it, we are faced with at least many different possible options, in the sense of what would be physically possible to happen provided that appropriate signals were sent from either the brain or the relevant small portion of it. I take it that it is from among these physically possible options that we attempt to make a rational decision. I will now show how the apparent conflict between the claim that we should do otherwise implies that we could do otherwise and the truth of determinism can be resolved by taking note of the distinction between this last sense of 'can' and the sense which includes all of the details of the brain.

Consider in the foregoing regard Kant's dictum from his *Critique of Pure Reason* (1787/1929, p. 473) that 'ought' implies 'can.' I wish to claim that the sense of 'can' in this dictum is best interpreted as referring to the sense whereby we 'can' do something if we at least typically succeed in doing it when we try to do so. In particular, it can be noted that the illocutionary aspect of 'ought' involves an attempt to persuade a person to act a certain way, and thus may imply that they were not going to act in that manner anyway. It follows then that the introduction of new causes, at least by introducing new information by non-coercive verbal means, is compatible with Kant's dictum. Also, Kant certainly did not wish to claim that people always act as they ought; which can be explained either in terms of a lack of pertinent information or because the person is using too narrow of a point of view. It should be emphasized that the preceding points are not meant as an exegesis of Kant's actual thought, and it is clear from the context that Kant took himself to be actually presenting an argument for indeterminism of the will here.

It can next be pointed out that, assuming the truth of determinism, if all of the minute details of the brain were to be taken into account then only one potential course of action would actually be physically possible, the one which was causally determined to occur. This does not mean that we cannot make rational decisions if determinism is true—at the end of the chapter I will argue that we can—but rather that this rational decision-making process is itself fully causally determined. It does mean though that if 'could' is construed as meaning 'physically possible' in the last sense, we could not (in at least this sense of 'could') have done otherwise than how we in fact act.

It is true that still other senses of 'can' have been cited as being the relevant one for ascriptions of the ability to do otherwise which is relevant for ascriptions of moral responsibility. Dennett (1984, Ch. 6), for example, claims that an 'epistemological' sense is the relevant one here; that being that an actual course of action is free so long as we could have done otherwise "for all we know." Counter-examples, in both directions, are obvious concerning the claim that this is the relevant sense though. The high jumper who thinks that they can jump seven feet but who is physically unable to do so cannot physically perform a course of action of a type which they think they are physically capable of. Also, the runner who thinks that they cannot physically-possibly run a four-minute mile but who goes on to do it physically, can physically perform a course of action of a type which they think they are physically-incapable of. If 'does' implies 'can,' which certainly at least sounds like a plausible restriction to place of the sense on 'can' presupposed by ascriptions of 'freedom' to actual courses of action (although there will be a 'twist' on this principle for the 'ability' sense of 'can' which I will discuss next), then it would follow that the epistemological sense cannot be the relevant one here.

As I just noted, still another sense of 'can' which is sometimes invoked here is the 'can' of general ability. In this sense, it is claimed that an agent 'can' perform a course of action of a given type if they have a general ability to do so, even though this ability may or may not be actually demonstrated on any particular occasion. For example, Austin (1961/1979, p. 205) in “Ifs and Cans” gave an example of trying to sink a putt during a game of golf, whereby a usually proficient golfer (who would have the general ability to sink such putts) on this occasion misses. The question is then raised as to whether or not they 'could' have made it. Austin says that they could because of their general ability to make such putts, even though on this particular occasion they failed.

It should be noted that the principle that 'does' implies 'can' could be challenged in the context of the 'can' of ability. This is because, to change Austin's example slightly, if the golfer was to make a hole in one, we presumably would not say that they had a general ability to make such shots; saying instead that it was due to luck. Actually, ordinary English may work both ways here though, since one might wish to reply to a dispute over whether an agent possessed a given ability, that since they succeeded in doing it, they must have been able (but perhaps 'able' is being used in two different senses here). In any event, I think that the crucial observation to make here is that if an agent fails when they are trying to perform a possible course of action of a given type, even though under this sense of 'can' they "could do it," we would not hold them to be morally responsible for the failure. For example, if, for some strange reason, the only way to save someone's life was to make the putt in Austin's example, and if the golfer, although both trying to make the putt and being usually proficient in making similar putts, missed on this occasion, I do not think that anyone would say that they were in any way either at fault or morally responsible for the resulting death. In the absence of other plausible candidates for the sense of 'can' which is relevant to ascriptions of 'freedom' to possible courses of action, I will conclude that the last sense of 'physically possible' which I just analyzed is in fact the relevant sense.

I now wish to close this section by means of critically examining a purported counterexample, originally due to Frankfurt (1969), to the claim that an actual course of action is only 'free' if I could have done otherwise should be dealt with. Frankfurt's purported counterexample to this principle essentially involves a case of causal over-determination, whereby, if for some reason an agent should not 'freely' decide to perform a course of action of a given type, some other 'force' (the nature of the 'force' does not matter here) would then come into play and cause the agent to perform a course of action of the given type anyway. However, recalling the distinction which I made at the beginning of this chapter between a course of action being 'voluntary' and a course of action being 'free,' it would seem that Frankfurt has just given an example of a voluntary course of action here (which, as Locke noted with his locked room example, is compatible with not being able to do otherwise), but it is far from clear to me that he has also given an example of a free course of action. In particular, it can be noted that under each of the different senses of 'freedom' which I have analyzed, an actual course of action is only characterized as being 'free' if an agent has both the ability and opportunity to do otherwise. However, in the case which Frankfurt has presented, the very exercising of an agent's ability to cause a situation of a given type to exist, denies the agent the opportunity to have done otherwise. Thus, the agent would not have both the ability and the opportunity to do otherwise here.

Before making use of the sense just developed of 'could' as 'physical possibility with all of the background conditions kept the same' in my investigation of the justifiability of ascriptions of moral responsibility to agents, I wish to first turn to both an analysis of the absolute sense of 'freedom,' and also to a discussion of the issue of whether or not agents can be legitimately characterized as being rational if determinism is the case. I will be making use of the distinctions between different senses of 'could' in both of these treatments.

Section Three Absolute Freedom

In this section I will both present an analysis of the sense of 'freedom' as an absolute ability to will in different ways even when all background conditions remain fixed and will also critically examine the presuppositions inherently made by attributions of this sense of 'freedom' to agents. In this sense, an agent is held to be 'free' if and only if, given all of the antecedent causal conditions in their background, it is still physically possible for them at least to try to either perform or not to perform a possible course of action of a given type. In other words, the issue of whether an agent is 'free' or not is pushed back one step from the issue of whether they could have either performed or not performed a possible course of action of a given type if they had so chosen (which was the sense characterized by physical freedom and liberty), to whether they have the ability to choose to perform it.

At least on the surface, the absolute sense of 'freedom' just defined would seem to be broader than that of either physical freedom or liberty, since it would seem that an agent could at least try to perform any of many distinct possible courses of actions which were either externally blocked or where there were external coercive factors present for not performing them. Lack of such freedom, also at least on the surface, might seem to correspond to cases of either phobias (where we are unable to even try to perform a possible course of action of a type which we possess the phobia against) or psychological compulsions (where we are unable to prevent ourselves from trying to perform a possible course of action of a type which we possess the compulsion towards), and in the absence of either of these, it might seem that we would be free either to perform or not to perform a possible course of action of the type in question. I will be shortly raising certain difficulties, including one involving a regress, for the true justifiability of these initially plausible claims though. However, it will be useful to review first the four-fold distinction which I drew earlier between positive and negative internal compulsive and coercive factors.

It can be recalled that under my four-fold distinction between types of internal compulsive and coercive factors, phobias fell under the category of negative internal coercive and compulsive factors, and psychological compulsions fell under the category of positive internal coercive and compulsive factors. When phobias and psychological compulsions are coercive then they make it very difficult for us respectively either to choose or to refrain from choosing a possible course of action of a type characterized respectively by the phobia or psychological compulsion, and when they are compulsive they make this be physically impossible. For example, typically in the cases of drug addictions, or such 'compulsive' behaviors as kleptomania or pyromania, the agent is merely being internally coerced psychologically to act a certain way. Here, given a strong enough external coercive factor (such as, for the kleptomania or pyromania cases, the presence of a police officer), the agent would have chosen otherwise.

It may be noted that the proper classification of other cases of internal coercive and compulsive factors—particularly those involving hypnotic 'suggestions' or 'brainwashing'—need not be nearly as obviously clear-cut as in the foregoing cases. However, as I also noted before, the key question to ask always is whether, given a strong enough reason, the agent could be externally coerced into acting contrary to the phobia or psychological compulsion. If they can be so coerced then the factor is just internally coercive, if not, it is internally compulsive. Thus, it might appear that the phobias and psychological compulsions play analogous roles to those played by external compulsive and coercive factors with respect to the concepts of 'physical freedom' and 'liberty.' That is, they may appear to constitute physical constraints in the absence of which we can be said to be absolutely free. However, the issue arises as to whether, even here, we are examining the issues closely enough, and I will now raise two distinct problems for the position.

First, I wish to show now that it is possible to raise a regress argument with respect to the absolute sense of 'freedom' by means of continuing to push the issue of whether we could have chosen otherwise further steps back from the decision per se to choose to perform a possible course of action of a given type. In particular, I wish to claim that each time that it is claimed that an agent is performing a free choice, one can raise the issue as to whether or not the decision so to choose was itself free. For example, we saw that if it is claimed that an actual course of action is free when performed without either external compulsion (physical freedom) or external coercive factors (liberty), one can still raise the issue as to whether to try to perform the course of action was itself free or not (absolute freedom).

In particular, one might take note of the concept of a 'volitional ability,' which was introduced by Gert and Timothy Duggan (1979) in this regard. In Gert and Duggan's language an agent is said to possess such an ability towards a possible course of action of a given type when they do not possess either an internal coercive or compulsive block (e. g., a phobia) against pursuing a possible course of action of the type in question. Such an ability is then contrasted with a 'voluntary ability' which would correspond to the physical ability to pursue a possible course of action of a given type once an agent has so chosen. An agent would only be characterized as being free to pursue a possible course of action of a given type if they had both a volitional ability and a voluntary ability to pursue it.

Notice that the regress need not stop here though, since one can also ask whether the agent was free to freely choose the course of action or not, from whence the regress can continue to be pushed back indefinitely. This point has been made by a number of classical philosophers, including Jonathan Edwards

(1754/1957) and Schopenhauer (1841/1960). Schopenhauer, for example, notes the danger of a regress occurring as follows:

> The empirical concept of freedom signifies: "I am free when I can do what I will." Here in the phrase "what I will" the freedom is already affirmed. But when we now inquire about the freedom of willing itself, the question would then take this form: "Can you also will your volitions?", as if a volition depended on another volition behind it. Suppose that this question is answered in the affirmative, what then? Another question would arise: "Can you also will that which you will to will?" Thus we would be pushed back indefinitely, since we would think that a volition depended on a previous, deeper volition. (Schopenhauer, 1841/1960 p. 6).

Schopenhauer goes on to note that we are at least typically much more clear about the consequences of an act of willing than its causes, and thus questions how we can be at all sure that the act itself is not causally determined. *A fortiori*, it would seem that when the issue of whether an act of willing was free or not is pushed even more steps back it is not at all clear that our introspective evidence of what is going on is incompatible with causal determinism. It is as if decisions to will or not will particular possible courses of action just enter our conscious mind while we are ignorant of the true nature of the causes. A good example here is that of the compulsive handwasher who is under the delusion that their hands are always dirty even when it is pointed out to them that they were just washed. This is an important point, and I will be exploring some of the implications of it in more detail in Chapter Five in my discussion about responsibility and the retributive theory of punishment.

A second point here concerns the detail with respect to which the physical situation of an agent is to be described in determining whether or not they are free to choose otherwise. In particular, it can be noted that in talking about phobias and psychological compulsions, I was only bringing in certain causes and not all of the antecedent conditions in an agent's causal background. Thus, the question arises as to whether, given the rest of the antecedent conditions in an agent's causal background, the actual courses of action of everyone are, in an important sense, comparable to those of the phobic and psychologically compulsive agent; i. e., that given all of the conditions, they could not have acted otherwise.

Elizabeth Beardsley (1960) has called the resultant moral attitude towards agents when all causal antecedent conditions are brought in 'ultimate moral equality,' and I think that there is much to be said for this attitude, which has also been espoused by Walter Kaufmann (1973) among others. In fact, assuming the truth of determinism, I do not see how taking the attitude may ultimately be legitimately avoided. I should note though that there may be other comparable concepts concerning how best fairly to deal with agents from a consequentialist perspective which can be justified even if determinism is true, and in fact I will be developing some of these concepts in Chapter Five and in Part Two. There are obvious connections between the issues just discussed and those concerning ascriptions of rationality since cases of phobias and psychological compulsions are often deemed to constitute irrational conduct. In fact, this may seem to under-cut my claim that there is no sharp dividing line, at least in terms of their causal determination, with courses of actions of other types. In order to show that my claim can still be defended in spite of this point, it is necessary to examine both the issue of whether or not determinism is compatible with ascriptions of ration-ality and also of what marks the distinction between rational and irrational courses of action. As a preliminary to this examination I will make a few remarks on the subject of 'prediction.'

Section Four Prediction

The concept of 'prediction' plays a key role in both my analyses of "deliberation' and 'rationality' in this chapter and also with respect to several issues discussed in Part Two. The issues in Part Two include predicting probable societal consequences of enacting various alternative systems of laws and the predictions of potential lawbreakers in considering the probable consequences if they break the laws. There are obvious tie-ins between this last issue and the topic of deterrence. The subject of prediction is multifaceted with respect to several distinct issues, including the distinctions between what is predictable in principle versus what is predictable 'in practice,' prediction in deterministic versus indeterministic systems, and issues concerning what occurs when there is feedback from the fact that a prediction has been made to the system with respect to which the prediction is being made. I will now deal with each of these issues separately.

For a deterministic system prediction the subject of what is predictable 'in principle' is reasonably straightforward. A major, and, in the light of quantum mechanics, questionable assumption here is that the laws of physics (as they ideally are and not necessarily as we claim to know them) are deterministic and not just probabilistic in character. Given this assumption, the prediction then is what follows for a given time and situation type in the future from applying these laws of physics to a complete set of environmental initial conditions in the present. A classic statement of this in principle position was given by Pierre Laplace:

> An intelligence that, at a given instant, could comprehend all the forces by which nature is animated and the respective situation of the beings that make it up, if moreover it were vast enough to submit these data to analysis, would encompass in the same formula the movements of the greatest bodies of the universe and those of the lightest atoms. For such an intelligence nothing would be uncertain, and the future, like the past, would be open to its eyes. (Laplace (1825/1995, p., 2)

If the laws of physics are truly indeterministic in character (as is held by modern quantum mechanics) even the 'in principle' predictions become probabilistic in character. It is noteworthy that this may be true of the macrocosm and not just the microcosm. A good example illustrating this point is the case where a microscopic event is amplified, as when a Geiger Counter clicks in response to the absorption of a gamma ray. I will now turn to my discussion of the 'in practice' case, which as I noted in Chapter Three in my discussion of objective and subjective senses of 'best,' is the most relevant case to the extent that ethical decision-making is a practical system.

Obviously our knowledge is typically imperfect with respect to both the laws of physics and environmental initial conditions. Thus, in making predictions here we 'make do' with respect to both of these factors, although depending on what is at stake and time constraints we may make more or less of an effort to gather relevant environmental information or even to gain a better understanding of the relevant physical laws. I might note that Wilfred Sellars (1963, p. 6) calls the internal representation of the environmental initial conditions the 'manifest image.' Some cases of 'in practice' prediction are completely reliable and straightforward. Good examples here include predicting planetary orbits or the fact that the sun will rise tomorrow. Complexity of initial conditions can make matters very difficult to predict though, as in the case of chaos (James Gleick, 1987). A good example of trying to predict a chaotic system is the case of weather prediction, in particular in situations where a front is predicted to come close to the region at the time when the weather is being predicted.

Predictions concerning human actions (typically of other people, but sometimes even ourselves) possess a number of further subtleties. Even here though some predictions are quite straightforward, particularly those concerning habitual activities; e. g. parts of one's daily routine, such as brushing one's teeth in the morning. Other straightforward cases involve predictions from relatively fixed personality traits, such as whether a person is in general selfish or generous. In cases where people have a hard time making up their minds though, the situation is different. A good example of such a case involving a conflict between what is called for from different points of view is Jean Paul Sartre's (1946/1956) famous example from "Existentialism is a Humanism" of one of his students trying to decide whether to go to England and join the free French forces or to stay home and provide for his aging mother. It is hard to predict our own future decisions in cases like these, let alone those of someone else, and, as Sartre emphasizes, the resulting act of decision-making can be full of angst.

In cases where the act of making a prediction can affect the results being predicted even more complications occur. For one point, if a person with respect to whom a prediction is being made learns of the prediction they may deliberately do something else so as to thwart it. For example, if a person learns about a prediction that they will die in a car accident on a given day they may deliberately avoid being in a car on that day. It is also possible to bring in game theory here, as John Von Neumann and Oskar Morgenstern (1944) do. As Von Neumann and Morgenstern point out, much depends on whether the other agent is a competitor, as in chess or poker, or a cooperator, either in the case of formal partners such as in bridge or in informal alliances such as in risk or monopoly. They also distinguish between games involving perfect knowledge (e. g., chess), those involving a chance element (e. g., backgammon), and those involving partial ignorance (e. g. some card games). There are further complications when we can predict that the competitor will try to take our predictions into account as Von Neumann and Morgenstern (1944, Ch. 4) discuss for the case of bluffing in poker.

As I pointed out in Chapter One, to some extent life can be viewed as a game, and there are obvious parallels between making predictions in the 'game of life' and those of the games discussed by Von Neumann and Morgenstern. This is true even though the stakes with respect to the consequences of winning and losing are at least typically much more serious in the game of life than in actual games. Real life cooperative examples include cases where we can 'count on' a person or group of people to play a cooperative role, as in the cases of personal friends, business cartels, or allies in war. That is, we can make a prediction that the person or group of people will act in such a manner that they assist us in accomplishing a goal in question. In contrast, competitive cases would be situations where we can count on someone or a group of people at least to attempt to thwart us in carrying through with our plans. Examples here include personal rivals, competing businesses, or wartime enemies. Clearly there are also 'in between' cases as well which often are even harder to predict in practice.

It can also be pointed out that some foundational issues have been raised concerning limitations on predictions about formal systems which are adequate for number theory. For example, J. R. Lucas (1961) argues for the existence of absolute freedom based on implications of Gödel's theorem on such systems. However, since the focus of this book is the 'in practice' case, I will not develop this subject further other than to note that it has resulted in a large and contentious literature; see Douglas Hofstadter (1979, Ch. 15) and Judson Webb (1980, Ch. 4). I will now turn to my discussion of rationality.

Section Five The Compatibility of Rationality with Determinism

In this section I will first present analyses of the concepts of 'rationality' and 'irrationality. I will then, making use of these analyses, defend the claim that ascriptions of human rationality are compatible with determinism. I will also show that these ascriptions are compatible with certain roles for indeterminism in our decision-making procedures. Since both my analyses of 'rationality' and of 'irrationality' are strongly influenced by concepts presented by Dennett (1984), it will be useful to summarize what Dennett has to say on the related concept of 'deliberation' prior to my discussion of rationality and irrationality per se.

As Dennett notes, 'deliberation' can be analyzed in terms of three components—the evaluation of the different consequences of a series of at least apparently physically possible but mutually incompatible potential courses of action; the ranking of the relative merits of these options by some system; and the subsequent opting, based on this ranking, of the pursuit of a possible course of action of a given type. With regard to the first component here, a deliberating agent must possess something akin to Sellars' (1963, p. 6) 'manifest image' of their environment together with the ability to predict (in the sense of 'in practice' prediction just discussed) what changes will occur in that environment in response to undergoing different potential courses of action. With regard to the second component, the decision-making process for deliberation per se can be based on any ranking criterion whatsoever. However, in view of my claim that, even in non-moral contexts, we ought to do what is best, the question arises here as to what the best means of deliberation is. This issue though is obviously very closely tied in to the subject of the nature of rational deliberation, and thus I will postpone discussing it until after my analyses of 'rationality' and 'irrationality.' Finally, regarding the third component of actually opting for the pursuit of a particular potential course of action based on the foregoing decision-making process, I wish to merely point out that this raises 'mind - body' issues concerning how there can be causal connections between internal 'mental states' and bodily movements. However, I will not go into these issues in this book. I will thus move on now to my analysis of 'rationality,' which as I noted is also closely connected with an analysis provided by Dennett.

In order to ascribe 'rationality' to an agent (or, for Dennett, possibly an animal or even a machine), the agent must first possess something akin to interests; which it can be recalled I analyzed in Chapters Two and Three in terms of needs and matters of mere desire. It should be emphasized that I am not confining my usage here to moral interests, inasmuch as it is not always irrational to be immoral; e. g., if one is not endangering oneself in the process. The degree of rationality (note that by speaking of 'degrees of rationality' I am assuming that the concept of 'rationality' is not 'all or nothing,' and to some extent this may go against ordinary usage) of the agent can then be judged in terms of how well their actual and potential courses of action coincide with the optimal furthering of either their individual interests or those of a wider group of individuals.

Dennett also makes some intriguing points concerning possible internal workings of rational decision-making. As I noted in my summary of Dennett's analysis of 'deliberation,' a deliberating agent must possess a manifest image of their environment along with the ability to predict impacts on that environment of different potential courses of action. If the agent is also perfectly rational (and assuming here an egotistical point of view), then according to Dennett they will pick that potential course of action whose causal consequences on the environment most closely coincide with their own interests and desires. An apt metaphor which Dennett uses in this connection is that of a game. In particular, explaining how some moves are forced, how sometimes there is only one non-suicidal move (i. e., only one rational move) and how sometimes we have a great deal of 'elbow room' among different at least apparently equally-rational moves. Of course, the rules of the 'game of life' are much less fixed than games like chess, and it is less clear-cut what it means to 'win' the game. Still, there would appear to be a number of relevant parallels between the two cases.

I wish to make two amendments to Dennett's analyses here. The first amendment is that I wish to claim that ascriptions of rationality are at least compatible with using a broader viewpoint than a purely egotistical one in making decisions. The second amendment in turn involves the nature of decision procedures used under any of these viewpoints. In particular, I would question whether ascriptions of responsibility presuppose the utilization of the decision-making procedure of maximizing expected utility. I will develop the first amendment in some detail now, and will then move on to develop the second amendment.

Unlike Dennett, I think that a potential course of action may be characterized as being 'rational' whether it is in the interest of just a single individual or a wider set of individuals who we care about. For example, I think that it is clear that a parent who rushes into a burning building to save their child is not acting irrationally, although they are deliberately putting their own life at risk. However, courses of action involving self-sacrifice would only appear to be rational if they are both performed in order to help other agents and when also the good to be achieved is comparable in scope with the sacrifice involved. It also follows that, inasmuch as I argued in Chapter Three that while consciousness (and hence life itself) is an intrinsic good, non-conscious physical objects at most possess only instrumental worth, risking one's life just to try to save property (whether one's own or someone else's) is not rational unless basic necessities for life are involved. In summary, my claim is that in acting rationally an agent both must be utilizing either the moral point of view or some narrower point of view (e. g., egoism or any other form of provincialism) and must also choose to pursue the best potential course of action from this point of view (either with or without the fairness constraint given in Chapter Two) given the agent's current knowledge of the overall situation.

The second amendment which I wish to make to Dennett's analysis is that the determination of what is rational is relative both to stakes that an agent has in a given situation and to time constraints for making the decision. One key issue here concerns whether a decision is made under certainty of the consequences, risk (where at least the subjective probabilities of potential outcomes are known), or under uncertainty of outcomes (where even subjective probabilities of different potential outcomes are not known). If a decision is made under certainty then we should, if we are to act rationally under the relevant point of view, choose our best potential course of action, again with or without the fairness constraint. The situation is more subtle with respect to decisions made under either risk or uncertainty since knowledge is incomplete in these situations, and thus much will depend on the nature of the downside stakes if we turn out to be mistaken. If there is a great deal at risk (e. g., a life-threatening situation) then it may be rational to use either the maximax strategy (whereby agents "go for broke" and choose potential courses of action where, if the consequences go in their favor, they are the best well off) or the maximin strategy, where they try to "hold their potential losses."

An added issue here, which is also clearly dependent on both stakes and times constraints, concerns how far into the future (i. e., whether to use a short-term or a long-term outlook) to predict probable consequences of different potential courses of action. For example, if the long-term effects are essentially the same no matter what an agent chooses (e. g., for most plausible scenarios, in cases of choosing what to order from a menu at a restaurant), then clearly the agent need not worry too much about long-term effects. In contrast, if the causal effects may well escalate over time; e. g., if our contemplated assassination of a popular political leader may well lead to political instability in a country) then clearly much more attention needs to be paid to those long-term consequences, even from a purely-egotistical point of view. I will be having much more to say on the subject of causal consequences of potential courses of action in Chapter Six, and thus I will postpone a more detailed discussion of the topic until that chapter.

Before leaving the topic of the nature of rational decision-making procedures, I wish to take note again of a point which I originally raised in discussing the ethical theory of Rawls in Chapter Two. This point is that the cases where it is most appropriate to use a maximax strategy to either gain or not jeopardize a commodity (e. g., one's life savings, one's life, or one's health) are also the same cases where it is appropriate to use a maximin strategy to protect the commodity. For example, it is appropriate to use a maximin strategy with respect to decision-making with potentially life-threatening consequences, and similarly, if the only way to save my life is to permit something which will probably cause me to die (such as an extremely risky operation), I may still be justified in doing it under the maximax strategy. In contrast, the strategy of maximizing expected utility deals neither with cases where we are so far ahead financially, or otherwise, that a potential loss does not bother us much, nor where failure to achieve an otherwise unreachable maximum is thought to be unacceptable, and where we are thus willing to risk everything in order to have at least some chance of obtaining it. This completes my discussion of the nature of decision-making in the context of rational deliberation, and I will thus now turn to an analysis of 'irrationality.'

Since my analysis of 'irrationality' will make integral use of the concept of an 'intentional action,' I will begin by making a few remarks on that latter concept.

As has been pointed out by Anscombe (1957/1963, Sec. 6), and later emphasized by Davidson (1980, Essay 5), the characterization of an action as being 'intentional' is relative to a particular description. In particular, an intentional course of action can be construed as the purposive pursuit of the existence a given type of situation under some particular description of the situation, although not necessarily under all possible descriptions of the situation. It should be emphasized that an action that is thus characterized as being 'intentional' under one description (say, shooting what one takes to be a deer) may not also be characterized as being 'intentional' under another description (say, shooting a person). This point will be of importance in my analysis of excuses involving ignorance in Chapter Six.

As a working definition of the 'irrational' then, I propose the following. Opting for a potential course of action is to be deemed 'irrational' if and only if the potential course of action was intentionally chosen under a given description such that there was also an alternative potential course of action which was clearly superior to the first under another description that the agent was also cognizant of. It is assumed that the same point of view (e. g., egoism or the moral point of view) is being used throughout here. Thus, courses of action chosen at random for the purposes alluded to by Dennett would not be deemed 'irrational.' An example of a course of action that would be deemed 'irrational' here would be that of an agent who, say in the context of playing a game of chess, makes a particular move even though they are cognizant at the same time that another possible move would be clearly superior and if they also desire to win the game.

Irrational courses of action may also seem to occur with respect to cases of what is known as 'weakness of the will.' These courses of action are like the irrational courses of action just discussed (i. e., a less than optimal course of action is performed even though the agent is cognizant at the time that another one would be superior), except that the course of action is not consciously chosen, but instead is performed even in spite of a conscious decision to do otherwise. It can be questioned as to whether such a course of action is really 'voluntary' (in particular if 'voluntary' is defined in terms of being caused by conscious 'acts' of the will) or not though, and if the ascription of rationality and irrationality is restricted to voluntary courses of action, then this sense would obviously be moot.

'Rational courses of action' can now be defined as being all those potential courses of action which are not irrational. 'Rational deliberation' can then be defined as being all deliberation which is based on rational principles. The concept of a 'rational course of action,' thus defined, does not "home in on" a single potential course of action whereas the concept of 'the best possible potential course of action' does. A complication does arise here when we speak, as I allow, of some potential courses of action as being more rational than others. Even here one must be wary of the concept of 'the most rational course of action' though since this will vary depending upon whose interests an agent is looking out for. For example, an act of self-sacrifice may not be the most rational for an agent, even if it does produce the greatest overall preponderance of goods over harms, when the agent is working under the narrow point of view of egoism. This completes my analysis of 'rationality' and 'irrationality,' and thus I will now turn to the subject of showing that ascriptions of these concepts can be compatible with the truth of determinism. I will begin my discussion by showing, as Davidson (1980, Essay 1) and Fred Dretske (1988, Ch. 4) have argued, that reasons may serve as causes. I will first give a brief sketch of Davidson's and Dretske's arguments, and will then offer a few amendments of my own.

Davidson begins his argument that reasons serve as causes by pointing out that, even though reasons may not be germane as constituting causes for actions under all of the possible descriptions of the actions, so long as they are a relevant rationale under at least one description of the action (in the manner previously discussed), they can constitute a cause. Ontological commitment issues concerning the teleological aspects of reasons are finessed by means of an analysis in terms of beliefs and desires which are physiologically grounded. In particular, Davidson analyzes the concept of 'acting for a reason' in terms of what he calls the 'primary reason' for the action in question. Primary reasons are in turn held to be constituted by both a 'pro attitude' (e. g., a desire, which Davidson uses in a wide sense so as to include such other propositional attitudes as wants, urges, goals, intentions, and feelings of duties) on the part of the agent plus a belief that the type of action under a particular description will constitute the fulfillment of that pro attitude. The apropos beliefs and pro attitudes are then grounded in physical existents by means of analyzing them dispositionally, whereby the dispositions correspond physically to various standing psychological states which possess physiological groundings. However, Davidson ducks issues concerning the nature of these groundings. It is held then that the dispositions can then be activated by a change in our physical environment (e. g., if an opportunity to fulfill a desire occurs) which we psychologically "take note of"; i. e., the environmental change causes a change in the belief state.

Dretske in turn, like Davidson, presents an analysis of how reasons can serve as causes in terms of beliefs and desires which are physiologically grounded. Unlike Davidson, Dretske also includes a relation to a representation of needs. Dretske is also more elaborate than Davidson on the nature of the physiological grounding. In particular, Dretske presents a representational analysis of beliefs, desires and representations of needs in terms of what he calls "type three representations," which are defined as being natural systems which possess intrinsic indicator functions. The 'indicators' of the systems are defined as being items that constitute reliable signs for whatever they are indicators for, in the sense that the presence of the indicators is causally determined by the existence of what they are indicators for. Physiologically-grounded beliefs, desires and representations of needs are then claimed to serve as 'structuring' rather than 'triggering' causes, in the sense that they are held to determine what structure an effect (e. g., a course of action) will take as opposed to 'triggering' its occurrence. I am not necessarily endorsing either of these account except to point out that they show that plausible accounts exist for grounding reasons as causes, and that similar accounts can be fleshed out in much more detail than sketched here.

Mention should also be made in this regard of various linguistic issues concerning how meanings (semantics) can be mimicked by syntax. In particular, the work of H. P. Grice (1957) can be cited in this regard, where an attempt was made to reduce meaning, in the semantic sense, to what Grice calls 'non-natural' meaning (as opposed to natural indicators), which he analyzes in terms of the intentions of the speaker and the listener. Assuming that intentions at least can be psychologically grounded, then it would seem that such an analysis would lead in principle to a reduction of semantic meaning to physical existents. It should be noted that a large literature has grown up both attacking Grice (e. g., Paul Ziff, 1967, and Searle, 1970, although Searle is somewhat sympathetic to the general enterprise), and also defending at least the broad scope of his analysis (e. g., Dennett, 1987 and Steven Stich, 1983). However, both for reasons of space, and because I have nothing in particular new to add to the debate, I will merely refer to it and neither summarize it or criticize it here.

Before moving on to make some concluding remarks for the chapter, I wish to take note of two amendments which I believe ought to be made to the foregoing accounts of both Davidson and Dretske. First, I wish to point out again that, along with being relative to beliefs and desires, rationality is also relative to stakes. Thus, both Davidson's and Dretske's accounts need to be amended so as to take cognizance of the fact that the rationality of a potential course of action is relative to an agent's stakes (either upward or downward) in different possible outcomes. The second amendment concerns the width of the point of view used in rational decision-making. Again, as I previously pointed out, this may involve either a narrow (e. g., egoist) or a broad (e.g., moral) point of view, and it needs to be emphasized that pro attitudes thus need not be selfish in character. For example, one can have a desire to help others and still be rational. I will now turn to a discussion of the possible role of indeterminacy in making choices which are equally strongly backed up by reasons in different directions.

Sometimes, say, in the context of the chess example discussed in Chapter One, if a chess clock is being used, we are under time constraints to make a move. In these sorts of cases it may be necessary to use a heuristic shortcut instead of actually deriving the truly optimal solution, assuming that there actually is one. This, according to James (1884), Dennett (1984, Ch. 5), and Kane (1985), is one type of situation where it is rational to choose at random from among a number of at least seemingly equally-rational alternatives. However, as Dennett also points out, it makes no practical different here as to whether one's decision-making procedure is only pseudo-random (actually deterministic) or truly random, such as by amplifying the results of a quantum process. Hence, the whole issue of indeterminism (at least where this is held to be compatible with, or even a prerequisite for, ascriptions of rationality and moral responsibility) versus determinism may just involve pseudo-issues, since even if indeterminism is true it would appear to add nothing to solving the problem. I will return to discuss this subject in somewhat more detail when, in Chapter Five, I present my arguments against the efficacy of our common-sense notions concerning when ascriptions of moral responsibility are justified. Thus, I will now close this chapter by showing how the preceding analysis of 'rational decision-making' can resolve at least an apparent paradox to the position of act consequentialism, which the position of determinism may seem to present.

The apparent paradox for act consequentialism raised by the position of determinism can be stated as follows. It would seem that act consequentialism must assume both the truth and the falsity of determinism. It would seem that act consequentialism must assume the truth of determinism since, in comparing the relative worths of the consequences of different potential courses of action, it must assume that these consequences are causally fixed indefinitely far into the future. And yet, act consequentialism would seem to also have to assume the falsity of determinism since it assumes that, at the moment of rational deliberation among different potential courses of action, the actualization of a course of action of more than one type is in fact physically possible. The question then can be raised as to how other agents' courses of action can be accurately predicted, as required for the determination of the consequences of those courses of action. I now wish to make a point from the preceding analysis of the nature of rational decision-making which will resolve this apparent paradox. I might also note that what I believe to be the solution to the paradox, that rational deliberation among different potential courses of action (including even the 'pseudo-random' picking of potential options) is perfectly compatible with determinism, will also defuse at least one of the historically prime motivations which have been given for holding the position of indeterminism, namely the belief that rational deliberation is not compatible with determinism.

According to my account of the nature of rational decision-making, we are faced with more than one open potential course of action in this decision-making, as stated in the foregoing paradox, only in the sense that the causally-determined deliberation process makes use of representations of these potential courses of action (in Dretske's physiologically-grounded sense) in the process of evaluating their relative merits. This would also appear to be the appropriate sense of interpreting Kant's claim that 'ought' implies 'can.' That is, I am claiming that Kant's usage of 'can' here is most plausibly construed as just referring to potential courses of action, as just analyzed, and not to that which is physically possible given absolutely everything in our background. Still, since only one of these potential courses of action (the one which is causally determined to be chosen) is in fact chosen by the rational deliberator, the whole process here is compatible with the truth of determinism.

Thus, the foregoing paradox can be resolved by noting that, rather than it being the case that the concepts of 'rationality' and 'determinism' stand in opposition to each other, in actuality ascriptions of rationality typically either presuppose the truth of determinism or are at least compatible with its truth, as in the cases where a pseudo-random decision-making procedure is necessary due to a time constraint. This completes my discussion of the free-will issue, and in my next chapter I will apply some of my conclusions here with respect to the issue of the justifiability of ascriptions of moral responsibility to agents for their courses of action.

Chapter Five
A Critique of Moral Responsibility and the Retributive Theory of Punishment

In this chapter I will make use of the concepts and arguments which I introduced and developed in Chapter Four, on the free will problem, in order to present a series of arguments that ascriptions of 'moral responsibility' and 'retribution,' at least as we normally use those terms, are never justified. I will first present analyses of our respective common-sense concepts of 'moral responsibility' and 'retribution' and will then present a critique both of a common-sense theory of psychology presupposed by both concepts and also of the internal self-coherence of the concepts.

Thus, the arguments of this chapter will be primarily negative, showing the non-efficacy of our common-sense theories of moral responsibility and retributive punishment. However, I should note that in Chapter Six I will show how a rationally-reconstructed 'causal' concept of 'responsibility' can be made to serve many of the same purposes as the common-sense notions. However, it will lack one key feature of the common-sense notion, in that agents will not be held to be either personally 'blameworthy' or 'praiseworthy' in a moral sense in virtue of their courses of action. Thus, I will be arguing in that chapter that, while the courses of action of agents can be criticized in terms of the nature of their consequences, we are not thereby also justified in making moral value judgments on the agents themselves. I should also note that in Part Two I will offer an alternative theory of punishment (or 'correction') to the one that is based on retribution. I will begin the chapter by analyzing 'moral responsibility' and will then move on to my analysis of 'retribution.'

Section One Moral Responsibility

In this section I will present an analysis of the common-sense theory of 'responsibility' which I shall term 'moral responsibility,' so as to distinguish it from a reconstructed causal sense of 'responsibility' which I will be developing in Chapter Six. A key distinction between the two senses will be that attributions of 'moral responsibility' will include ascriptions of moral judgments with respect to agents, while the attribution of 'causal responsibility' will be neutral with respect to these judgments. I will begin my discussion of 'moral responsibility' by making a few comments on the etymology of 'responsibility,' and will then show how a whole common-sense theory of human nature is implicitly assumed by the concept.

To begin, it can be noted that 'responsibility' is derived from the Latin 'respondere,' meaning 'to respond.' This shows at least an historical link with the concept of 'being answerable,' as in having 'to answer' for the consequences of one's courses of action. I wish to show now how a whole common-sense theory of human nature is implicitly being presupposed by this notion of 'being answerable.' First, it can be noted that under the common-sense theory of the nature of moral responsibility, agents may be held to be responsible for either acts of 'commission' or those of 'omission.' In the case of acts of 'commission,' it is held that agents are only answerable for the consequences of those courses of action which either were performed intentionally (i. e., 'on purpose;' that is, under the analyses of Davidson (1980, Essay 1) and Anscombe (1957/1963, Sec. 6), where the agent was consciously aware of the consequences of the course of action under the description for which they are held responsible for it), or were performed under circumstances where the agent at least should have been aware of the consequences even though, as a matter of fact, they were not; e. g., if negligence was involved. It is also held that the agent must have been 'free' to have done otherwise, in the absolute sense of 'freedom,' which I analyzed in Chapter Four.

In the case of acts of omission, the common-sense theory holds that responsibility is incurred whenever any sort of moral or legal obligation has been incurred—say, by means of either making a promise or entering into a contract—inasmuch as we are then held to be responsible for carrying out the obligation, in these cases, by either keeping the promise or fulfilling the terms of the contract unless a circumstance that constitutes an 'adequate excuse' contravenes. Our common-sense theory of what constitutes an 'adequate excusing condition' is rather vague. Still, it does seem to be clear, as Ross (1930/1988, p. 22) points out, that just utilitarian (at least in the positive utilitarian sense of maximizing the preponderance of goods over harms) criteria per se are not always held to be sufficient conditions by the theory. For example, the mere fact that some alternative potential course of action would have produced more good than that produced by keeping a promise is at least not usually taken by the theory to constitute an adequate excuse for breaking a promise. However, it can also be noted that if the difference in consequences is sufficiently drastic (such as if one can only save a child's life by means of breaking a promise), an adequate excuse may be deemed to be present.

It would seem that negative utilitarianism is more in line with common sense here than positive utilitarianism, inasmuch as the mitigation of harms is often taken to be an adequate excusing condition for such acts as breaking promises. Another alternative justification here would be one based on Ross's (1930/1988, p. 19) conception of '*prima facie* duties.' For example, in the case of breaking a promise in order to save a child's life, under Ross's system there would be a conflict between the *prima facie* duty of fidelity to keep promises and the *prima facie* duty of non-maleficience to preserve life. Clearly here the higher-order duty to preserve life would win out. In cases where there is no conflict between *prima facie* duties, under Ross's system though we would have to keep a promise. I will now turn to my analysis of what the common-sense theory holds is the meaning of 'moral responsibility' by means of first analyzing the related concept of 'legal responsibility.'

Much of the following analysis of 'legal responsibility' is influenced by a model discussed by Hart (1968, Ch. 6). In order for an agent to be held to be 'legally responsible' for the commission of a crime, at least three distinct criteria must at least usually be met. In the first place, an '*actus reus*' (wrongful act) must have occurred; i. e., some actually enacted law must have been broken. That is, some situation must have been brought into existence which was of a type either not in accordance with the types of situations whose existence is prescribed by the law, or included within the types of situations whose existence is prohibited by the law. It can be noted that this distinction between laws stated in terms of requiring the existence of certain types of situations and those stated in terms of prohibiting the existence of other types of situations is actually not all that fundamental. This is because, by the law of contraposition, the prohibition of the existence of certain types of situations is logically equivalent to the requirement that the only types of situations which may exist must belong to the logical complement of the foregoing class. For example, the 55 mile per hour speed limit can be interpreted as either prohibiting higher speeds or as requiring ones of 55 or lower.

It might be thought that cases of conspiracy laws would constitute counterexamples to Hart's first condition, since under these laws it is deemed to be illegal to just plan to commit a crime. However, it should be emphasized that what is actually deemed to be illegal here is the planning itself and not the crime which is being planned. Thus, in the case of a conspiracy to commit a bank robbery which ends up being thwarted, the conspirators would not be charged with the bank robbery itself but instead merely with conspiracy to do so, which would typically carry a lesser penalty. Also, since this latter act is itself of a type which is proscribed by the law, a law has in fact been broken here, albeit not the one which the conspirators were planning to break. Thus, this sort of case does not actually constitute a counterexample to the model.

The second criterion for 'legal responsibility' discussed by Hart can be stated in terms that either the legally responsible agent must have caused the law to broken (that is, pursued a course of action among whose consequences was that the law-breaking situation mentioned in the first criterion came into existence), or that, in the case of 'vicarious responsibility,' some other agent who they were 'responsible for' must have caused it to be broken. Thus, in the vicarious case, the responsibility is, in effect, transferred from the actual agent breaking a law (in the causal sense) to some other agent. Examples here would include cases where parents are held responsible for the consequences of the courses of action of their children and cases where employers are held responsible for the consequences of the courses of action of their employees. It should also be noted that the vicarious case is sometimes just talked about in terms of 'legal liability' and not 'legal responsibility' though, with the implication being that the agent being held liable must still suffer the legal ramifications of the wrongdoing even though, since they are not the direct cause, they may not, in some sense to be elaborated on shortly, be morally blameworthy of the crime.

The third criterion for 'legal responsibility' is a somewhat controversial one as Hart points out, and does not apply in cases of 'strict liability' (e. g., cases of parking violations). where the first two criteria alone are deemed to be sufficient. It involves the mental state (known as 'mens rea') of the agent who is being held to be legally responsible. Roughly, according to this criterion a legally responsible agent must have both intentionally and voluntarily caused the existence of the situation which was not in accordance with the law, and the agent must have also had both knowledge of the circumstances which they were in and foresight of the probable consequences of their course of action.

If all three of the just-given criteria for 'legal responsibility' are met (or just the first two criteria for cases of strict liability), then it is held that the agent in question is 'legally responsible' for the commission of the crime, in the sense that they are held then to be liable to the imposition of some type of penalty; i. e., punishment. That is, it is held that a court then has the 'right' to 'sentence' this agent to some unpleasant experience, such as incarceration in prison or being forced to pay a fine. It may also be implied here, to the extent that punishment is being viewed as 'retribution,' that this agent in some way 'deserves' to be punished due to the fact that they committed the crime. I will be elaborating on a number of these points, in particular on the one concerning the justifiability of punishment as retribution, both later in this chapter and also in Part Two in my chapters on the judicial and post-judicial systems. For present purposes though I wish to move on to my analysis of the concept of 'moral responsibility.'

My analysis of 'moral responsibility' will fairly closely parallel the analysis just given of 'legal responsibility.' There will be a few crucial differences though, notably involving the point that 'moral responsibility' can be used in either a positive or a negative sense—i. e., as either grounds for praise or grounds for blame—instead of just the negative sense which occurs with ascriptions of legal responsibility. I shall just be concerned here with the negative sense of 'moral responsibility' though.

Instead of an enacted law having to be broken (which was one of the prerequisites of legal responsibility), when it is held that 'moral responsibility' in the negative sense is incurred, some purported moral principle must have been at least intended to be broken. It can be recalled that in Chapter Three I justified the existence of moral principles, such as that we ought to tell the truth or keep our promises, in terms of their value apropos the resultant abilities of others to have at least relatively-fixed expectations concerning our future conduct in cooperative efforts. It should be noted though that it is not as clear-cut in the case of moral responsibility as it is with the case of legal responsibility that an agent actually succeed in following through with their intentions in a course of action. That is, while an agent cannot be held legally responsible for an intention to commit a crime if, for any number of possible reasons, they are thwarted from following through on their intentions, some would hold that they are still morally responsible. It is clear though that, as was the case with ascriptions of legal responsibility, the cause of a principle having been broken must have been a deliberate and intentional course of action of either the 'responsible' agent or some other agent whom they are held to be 'responsible for' in order for an ascription of moral responsibility to apply. Thus, in particular, an agent is not at least typically held to be morally responsible for the consequences of a course of action where they were trying to avoid the consequences but failed in doing so.

Instead of being held to be liable to the imposition of a government-sponsored penalty, as was the case with ascriptions of legal responsibility, in the case of ascriptions of moral responsibility, the agent in question may be merely held liable to some type of non-government-sponsored censure or rebuke—e. g., blame or some other form of penalty, depending upon the nature of the circumstances. For example, if an agent is either caught in a lie or in breaking a promise, then this is cause for rebuke on the part of the person being respectively lied to or to whom the promise was originally made. Since the automatic (i. e., without consideration of the consequences on the wrongdoer) imposition of a penalty under these circumstances would, in effect, constitute 'retribution,' it is necessary to also give an analysis of the common-sense theory (the retributive theory of punishment) which holds that the imposition of penalties under these guidelines is justified. It can be noted that such a theory is often invoked for justifying the imposition of either government-sponsored or non-government-sponsored penalties in response respectively to either lawbreaking or the breaking of moral principles. It can also be noted that it is typically more clear-cut in the government-sponsored case who is in charge of assessing and implementing these penalties.

Section Two Retribution

As was the case with 'moral responsibility,' it is useful to begin the analysis of 'retribution' by means of looking at its etymology—it being derived from the Latin 'retribuere,' meaning 'to pay back.' Thus, there is at least an historical link between the concept of 'retribution' and the notion that a wrongdoer 'ought' (in the original sense of 'being owed,' which shows an interesting link between the etymology of 'ought' and retributive theories) to be paid back for the consequences of their courses of action. I should emphasize that I will only be analyzing 'retribution' in the pure case, and not in contexts, such as in our own judicial and post-judicial systems, where retributive theories are mixed with other theories; e. g., consequentialist ones. My discussion has to some extent been influenced both by C. S. Lewis (1970, p. 287) and Anthony Manser (1962).

Basic claims made by purely retributive theories of punishment include the claims that a debt to society is incurred by a wrongdoer when they commit an act of wrongdoing, and that 'justice' (in the 'retributive' sense, sometimes also known as the 'commutative' sense, of repaying a debt) will not be done unless and until this act has been 'repaid' by means of the extraction of an amount of suffering on the part of the wrongdoer which is comparable in scope to that which the wrongdoer inflicted on others. The suffering may either involve the imposition of a harm, as with the imposition of pain in corporal punishment, or may involve the loss of a good, as with the loss of money with a fine, the losses of physical and other types of freedom during incarceration, or the loss of life with capital punishment. To capture the claim that this suffering is deserved, it is typically held that the punishment should, in some sense, 'fit' the crime, as captured by such expressions as 'getting even,' 'quid pro quo,' 'tit for tat,' or the Biblical (*Exodus* 21) 'an eye for an eye and a tooth for a tooth.' It is also sometimes held that the act of punishment in some sense 'annuls' the crime, in the sense of making everything even, or when it is said that a prisoner is "repaying their debt to society." In view of this last point, it is also held that we should not feel sorry for the person being punished since they 'deserve' it, and, so to speak, it 'serves them right.' Furthermore, it is held that, in view of this desert, the person being punished has no morally-justified grounds of complaint for being punished.

It is possible to distinguish between two distinct versions of the retributive theory of punishment at this point; the first of which is act-oriented and the second of which is motive-oriented. The first version, which I take to be the older theory, can be found in the 'eye for an eye' quote from the Bible if this is literally construed, and involves the claim that punishments should match the consequences of actions in severity. One merit of this position is that a person must have actually committed a crime before it is claimed that they deserve punishment, and thus it never calls for punishing the innocent. Looking ahead, it should be noted that I will give an alternative consequentialist rationale for this restriction in Chapter Seven, and thus the possession of this feature need not constitute a superiority for this version of the retributive theory over the consequentialist system which I am advocating.

There are several major difficulties for the act-oriented version of the retributive theory. For one point, it is not at all clear how to match such crimes as rape, slander, or the production of illicit pornographic materials with matching punishments. In fact, if the matching 'punishment' is construed literally in these cases, there can even be perverse results which are reminiscent of the counter-example to the first version of Kant's Categorical Imperative which I gave in Section Four of Chapter Two. Examples would include such cases as a pornographer or rapist actually enjoying (or worse, committing the crime in order to receive) the matching 'punishment.' Also, since motives are completely ignored in this version, such cases of taking a life as negligent homicide, euthanasia, and intentional deliberate murder will all be classified the same way, with capital punishment being called for in all of the cases. In the case where the consequences of a crime escalate (e. g., where a fire started by an arsonist gets out of control and destroys a city block), questions can be raised as to whether it is fair to hold the arsonist completely accountable.

It might be thought that the foregoing difficulties with the act-based retributive theory could be avoided with the motive-based version of the theory. In particular, this may be thought since the motive-based version is based on matching the motives behind an action instead of the consequences of the action for determining the proper punishment. Thus, under this version the first-degree murderer will be held to deserve a more severe punishment than the person guilty of negligent homicide or euthanasia inasmuch as they acted deliberately and with malice, in the sense of ill-will. However, it can be noted that punishing the innocent can be justified here in a case where someone had the intention to commit a crime but was thwarted in their attempt to carry it out. The two versions of the retributive theory are not always carefully distinguished, and hence the fact that each version separately possesses quite-clearly unacceptable consequences may be missed by conflating the versions together.

Two points of contrast can be noted at this point between retributive and consequentialist theories of punishment concerning the temporal orientation of the theories. From the temporal perspective of the act of punishment itself, retributive theories are past-oriented inasmuch as it is held that what justifies the act of punishment is the consequences of the actual act of wrongdoing regardless of any positive effects of the punishment on the agent being punished. In contrast, as I will show in detail in Chapter Seven, consequentialist theories of punishment (or alternatives to punishment) justify the act of correction in terms of its consequences on the future actual and potential actions of the agent being corrected. When it comes to looking at causes of acts, (i. e., motives) though, non-motive-based retributivists claim that these are not relevant since only the consequences of the act should be matched with the penalty. In contrast, I will show in Chapter Seven that for consequentialist theories the issue of what the nature of the motives were behind an act of wrongdoing is going to be one of the most important factors in determining what correctional follow-through is appropriate. Before touching on some further critical points with regard to retributive theories, I wish to take note now of a few points of contrast between the concept of 'retribution' and two related concepts, those of 'revenge' and 'restitution.'

In spite of some of the connotations of such phrases as 'getting even' or 'tit for tat,' it is important to distinguish between the senses of 'retribution' being characterized so far and 'revenge.' For one point, it can be noted that revenge is typically taken by someone directly emotionally involved with respect to the original act of wrongdoing, such as either the victim of the crime or someone else having a personal interest in the victim's case, such as a relative. Also, typically this person will take a personal satisfaction in the act of vengeance, in a sense having been put into an unbalanced psychological state (i. e., that of bearing a 'grudge,' this being a feeling of resentment and also of entitledness directed at the perceived perpetrator of the wrong) by the original act of wrongdoing. It is also held that the balance is only restorable, and hence the 'grudge' removed, by the act of vengeance. In contrast, in the case of retribution, the act of retribution is typically carried out by an emotionally-neutral (i. e., 'disinterested') third party to a dispute, typically an agent of the government. Thus, the direct emotional involvement of vengeance will be missing in cases of retribution, and it can even be noted that otherwise there would be a 'conflict of interest' in the determination of a just punishment. Still, there is something in common between cases of revenge and cases of retribution at least to the extent that it is claimed in both cases that the suffering inflicted on the wrongdoer is deserved on a personal level due to what the wrongdoer did in the past. In view of the claim of this personal desert, it is thus also held in both cases that a debt has been incurred by an act of wrongdoing and that it will not be repaid unless and until a comparable amount of suffering has been inflicted on the wrongdoer.

Retribution also needs to be clearly distinguished from the institution of restitution. As in retribution, restitution involves a wrongdoer in a sense 'righting a wrong,' but in this case by way of paying the victim a benefit that is either comparable in scope to the harm that done to them, or, if possible, by means of repairing the damage by way of restoring circumstances to the way they were before the act of wrongdoing. Thus, two important differences can be noted between the institutions of retribution and restitution. One difference is that the direction of the debt to be repaid is the opposite in restitution from what it was in retribution; being from the wrongdoer to society rather than the other way around. A second difference involves the fact that the institution of punishment as retribution does not attempt to restore circumstances to the way they were before the act of wrongdoing (as restitution does), but instead tries to balance states of affairs out by means of causing the occurrence of another bad situation, the punishment of the wrongdoer. This last fact sometimes leads to a common-sense criticism, perhaps on utilitarian lines, of the institution of retribution, but notably not also of restitution, when it is said that "two wrongs do not make a right."

Inasmuch as there may also be an implication from the foregoing characterization of retribution that we should be free to do wrong so long as we are also willing to 'pay the consequences,' a second criticism can also be raised in this regard. In particular, it may sound as if under the retributive theory of punishment agents would be justified in committing crimes if they were also willing to receive the punishments. That is, it may be thought that not only is it being advocated "don't do the crime if you can't do the time," but it would also seem to be being advocated "feel free to do the crime if you can do the time." Thus, under this construal, punishments may be seen from the viewpoint of lawbreakers as being 'costs of doing business,' where the penalties involved are treated, in effect, like a tax. In contrast, under the consequentialist approach it is held that criminal courses of action are still wrong whether the 'consequences' are later 'paid' or not.

A difference with the deterrence theory of punishment can also be noted here. Punishments which people are willing to receive as a cost of committing a crime are obviously not serving as a deterrent. Thus, under the deterrence theory of punishment still stronger penalties would have to be at least sometimes threatened than those called for under the retributive theory. Still, as I will argue in Chapter Eight, only the minimal effective penalty would be justified. It can also be noted that the 'getting even' associated with retribution tends to possess a built-in mechanism for self-perpetuation, inasmuch as one party's 'act of avenging a wrong' or 'retaliation' may constitute the origin of another party's 'grudge,' which they feel needs to be 'avenged.' The result may be an ongoing cycle taking place over a period of many years, and it may never be clear as to who actually started the process going.

Notice that in the preceding account of the nature of retribution, it is agents who are personally characterized as being 'bad' (and hence 'deserving of punishment') and not just their courses of action or their characters. Otherwise the justification for the punishment would be a consequentialist one. Thus, a 'moral judgment' is being made with respect to wrongdoing agents here, with the claim that they are 'bad' in virtue of what they have done and that states of affairs can only be made 'right again' if they are made to suffer bad consequences themselves which are comparable in degree to those which they caused on others. I shall now turn to a critique of the common-sense theory of human nature which is presupposed by the classical conceptions of 'responsibility' and 'retribution' just analyzed. My critique will consist of three parts. The first part will be based on certain aspects of the free will problem which were discussed in Chapter Four. The second part will be based on the claim that the theory itself is either syntactically or semantically ill-formed inasmuch as it predicates values on agents per se instead of predicating them of relations between the existence of separate situations and the agents. The third part in turn will involve helping to motivate the plausibility of the claim that we are not 'morally responsible,' in the common sense notion of that phrase, for the consequences of our courses of action by considering the case of an amnesiac.

Section Three Argument from the Free Will Problem

My argument from the free will problem against both the justifiability of ascriptions of moral responsibility and the use of punishment as retribution will be posed in the form of a dilemma. One horn of this dilemma will assume the truth of determinism, while the other half will assume the truth of indeterminism. Since these two horns exhaust the logical possibilities concerning the possible nature of the world, it follows that one and only one of them must be the case. However, I will argue that neither possibility can account for the justifiability of either ascriptions of moral responsibility or the use of punishment in a purely retributive sense. Hence it will follow that these respective senses of the terms 'responsibility' and 'punishment' are without legitimate application.

I will begin my argument by means of examining the first horn of the foregoing dilemma, and will thus now assume the truth of determinism. In the first place, it should be emphasized that, as I showed in Section Four of Chapter Four, determinism is compatible with agents possessing the ability to make rational decisions. Thus, positing the determinist position clearly does not entail that people will in any way have to act irrationally. Having noted the compatibility of determinism with rational decision-making, I wish to also take note of a connection which is often thought to exist between the attribution of rationality to agents and ascriptions of moral responsibility to them. This purported connection is that rational agents ought to be held to be morally responsible for the consequences of their intentionally and deliberately chosen courses of action. In contrast, irrational agents (it can be recalled that I analyzed the concept of 'irrationality' in Chapter Four in terms of deliberately choosing options which are known to possess less than optimal consequences from the same point of view), such as those who are judged to be insane, may at least often be excused from ascriptions of both legal and moral responsibility.

It should be emphasized in the foregoing regard that people who have been deemed to be insane are often not allowed to possess all of the 'freedoms' and 'rights' (e. g., using the distinction developed in Chapter Two, mere privileges, although obviously not any truly-irrevocable rights) traditionally accorded to those who are deemed to be fully rational. In fact, allegations of insanity are often used as grounds for revoking many traditional 'rights,' such as voting rights, and even more freedoms in cases of forced confinement to an institution. It should be emphasized though that such confinement need not be viewed as constituting punishment, although I will raise the issue later in Part Two as to whether the rationale for confinement—either for the individual's own self-protection or for the protection of others—is really any different in kind from certain consequentialist justifications for correction. In any event, the issue does arise at this point as to whether or not a full-fledged dichotomy made in the foregoing way between those who are judged to be morally responsible for their actions and those who are judged to be morally irresponsible can be justified. I will present two arguments that it cannot be here. I will show that the first argument, while instructive, possesses a fallacy. However, as far as I can see, the second argument is sound.

To begin my first argument, it can be noted that if we are to be held to be morally responsible for our courses of action, in the negative sense of being blameworthy, then it is implied that we should have done otherwise. Note can also again be made of Kant's principle that 'should' implies, 'can.' The question arises though as to which sense of 'can' is the relevant one here. If it was that of the 'physically possible while keeping all initial conditions the same' sense, then it would follow that, if determinism is true as I am now assuming, 'can' implies 'will.' In this case it would follow both that we could not have done otherwise, and also that it is the case that we should not have done otherwise. However, I have previously argued that at times we should have acted otherwise than the way we do in fact act, and if this claim is to be maintained, then it follows that another sense of 'can' must be the one that is germane here.

To resolve the foregoing paradox, it can first be recalled that in Chapter Four I distinguished between what we are able to do given the background conditions of all of the minute details of our brains, and what we are able to do provided that appropriate signals emerge from a certain small portion of the brain. It would seem then that if 'can' and 'should' in the preceding argument were to be interpreted as referring to this latter sense instead of the sense where all initial conditions are kept the same, then determinism would be compatible with both the claims that we should and could have done otherwise. This would mean then that when we claim that we should have acted otherwise it would have been better (from the same point of view as 'should' is being used) if either our decision-making procedure had been set up differently, or if we had access to more complete information on which to base the decision. This claim is of course consistent with the truth of determinism since nothing has been said in it that in any way denies that we were causally determined (by the information and the decision-making procedure we did have) from making the less than optimal decision that we in fact made. Hence, a fallacy was incurred by the alleged paradox when it failed to make this distinction in senses of 'can.'

In spite of the existence of the fallacy which I just pointed out in the preceding argument, I believe that a valid argument can still be constructed to show that using the first sense of 'can'—that which is physically possible given all of the minute details of our brains—ascriptions of moral responsibility are never justified. This is because, in this sense of 'can,' we could not have acted otherwise than we in fact acted. I should note though that with respect to the causal sense of 'responsibility,' which I will be developing in detail in Chapter Six, and where, unlike the case with the common-sense concept of 'moral responsibility,' ascriptions of blameworthiness will be missing,' the second sense of 'can' (which corresponds to what is physically possible if we try) will be the relevant sense. To return to my argument against the common-sense theory of moral responsibility though, it can first be noted, as Dennett (1984, Ch. 2) points out, that the same decision-making system which can be characterized as being rational (i. e., goal-directed), can also be described, by my deterministic assumption, in completely mechanistic terms. That is, the complete explanation of what is going on in the system can, at least in principle, be given just in terms of physical mechanisms, and no non-mechanistically-reduced teleological language is used. Good examples illustrating this point can be found in the field of artificial intelligence, such as with chess-playing computer programs that have beaten world grand masters in chess.

The key point in the argument is to observe now that, assuming the truth of determinism, since the decision-making system of an agent can be described deterministically as a mechanical system, it follows that when 'can' is used in the sense referring to that which is physically possible given all of the minute details of our brains, we could not have done otherwise. Thus, using 'could have done otherwise' in this last sense, together with the 'desert' sense of 'fairness,' (which it can be recalled from my discussion in Chapter Two is a sense of 'fairness' which cannot be justified under consequentialism, but which is the primary sense under the retributive theory), the question can be raised as to how it can be fair to hold people to be 'morally responsible,' in the sense of being blameworthy, for those courses of action where they could not have done otherwise. Under the 'desert' sense of 'fairness' it would seem that the imposition of something bad here (the penalty associated with being held to be morally responsible) would be unfair since it was not personally deserved. It is of course assumed here, as sounds plausible, that if an agent could not have done otherwise with respect to a course of action then that agent does not deserve to be held personally blameworthy for the consequences of the course of action.

This finishes my discussion of the first half of the dilemma I posed, where the truth of determinism was assumed. It would seem that if that assumption is merited, then ascription of 'freedom' to agents, in the absolute sense whereby they are held to be personally blameworthy for at least the consequences of some of their courses of action, would not be justified. To complete my argument, I will now assume the truth of the logically complementary position to determinism, indeterminism, and see whether or not ascriptions of 'freedom' in the sense just discussed are in turn ever justified if that position truly characterizes the nature of the world.

Recall that literally the position of indeterminism just means that the occurrence of some events, including presumably some involved with the causation of human courses of action, are at least not completely causally determined by causally anterior events. As I also mentioned, this position is consistent with the types of events occurring being causally constrained to a limited set of possibilities, or even for there to be a probabilistic weighting among these possibilities. In other words, these events must possess, to at least some extent, a 'spontaneous' element to them. Next, it can be pointed out that even while 'spontaneous' does not literally mean 'random' (i. e., possessing no order; there being no method of completely describing a random series of events short of specifying each of the individual members), the latter property can be seen to follow from it by means of taking note of Leibniz's principle of sufficient reason that nothing exists unless there is a sufficient reason for its existence. That is, in the absence of causal determination, no reason can be present for choosing to cause the occurrence of an event of one type as opposed to an event of some other type, and thus determining a ranking.

It is true that a number of philosophers have denied the validity of this last entailment (e. g., Richard Taylor (1966, Ch. 8), Charles Campbell (1957), and Chisholm (1976, Ch. 6)), and have claimed that a free agent can 'perform' or 'initiate' an action in such a way that it is both the case that, given everything in their causal background, they still could have done otherwise, and where they were choosing for a reason and not randomly. But if, as I argued in Chapter Four, reasons serve as causes, it would seem that the following dilemma can be pressed here. If the agent is ultimately choosing for a reason, then the choosing is caused by the reason. If the agent is not ultimately choosing for a reason (perhaps in the case of choosing between equally rational, in the sense of being backed up by equally-compelling reasons, potential courses of action), then the ultimate opting involves choosing at random. Having already argued that in the deterministic case (which includes choosing for a reason) ascriptions of moral responsibility are never justified, I wish to argue now that such ascriptions are never justified for the indeterministic case as well.

If the preceding dilemma on the nature of indeterministic choosing is granted to have persuasive force and it is thus conceded that ultimately indeterministic choosing involves choosing at random, then the question can be raised as to how ascriptions of moral responsibility can be justified for courses of action which were thus just picked at random. As in the deterministic case, I will use the 'desert' sense of 'fairness' in my argument here. In this sense of 'fairness,' it would seem that ascriptions of moral responsibility in the foregoing circumstances are inherently unfair since an agent has no control over random outcomes. Thus, an agent choosing at random in these circumstances would not deserve to be held blameworthy when the consequences of their decisions possess untoward characters; it can be recalled that in Chapter One I designated the term 'untoward' to refer to any intrinsically bad type of situation. It should also again be emphasized that a course of action picked at random need not be irrational. This is because, as I pointed out earlier, there can be rational reasons for sometimes choosing from a limited set of apparently equally-rational alternative potential courses of action at random; in particular, if there are time constraints involved and there is not that much at stake.

It can be observed that the foregoing dilemma between deterministic and indeterministic choosing can be raised at more than one level of the decision-making process. In particular, it can be raised in terms of the choice of motives, ends, or means. It can also either be raised abstractly, in terms of the abstract nature of decision-making procedures, or physically, as in terms of the neurophysiology of the nervous system. In each case though the dilemma remains the same. Either the choice, at whatever level was involved, was deterministic or indeterministic. In the deterministic case the choice was completely caused, which I have argued absolves the agent of moral responsibility. In the indeterministic case, the choosing would ultimately be done at random, which I also have argued absolves an agent of moral responsibility.

It would seem then that the retributive theories of moral responsibility and of punishment self-destruct on their own terms. This is because, using the very sense of 'fairness' apropos to the theories, it can be shown that, regardless of whether determinism or indeterminism is the case, holding an agent to be morally responsible for the consequences of their courses of action is 'unfair' in this sense. It would also seem that, while rationality is compatible with the truth of either determinism or indeterminism, neither position can be used to justify ascriptions of moral responsibility in the sense of moral blameworthiness. This completes my critique of retribution based on the free will problem, and I will now turn to a discussion of what I take is either a syntactic or a semantic incoherency in the concept. I might remark that the argument is a bit abstruse and thus may be skipped over in an initial reading.

Section Four A syntactic or Semantic Incoherency in Retributive Theories

In Chapter Two I presented an argument that values are supervenient properties; i. e., are not observable properties of situations per se but rather possess their properties in virtue of other, typically observable, properties. I also argued that the proper subject matters of value judgments are either situations in virtue of their relations to conscious agents or these relations per se. As I mentioned in that chapter, I find it to be completely arbitrary as to which of these two construals for the supervenience relations is to be chosen. Thus, inasmuch as we are dealing with a rational reconstruction of the concept of a 'value' here, I see no overwhelming rationale for picking one possible reconstruction over the other. In any event, I wish to argue now that, depending on which of these construals of the supervenience of values is taken, retributive theories of punishment will be respectively either semantically or syntactically incoherent when they characterize agents per se as being 'bad,' and hence as deserving of punishment.

Before applying my analysis of the proper subject matter of values to the issue of retribution, it will be instructive to first analyze a parallel case in Moore's analysis of the garbage world which I described in Chapter Three. In this case the syntactic error is, depending on the interpretation of the retribution case, either the exact converse of, or somewhat more complexly related to the retribution case. It can be recalled that in his garbage world example, Moore raised the issue as to whether a 'garbage world' would be intrinsically worse than an extremely beautiful world even if no one could ever, even in principle, be consciously aware of either world. As I noted in Chapter Three, it follows then that in characterizing such as 'garbage world' as being intrinsically worse than the beautiful one, what is being characterized as being 'good' or 'bad' does not involve a relation to a conscious agent, since this is explicitly excluded. But then, according to my analysis of the proper subject matter of values in Chapter Three, it would seem that a syntactic error is occurring with this claim since the first-place argument (the agent argument) in the relation which must be present in order for a value to supervene on a situation is missing here. It can be pointed out that this is true under either of the two interpretations which I presented for the nature of the supervenience of values.

I will now show a connection between the syntactic error just pointed out with respect to Moore's 'garbage world' example and what occurs in the syntax and semantics of retributive theories of punishment. The key point here is that act-based purely-retributive theories inherently justify punishment in terms of 'getting back' at an agent for what they have done in the past. This is opposed to the looking ahead to the future which is characteristic of consequentialist theories of punishment. Thus, it is agents themselves who are characterized as being 'bad' (and hence as 'deserving' of punishment) and not just their courses of action or their characters. In fact the agents are held to be bad solely in virtue of their past courses of action. Thus, the issue of the coherency of the claim that values can supervene in this manner on agents per se in virtue of their past courses of action would seem to lie at the very heart of the debate between retributivists and consequentialists. This is the case since, as I just noted, act-based retributivists would typically claim that a person is bad, and hence deserving of punishment, solely in virtue of a course of action that they pursued in the past. In contrast, consequentialists would instead claim that the person should be punished because of present dispositions to potential courses of action which the pursuit of the past course of action constitutes evidence for.

It may be disputable as to whether or not a relation genuinely exists between agents and their past courses of action, inasmuch as the second-place argument (the past course of action) at least no longer exists when the act of retribution is invoked. It should be emphasized again that the person being punished is being held to be bad solely in virtue of past courses of action according to the act-based retributive theory, and not present dispositions to potential courses of action. If a genuine relation is not held to exist, (due to the present non-existence of the past course of action), then a syntactic incoherency is taking place which is straight-forwardly the converse to the one occurring in Moore's 'garbage world' example. This is because, in contradistinction to that case where the first-place argument (the agent argument) was missing from the relation that values supervene on, in this case the second-place argument (the distinct situation argument) would be missing; the agent per se being termed 'bad.'

If instead a genuine relation is held to exist between an agent and a past course of action, the situation is somewhat more complex, with the incoherency being semantic instead of syntactic. It is true that under this construal arguments for both argument places are present. However, it is the first-place argument (the agent argument) which is characterized as possessing the value in virtue of the relation instead of the second-place argument, the distinct situation argument which in this case is the past course of action. Inasmuch as agents are not situations, a semantic incoherency is thus occurring here.

To summarize, it would seem that either syntactic or semantic incoherencies are inherent in the claims made by retributive theories of punishment. This is because what is predicated as being 'bad' by these theories is neither a relation between an agent and a separate situation (as would be the case if the agent's relation to their character or courses of action were being so characterized), nor a situation distinct from the agent, as would be the case if the agent's character or courses of action per se were characterized as being 'bad.' While the incoherencies involved differ in character, in the former case being syntactic and in the latter case being semantic, the important point is that incoherencies are present under either account.

It could of course be objected at this point that either the syntax or semantics of value statements used to characterize conscious agents per se are simply different from the ones occurring in other uses of the terms. In particular, it might be noted that deontological ethical theories often make ascriptions of moral values to agents themselves, as Kant (1785/1959, p. 9) for example, does in his discussion of the 'good will.' Sometimes the terms 'moral goodness' or 'moral evil' are also invoked here (as in characterizing Hitler or Osama bin Laden as "just being evil"). However, I do not find usages of these terms to be overly consistent, and suspect that what is usually being meant is that the person being so characterized has either done something extremely good or extremely bad, or that they have character traits (which can be fleshed out in terms of dispositions for action) for doing so.

The issue arises then as to what is held in common between the value term usages just given with different syntactic or semantic features other than the fact that the same word is being used. If no common elements can be pointed to here—and I see no obviously-plausible candidates for such elements—it would appear that the use of the terms to characterize conscious agents per se is simply stipulative. As I argued earlier, the temptation to think otherwise is the result of either a syntactic or semantic misuse of value language arising from a confusion from the surface grammar of value statements (that values are non-superveniently predicable of situations per se) to a misidentification of the nature of their possible objects. I will now turn to one final argument against retribution which should help to make the conclusions of the foregoing arguments appear *prima facie* at least somewhat more palatable, this being from a hypothetical case involving amnesia.

Section Five Argument from Amnesia

In this section I will analyze a situation that was first posed by Locke (1690/1959, Bk. 2, Ch. 27). I believe that is one the most clear-cut cases that can be given whereby an agent's set of present properties are completely independent of past ones. I will then ask whether it is still at all plausible to hold that the agent deserves punishment solely in virtue of what they did in the past. Citing this example will not constitute an argument per se against the internal coherency of retributive theories of punishment, such as the one just presented. Instead it should show that it is not at all as clear-cut that our moral intuitions always side with retributionism, as might otherwise be thought.

Consider now the case of a permanent amnesiac who committed a serious crime before they lost their memory. Also imagine that since losing their memory they have been an ideal citizen. Furthermore, imagine that they have never been punished for their past crimes, and that it has been recently discovered that they are the guilty party. The question which I wish to raise now is whether this person still deserves to be punished solely in virtue of what they did in the past and in spite of the fact that they have no memory of their past courses of action.

A pure retributivist will clearly have to give an affirmative answer to the foregoing question, inasmuch as the concept of 'desert' is conceived of as being past-oriented. However, try putting yourself into the place of the amnesiac now. Not remembering your past courses of action, you will not, if punished for these courses of action, associate the punishment with the past courses of action. Hence, you will not recognize the alleged desert. But is the punishment still justified in spite of this? It would clearly be circular just to say so simply because that follows from purely-retributive theories of punishment, since it is the very legitimacy of those theories which is the subject at issue here. At least my moral intuitions here would be that punishment would not be justified. The basic reason behind this moral intuition is that no good would be accomplished by the act of punishment, and thus it can be asked what is the point behind it? While admittedly this answer does appeal to a consequentialist rationale, it also shows that our moral intuitions need not at least always being in the retributivists' corner.

A defender of the retributive theory of punishment at this point might try introducing a variant on the foregoing case. In this variant a wrongdoer would deliberately induce amnesia in themselves so as to avoid punishment. In this case I suspect that many people would hold, even if they did not in the previous version, that the wrongdoer should be punished anyway. Of course, a consequentialist could try to defend punishment here for its deterrence value. If the sole purpose here was to make an example of one person for its deterrence value on others then, as I will be arguing in Chapter Eight, the punishment would not be justified. This is because the person being punished would then be used just as a means, contrary to Kant's practical imperative. However, as Rawls (1955) and Hart (1958/1961) have argued, the whole institution of punishment needs set rules which need to be enforced in order to be effective. Thus, if the threat of punishment, in accordance with these rules, is necessary in order to deter potential offenders it would be justified, even if the punishment seems to be pointless to the person after they have induced amnesia. I might also note that inducing amnesia in oneself in the foregoing circumstances is not a very attractive alternative, seeing that one will lose absolutely all of one's memories of the past with no chance to regain them. I would thus raise the question as to whether, even from the perspective of the retributive theory of punishment, it can be plausibly held that the wrongdoer has truly 'gotten away' with anything here.

Another possible objection which could be raised concerns whether we are dealing with the 'same person' in cases of amnesia before and after the loss of memory. If different people are involved, then one person presumably would not deserve punishment in virtue of the courses of action of someone else. In fact, Locke's (1690/1959, Bk. 2, Ch. 27) theory of personal identity contains the ability to remember past courses of action as being one necessary facet for personal identity, and thus Locke argues that a wrongdoer should not be held personally accountable for the consequences of courses of action which they cannot remember performing. In particular, Locke states that if punishment were to be instituted in such a case it would, from the wrongdoer's perspective, merely seem that they have "happened onto a sorrowful" course of life rather than they are being punished for some past misdeed. Presumably Locke's reasoning for saying this is that the person being punished cannot form associations between the act of being punished and their past courses of action. However, it should be noted that Locke's theory has been criticized by Joseph Butler (1736/1961, Ch. 1), among others, as being circular in that it presupposes what it is trying to prove; i. e., a memory is only considered to be genuine if it corresponds to a past state of the same agent. Thus, no independent criterion is being presented for determining what constitutes a genuine memory; i. e., you can only remember something if you yourself previously experienced what is being remembered.

I might also note that one could also consider the converse case to the foregoing where an agent possesses at least 'pseudomemories' (which are quail-tatively indistinguishable from genuine memories, only where their content does not correspond to what an agent experienced in the past), and then raise the question as to whether the agent would deserve punishment. While, according to consequentialism, some sort of treatment or follow-through (possibly even in a confinement setting) might be merited, it at least would not be retributive in character. Thus, some type of follow-through could be justified even if retribution is never justified, as I have been arguing.

I have just presented arguments from the free will problem, from the syntax or semantics of values, and from the case of amnesia that retributive theories of punishment are unjustifiable. For the remainder of the book I will take this conclusion to have been established. Thus, I will now turn to my next chapter, where I will be developing an alternative 'causal' sense of 'responsibility' which will be consequence-based.

Chapter Six
An Analysis of Causal Responsibility

In this chapter I will develop a consequentialist alternative to the retribution-based theory of responsibility which I criticized in Chapter Five. In particular, I will distinguish and develop three distinct consequentialist senses of 'responsibility,' which I will term respectively 'causal responsibility,' 'liability,' and 'culpability.' Unlike the retribution-based concept of 'moral responsibility,' these alternative senses of 'responsibility will be neutral with respect to any issues of moral desert being incurred by an agent as the result of the performance of an actual course of action. Instead, they will be based on strict causal lines, in terms of the causal consequences of an agent's courses of action. Since issues of moral desert are being ducked here, the criticisms which I raised against retribution-based theories of responsibility in Chapter Five will not apply. It will also turn out that these alternative causal-based senses will be compatible with the truth of either determinism or indeterminism. I will now briefly define the three consequentialist senses of 'responsibility' and will then develop each in detail.

In a nutshell, 'causal responsibility' can be defined along strictly causal lines, in terms of whether or not an agent's actual courses of action constitute a necessary portion of a sufficient condition for the existence of a given situation. It can be recalled from Section Two of Chapter One that this is Bennett's (1988, Sec. 18) version of Mackie's (1974, p. 62) INUS condition for causation. Thus, the fact that an agent is causally responsible for the existence of a given situation does not entail that they did anything wrong. In fact, it is even compatible with the agent having performed their best fair potential course of action from the moral point of view.

Since I will be analyzing both 'liability' and 'culpability' in terms of the justifiability of introducing new causal factors into a situation in virtue of an agent's causal responsibility, it is useful to introduce the term 'accountability' to refer to both of these types of responsibility in both legal and moral contexts. I will be using 'liability' to refer to the claim that an agent has incurred an obligation to make good on damage either which they themselves caused, or which was caused by another agent whom they are vicariously responsible for. Such an obligation is clearly justifiable on consequentialist lines since no judgment is even being made about the agent's character. Instead, it is held that since someone has to make good on the damage, then the best fair candidate for doing so is either the agent causing the damage or someone else with whom they have either entered into a contract to assume the risk (e. g., an insurance company) or someone with whom they bear a special relationship; e. g., a parent.

The situation for 'culpability' is more subtle than that for 'liability,' since I will be using this term to make a claim about the character of the agent who is causally responsible. Thus, unlike the case of liability, ascriptions of culpability can only be transferred to other agents when those other agents are also at fault; e. g., in the case where they ordered the first agent to commit a crime. Even here though, since a consequentialist account is still being given, no claims are being made with respect to moral desert.

Roughly, my analysis of 'accountability' (and thus of both 'liability' and of 'culpability') will parallel the account of 'responsibility' given by Aristotle in Book Three of his *Nichomachean Ethics*, and which has been defended by Austin (1961/1979, p. 175), in his “A Plea for Excuses.” It is also influenced by Hart’s (1959/1990) *Causation in the Law*. In these works it is held that an agent is 'responsible’ for the existence of a situation of an untoward type (where it can be recalled that in Chapter One I analyzed such types of situations in terms of their possessing consequence which are prohibited by either a moral rule or by a legal statute) if and only if they are both causally responsible for the existence of the situation and they do not have an adequate excuse for this causal responsibility. In such circumstances I will term an agent to be 'accountable' for the existence of the situation. Then, depending upon whether it is deemed that the causally responsible agent must make good on the damages, or instead face other consequences to cause them to act differently in the future, they will also be deemed to be respectively either 'liable' or 'culpable.'

Thus, with a few exceptions (notably that of the vicarious case), causal responsibility will be a necessary condition for being held accountable. It will also constitute a sufficient condition for being held accountable in cases where it is both the case that the situation in question is of a type the existence of which violates either a legal statute or a moral rule and where any adequate 'excusing conditions' are absent. That is, in cases where either a legal statute or a moral rule is broken, the existence of causal responsibility for this situation will constitute *prima facie* grounds for the imposition of accountability. However, the presence of an 'excuse' can serve to either mitigate or remove entirely this connection.

Since two key aspects of my causal-based theory of responsibility involve distinguishing between active and passive senses of 'causation' and detailing the nature of excuses, I will divide up my remarks in the next two sections by first presenting a distinction between active and passive senses of 'causal responsibility,' and then investigating the subject of what constitutes an adequate 'excusing condition'; i. e., what types of situations make it be the case that an attribution of culpability, which was *prima facie* established causally, ought to be taken back.

Section One Active and Passive Senses of 'Causal Responsibility'

The following analysis of active and passive senses of 'causal responsibility' builds on the analyses of the active and passive senses of the 'consequences of a course of action' which were presented in Chapter One. Thus, I will be making use of the distinction between the consequences of courses of action which agents actively cause and those which they passively allow to happen. One key difference with my analysis in Chapter One though is that I will just be concerned with possible courses of action with consequences which are prohibited by either a moral rule or a legal statute; i. e., with acts with 'untoward consequences' as those were defined in Chapter One. While it is true that sometimes questions of causal responsibility are also raised with respect to the issue of determining the causation of positive situations (such as when we are concerned with assigning praise for doing something), nevertheless the foregoing restriction would seem to be justified in the context of the subject matter of the remainder of this book, since I will just be making use of the concept with respect to its usage in the judicial and post-judicial systems.

If an agent, by means of the pursuit of their courses of action, actively causes the existence of an untoward situation then I will deem them to be 'actively causally responsible' for the untoward situation, and will term the corresponding act, an 'untoward act.' It should again be emphasized that ascriptions of causal responsibility will neither entail any ascriptions of moral desert towards a person, nor in fact any claims about either their liability or culpability for the consequences of their actions. Of course these ascriptions may be relevant for establishing these latter claims though.

I also wish to introduce a corresponding concept for the passive sense of 'causal responsibility' for untoward situations which agents passively allow to come into existence; i. e., do nothing to prevent. In effect, agents thus perform ‘null acts’ (as defined in my discussion of action in Chapter One) with respect to the situations in question. By stipulation, I will deem such cases to be cases of 'passive causal responsibility,' and the corresponding acts 'passive untoward acts.' As with the case of active causal responsibility, ascriptions of passive causal responsibility will also not entail any judgments either of the moral desert of a person or of their accountability for the consequences of their actions. When the distinction between the active and passive senses of 'causal responsibility' is not germane to my analysis, I will simply speak of an agent as being 'causally responsible' for an untoward situation.

An obvious issue which arises concerning the analysis just given is that it appears *prima facie* to be much too broad. In particular, it would appear that under the analysis an agent might be held to be causally responsible for the existence of an indefinite number of future situations, where it may both be the case that with respect to most of the situations the agent had no idea that they were causally responsible for them, and where also the coming into existence of the situations in the future might be exceedingly difficult to predict. Feinberg (1970, p. 134) has termed this feature of causation the 'accordion effect,' although he places a restriction on his usage of the effect to just include causal consequences which are intended by an agent.

I am leery of placing a restriction, such as the one suggested by Feinberg, on my analyses of 'causal responsibility' and 'accountability' to intentional consequences. This is because to do so would entail that we not be held causally responsible or accountable for consequences of actions which occur out of negligence. Rather than unduly restrict the concepts of 'active causal responsibility' and 'passive causal responsibility' themselves, I will instead attempt to deal with cases where an agent is either actively causally responsible or passively causally responsible for an untoward situation, but where we are not justified in assigning blame to them, by placing a series of restrictions on ascriptions of accountability in terms of 'excusing conditions.' Before turning to my analysis of this subject though I wish to consider a series of cases where I think that it is clear that we would not wish to blame an agent for the causal consequences of their actions. In this regard, consider the following sorts of situations.

First, it can be noted that quite often the courses of action of several agents are each necessary parts of a sufficient condition for a situation to come into existence. This raises the issue as to who ought to then be held to be causally responsible. Here the concept of 'joint causal responsibility' can be introduced, whereby each of the agents can be held to be partially causally responsible for what took place. It can also be noted that sometimes the course of action of one agent, which constitutes a necessary condition for the coming into existence of a given situation, is temporally subsequent to a course of action of a second agent, where this second course of action also constitutes a necessary condition for the coming into existence of the situation in question. In many of these cases (at least where the first agent could not have predicted the course of action of the second agent) it would follow that the action of the second agent should absolve the first agent of any blame.

For example, consider the case where a child inadvertently leaves a toy in another person's path, and where that person subsequently trips and is injured. The injury would not have occurred if the toy had not been there, and thus under the foregoing analysis the child would be causally responsible for the injury. While it is true that we might claim that the child was at least acting negligently here (or, if one is concerned about the justifiability of ascriptions of negligence to children, one could change the example to involve an adult), even this need not be the case in other variations on this theme. For example, consider the case of a driver of a car being distracted by the sight of a pretty girl, and subsequently having an accident resulting in injury. If the girl had not been there the accident may not have occurred, yet surely this does not mean that the girl was acting negligently. Still another case might involve a car-owner who neglects to lock their car and where the car is subsequently stolen and is involved in an accident resulting in personal injury. While the car may not have been stolen if it had been locked and thus the accident not have occurred either, it is hard to see why a careless car-owner should be held accountable here; or even if they are held partially liable, it is at least questionable whether they should also be held culpable.

Indeed, examples can be given of even greater causal ramifications than these. In particular, consider cases where the consequences of a course of action escalate over time, or possess influences in the distant future. For instance, it might seem under the foregoing analysis that we would be causally responsible for the actions of our children, grandchildren, and so on, since they would not have even existed if not for certain of our past actions. Another example is that of the assassination of the Archduke Ferdinand of Austria. It is at least conceivable that if he had not been assassinated in Sarajevo that World War One would not have occurred. To push this point even further, what has been called the 'butterfly effect' can be noted here, which pertains to the claim in chaos theory that whether or not a butterfly flaps its wings in a particular way, may in the very distant future have very large effects due to a series of amplifications of effects of various consequences. As the story goes, for want of nail the battle was lost. Surely it might seem that there must be something wrong with a theory which holds the butterfly or the nail accountable for the loss of the subsequent battle.

The situation is still worse for the case of passive causal responsibility. This is because in this case if there was any potential course of action which an agent could have pursued which would have resulted in a given situation not coming into existence, the agent is thereby passively causally responsible for its existence. This criterion for passive causal responsibility would then result in such blatantly absurd consequences as highway designers being held passively responsible for not putting a curve in a road where a drunken driver runs off of it, inasmuch as if they had put a curve there the accident would not have occurred. In fact, it can be noted that given a long enough time period prior to the coming into existence of almost any untoward type of situation, the coming into existence of the situation could have been prevented if almost any given agent had expended all of their energies in so trying. Thus, it might appear that under this analysis, practically everybody could be held at least passively accountable for practically everything which happens temporally subsequently to their actions.

In order to deal with unwanted consequences such as the foregoing ones, clearly some restrictions need to be placed on when ascriptions of at least passive accountability should be assigned. I will take note of three conditions in this regard which were previously mentioned in my analyses of legal and moral responsibility in Chapter Five. These conditions are that (1) an agent must have either foreseen, or at least have been reasonably expected to foresee, the likelihood of the coming into existence of the untoward situation in question; (2) the agent must have been cognizant both of the circumstances which they were in and of their ability to prevent the situation from coming into existence; and (3) it must not be the case that by preventing the situation from coming into existence the agent would thereby be derelict with respect to some other at least as stringent duty.

I wish to take note now of a key difference between the active and passive cases of accountability with respect to the issue of who should bear the burden of proof for establishing accountability. Some would differentiate between the cases here by claiming that there is no actual duty to prevent harm (i. e., they would claim that the pursuit of a potential course of action with such consequences is merely supererogatory or morally praiseworthy), whereas we do have an actual duty (a duty of non-maleficience) not to actively cause harm. While I find that making this distinction is sometimes useful, I do not believe that it is truly fundamental. For example, consider such cases as where an agent just watches another person drown while being fully cognizant of their ability to save that other person. It can be noted that the end result in the passive case (namely death) is the same as when a death is actively caused, say by holding the victim's head underwater. Thus, inasmuch as I am defending a consequentialist system in this book, there is no apparent rationale to sharply differentiate between the justifiability of the two cases and hold that the agent is just exercising their right not to pursue a supererogatory course of action in all cases where an agent passively allows a death to occur.

Instead, I prefer to differentiate between the active and passive cases of accountability in terms of the issue of where the burden of proof should lie for determining accountability for the untoward situation. In the active case, if an agent has performed an untoward course of action, then I wish to hold that the burden of proof should be on the agent to show that the pursuit of their course of action was excusable. As noted, I will deal with the subject of what constitutes an adequate excuse here in my next section. However, in the passive case I wish to hold that an agent should not be found accountable for not having performed a passive untoward course of action unless another party has established the truth for all three conditions for ascriptions of such passive accountability previously mentioned; i. e., foresight, perceived ability and opportunity, and the absence of any overriding duty.

The foregoing restrictions on ascriptions of passive accountability are clearly justifiable on consequentialist grounds since otherwise the overall societal effect would be that we would always have to be on our guard lest we be held liable for missing an opportunity to prevent an untoward situation from coming into existence, and would have to be ready with excuses for our non-action. When the burden of proof shifts here, only the most flagrant cases of non-action will be worth pursuing by third party agents, and hence it will only be with respect to cases where it is obvious to us that we have both the ability and opportunity to prevent seriously-untoward types of situations from coming into existence that it will be incumbent on us to make sure that we act so as to prevent them from coming into existence. This concludes my discussion of the passive sense of accountability, and I will now turn to my discussion of excusing conditions.

Section Two Excusing Conditions

I will use the term 'excusing condition' to refer to the existence of a situation which ought to taken by an apropos authority figure to either limit or take back altogether a claim to accountability which has been *prima facie* established by the fact that an agent is causally responsible for the existence of an untoward situation. As I noted in my last section, as I am using the term, 'excusing conditions' only apply to the active sense of agent causation, and not also to the passive sense, since an agent only has the burden of proof to come up with an excuse when they performed an untoward act.

It should also be emphasized that the fact that an action was completely caused (as follows from determinism) does not by itself constitute a good excuse under a consequentialist system, such as the one that I am advocating, even if it may under a retributive theory. Two points can be made in support of this claim. First, as I argued in Chapter Four, the mere fact that an action was caused is compatible with the claim that another potential action would have been better from the moral point of view, and thus it is possible to criticize actual actions from the moral point of view. The second point, which I will be developing in more detail later, is that determinism is also compatible with the claim that the state is justified in introducing new causes (e. g., through the threat of punishment) into a situation so as to achieve new effects (e. g., less crime) in the future. The effect of an excuse here is to claim that, even though an agent performed an untoward act, there in fact was nothing wrong with the agent's decision-making from the moral point of view. Thus, no follow-through is in fact justified on the part of the state in such a situation.

I will now distinguish among a number of different types of excusing conditions. I make no claims that this listing is completely comprehensive. In each case the existence of the excusing condition, depending upon the details of the circumstances involved, will either completely absolve agents of ascriptions of accountability or at least constitute a mitigating factor in determining how to deal with the wrongdoer. I will then show how the excuses can be justified under the consequentialist rationale previously elucidated. This analysis will both parallel, but also build upon, the analysis of Aristotle in Book Five of the *Nichomachean Ethics*. There, Aristotle distinguished between two categories of excuses, those of coercion and those of ignorance. However, Aristotle did not distinguish between coercion and compulsion, as I did in Chapter Four. I will also discuss a type of excuse not mentioned by Aristotle, but which is discussed by Austin

(1961/1979, pp. 175) in his "Plea for Excuses." In this excuse an agent attempts to claim that an action was really justified in spite of its being prohibited by either a moral rule or a legal statute. I will begin my discussion by discussing excuses involving compulsion or coercion, and will then move on to discuss the other cases.

Excuses involving compulsion involve situations where an agent is physically unable to avoid breaking either a moral rule or a legal statute. It can be recalled that in Chapter Four I distinguished between types of compulsions both in terms of whether they were internal to or external from an agent, and also in terms of whether they were towards the coming into existence of one type of situation, or away from the coming into existence of another type of situation. It can also be recalled that I pointed out in Chapter Four that the distinction between whether a compulsive or coercive force is towards or away from the coming into existence of a given type of situation is not that fundamental, since one type of case can be redescribed in terms of the other. Still, it is possible to at least distinguish between these cases linguistically in terms of whether the compulsive situations are characterized positively or negatively. For example, the positive description that a prisoner is compelled to remain in their jail cell is equivalent to the negative description that they are compelled not to leave the cell. With the preceding characterizations in mind, I will now give examples of both internal and external cases of compulsions both towards and away from possible courses of action.

An example of acting under an external compulsive factor towards a possible course of action would be a case of being bodily forced to commit a crime, say a crime of trespass. An example of an external compulsive factor away from a possible course of action would be a case of being bodily prevented from the performance of a required action; e. g., being locked in a room when one is legally required to be elsewhere, as in court. An example of acting under an internal compulsive factor towards a possible course of action would be the case of striking a person during an epileptic fit. An example of internal compulsive factor away from a possible course of action would be a case where due to a physical disability an agent fails to perform a required action; e. g., in a school setting if the person with the disability is faced in a gym class with mandated exercises which they are physically incapable of performing.

Since we are only obligated to do what we are physically capable of doing (since, following Kant, 'ought' implies 'can'), it may seem that the courses of action performed under compulsion can be completely excused because the courses of action performed were in fact the best fair potential courses of action. Of course, this does not mean that other agents need be exonerated. In fact, if another agent is causally responsible for the existence of the compulsive force (as in the case just given of being locked in a room), typically culpability will be transferred to them. However, even with compulsive cases the issue as to whether the compulsive factor constitutes a complete excuse is not always clear cut. This is because a temporal complication sometimes arises with respect to cases where, while there is a time at which the existence of a prohibited type of situation could not have prevented, there was yet an earlier time when this was not so. For example, in a case of drunk driving, while an accident may be unavoidable by a driver while driving in a drunken state, at an earlier time they could have chosen either not to drink or not to drive after having been drinking. However, in these sorts of cases an agent may still be held accountable since they could have done otherwise if they had acted differently at the earlier time.

Excuses involving coercion parallel most of the points just made concerning excuses involving compulsion, aside from the fact that since coercive forces can be acted against if we try, coercive excuses tend to just constitute partial, or mitigating, factors rather than complete, or exonerating, excuses. As with the case of compulsion, if another agent is causally responsible for the existence of the coercive factor (as with the case of committing a crime at the point of a gun) then at least partial culpability will be transferred to them. An added point to make here is that besides the parallel distinction to the compulsive case, in terms of whether a coercive factor is towards or away from a particular possible action, as

I noted in my analysis of coercion in my discussion of moral freedom, a distinction can also be drawn which does not apply to compulsions; namely between positive and negative coercive factors. I will shortly argue that this distinction is relevant to the subject of the extent to which coercion is a mitigating factor, but first I will illustrate each type of coercion with an example.

An example of acting under an external negative coercive factor towards a possible action would be the just-mentioned case of committing a crime at the point of a gun. An example of acting under a positive coercive factor would be committing the same offence in order to receive a reward; e. g., a contract killer. An example of a negative external coercive factor against a possible action would be threatening a witness to a crime if they testify. An example of a positive external coercive factor would be a parallel case to the preceding one where a law-enforcement agent is bribed to "look the other way" when a crime is committed. An example in turn of acting under a negative internal coercive factor here would be where a person commits a crime in order to avoid negative withdrawal effects of a drug. A corresponding example of acting under an internal positive coercive factor would be the case of committing a crime while under the influence of the same drug. An example of an internal negative coercive factor away from a possible action would be a case where a claustrophobic agent succumbs to their phobia and does not show up at a required court appearance. Finally, a parallel example of an internal positive coercive factor would be the case where an agent with a drug addiction pursues the drug which they are addicted to rather than taking proper care of their child.

Several somewhat-related points can now be made on the subject of the connection between different types of coercive factors and excuses. One point is that negative coercive factors tend to involve pressures away from specific possible courses of action, and positive coercive factors tend to involve pressures towards specific possible courses of action. It can also be noted that many negative coercive factors appear to be quite strong as excusing factors. For example, the fact that a crime was committed at the point of a gun appears as a strong excuse, where culpability would be transferred to the gun pointer. In contrast, many cases of positive coercive facts do not appear to even be mitigating excuses. For example, the fact that a hired killer is, in effect, being bribed to kill, would not normally be seen to even mitigate the crime. At least a partial explanation of the foregoing difference involves the fact that negative coercive factors tend to involve necessities of life or at least risk to these necessities. Thus, the doctrine of necessity, as explicated in Chapter Two, can be invoked to justify acting in the coerced manner. Since, in contrast, positive coercive facts, by definition, involve goods and not harms, these coercive factors constitute matters of mere desire and not necessities. Thus, when an agent is tempted to commit an untoward act in pursuit of one of these goods (positive coercion) such an act would not be justified since, as I argued in my discussion of negative utilitarianism in Chapter Three, not causing harm takes precedence over causing good.

This completes my discussion of excuses involving compulsive and coercive factors. I will thus now turn to my discussion of excuses involving ignorance of facts. In my analysis I will be making use of the distinction which I developed in Chapter Three between 'absolute rightness,' where a course of action has the best fair consequences all things considered, and 'objective rightness,' where a course of action just has the best fair consequences relative to an agent's knowledge. The net effect of an excuse involving ignorance of fact then involves the claim that even though an agent's course of action was not absolutely right, since there was a still better fair potential course of action open to them, it was still objectively right since the agent was not cognizant of what this better potential course of action was. This latter fact is then held to constitute at least a partial excuse for the agent's actions.

As in the cases of acting under compulsive or coercive facts, as Aristotle notes, it is also possible to distinguish among several different types of cases of acting under ignorance of fact. These includes ignorance of either an agent's abilities or lack of abilities; ignorance of who an agent is dealing with (either the person's true identity, something about their condition, or even the fact that they are a person as in the case of a hunter mistaking another person for a deer); ignorance of the true nature of an instrument which an agent is using; ignorance of an agent's actual environmental circumstances; and finally ignorance of what effects will follow from a given course of action. The key issue, with respect to each of these cases, in determining whether the excuse constitutes a complete excuse or merely a mitigating circumstance, is whether or not negligence was involved. Thus, before presenting examples of the various types of cases of ignorance, both where the ignorance constitutes a complete excuse and where it serves merely as a mitigating factor, a digression is necessary into the subject of negligence. Along the way I will also be making some positive remarks on the nature of an intentional action.

'Negligence' can be defined in terms of agents intentionally pursuing courses of action with untoward consequences where, even though the agents themselves do not realize that the courses of action will have these consequences and hence do not take precautions to prevent them, the occurrences of the consequences is still 'reasonably foreseeable.' It is difficult to give precise criteria for what it means to be 'reasonably foreseeable,' other than to note a clear link with the subject of 'rationality' in general. Thus, for present purposes I will leave the boundaries of the concept vague except to emphasize again the connection between the concept of 'rationality' and stakes; i. e., that there is a correlation between the strength of the obligation to make sure that one is not mistaken in a belief and the extent of the downside consequences if one should turn out to be mistaken. Inasmuch as in cases of negligence agents are causally responsible for the existence of untoward types of situations, and, inasmuch as they ought to have foreseen that these situations would come into existence, it follows that they ought to be held at least partially accountable for the consequences of their courses of action. It can be pointed out that for the legal case this partial accountability usually is handled by reducing a charge, such as in cases where a murder charge is reduced to another charge such as that of either manslaughter or negligent homicide. Since my analysis of 'negligence' has made crucial use of the concept of being an 'intentional action,' a brief digression is required into that concept as well.

I will now present a brief synopsis of a well known analysis of 'intentional courses of action,' first put forward by Anscombe (1957/1963, Sec. 6) and then developed in detail by Davidson (1980, Essay 5) among others. According to this analysis 'intentional courses of action' (which are the only 'actions' under Davidson's system) are construed as being purposive pursuits of given types of situations under some particular descriptions of those situations. Thus, it can be noted that not all intentional acts of wrongdoing (i. e., acts which are intentional under at least some description) will also be intentional under the description by way of which their consequences are proscribed by a rule; e. g., a moral rule or a legal statute.

Using the preceding analysis, two distinct types of cases of intentional rule-breaking can be distinguished. The first involves cases of intentionally causing proscribed situations under the same description as the way the rule proscribes the situation. The second involves cases where the acts of rule-breaking are only intentional under other descriptions. Inasmuch as the first type of case does not constitute a case of negligence, I will only be dealing with cases of intentional rule-breaking which are intentional under other descriptions than those proscribed by a rule; i. e., which are performed under ignorance in one of the senses previously distinguished. This completes my analyses of 'negligence' and 'intentionality,' and I will now return to my discussion of how negligence may be involved with respect to these different types of ignorance of fact.

The first type of ignorance of fact which I will discuss involves ignorance of either one's abilities or lack of abilities. Apropos examples of acting under ignorance of an ability would include cases of either an epileptic or a person with an uncontrollable hand tremor striking another person uncontrollably; during the course of the epileptic fit for the first case. An example in turn of acting under ignorance of one's lack of ability here would be the case of an agent who has just suffered partial paralysis (say, from polio) but who is not yet cognizant of this fact. Because of the paralysis, they may fail to perform a given course of action which they have a *prima facie* obligation to perform. Assuming that negligence is not involved in these examples (i. e., in accordance with my analysis of 'negligence' just given, the person could not be reasonably expected to know about the respective ability or lack of ability), it would seem that the fact that the agent was acting under ignorance of either an ability or a lack of ability in these cases could even constitute a complete excuse.

An example given by Davidson (1980, p. 46) of acting under ignorance of fact concerning who one is dealing with is the case of Hamlet's killing of Polonius, where Hamlet does not realize that the person who he is deliberately killing is Polonius instead of his uncle. While the killing is an intentional killing under some descriptions of the murder victim, it is not an intentional killing of the victim under the description of being named 'Polonius.' It may still be questionable as to whether the ignorance constitutes even a mitigating excuse since it may be thought to be equally wrong to intentionally kill anyone. An example which would constitute a complete excuse in at least some circumstances might be one of 'friendly fire' where a soldier mistakenly shoots a soldier of the same side believing them to be the enemy, and if no negligence is involved. The example could also be cited of a hunter who mistakenly shoots another person, having mistaken them for a deer. Inasmuch as negligence would clearly be involved in this last example, it follows that the ignorance of the actual identity of what is being shot at would merely constitute a mitigating factor, or partial excuse, and not a complete excuse.

An example of acting under ignorance of fact concerning another agent's condition would be a case where an agent causes the death of a hemophiliac by causing them to bleed, assuming that the agent was merely trying to bloody the nose of the hemophiliac, being ignorant of the hemophiliac condition, and not trying to kill them. While possibly it could be claimed that at least some crime has been committed, it certainly would not be a case of first-degree murder.

An example of acting under ignorance of fact concerning the true nature of an instrument where this constitutes a complete excuse would be a case where, unknown to the parent, the painkilling pills which a parent gives to their child have been tampered with in a not readily distinguishable manner and are actually poisonous. Here the parent would not be accountable for a subsequent death, although presumably someone else may be; e. g., whoever poisoned the pills. An example in turn where an agent's ignorance merely constitutes a mitigating circumstance would be that of a person playing with a loaded gun which they think is unloaded and where another person is shot as a result. In most plausible scenarios negligence clearly would be involved in this last case due to the nature of the negative stakes involved if the agent was mistaken about the gun's actual condition, and since there should be no strong positive reason to be playing with the gun in the first place.

As an example of acting in ignorance of facts concerning an agent's environment, the case can be cited of a driver being unable to stop on an icy road where they end up injuring a pedestrian. Depending upon further details of the case (e. g., whether there was any visible evidence of the icy conditions and whether the driver was driving over the posted speed limit) ignorance of the environmental conditions may either constitute a complete excuse or merely a mitigating circumstance due to the existence of negligence. It can also be remarked that sometimes the fact that one agent acts under ignorance of fact concerning an environmental condition may cause accountability to be shifted back to another agent who caused the particular condition to exist in the first place. This causation may either be a result of negligence or even be deliberate. An example of negligence would be the case which I previously mentioned where a child leaves a toy on a set or stairs and where another person later trips over the toy and as a result is hurt. A good example of a deliberate case would be that of a booby trap. While a second agent may actually cause the booby trap to go off, since this result was only foreseen by the first agent who set up the booby trap, and not by the second agent, accountability is shifted to the first agent.

I will close my list of examples of excuses involving ignorance of fact by citing cases involving ignorance of the effect of a potential course of action. Many of these cases can be subsumed under ignorance of fact concerning either an environmental or agent condition, as in the cases of the hemophiliac and the loaded gun previously-discussed. However, there are also cases where, even given this information, a person is ignorant about what consequences will follow, possibly due to ignorance of laws of science.

Each of the foregoing types of excuses can be justified under my system since, as I noted in my discussion of Lewis's (1969) concept of 'objective rightness' in Chapter Three, in practical terms we are only obligated to choose what at the time is considered to be our best fair potential course of action in light of available information. However, as I also pointed out in Chapter Three, there may be an obligation, at least when very much is at stake involving negative downsides, to attempt both to maximize the relevant information if sufficient time is available and to utilize this information so as to predict the relative likelihoods of various possible consequences of different potential courses of action.

I would like to now close my section on excuses by briefly discussing two cases involving the relationship between rules and excuses. The first case involves ignorance of the rule and the second involves cases where an agent either believes that a rule is unjust or that an exception to a rule is justified on a particular occasion. Consider now the case where ignorance of a rule (either a legal statute or a moral rule) is offered as an excuse. While it is true, as Aristotle notes, that ignorance of a rule is not usually to be taken as a good excuse, there are even exceptions here, in particular if the rule has not been promulgated. If someone was negligent in not taking due care to ascertain what the rule is on a particular occasion, they would still be held accountable for breaking the rule. However, if there was no way in which they could, by reasonable means, ascertain the nature of the rule, then this would be a good excuse.

Consider in this last regard knowledge of traffic regulations. If I travel to, and then plan to drive in, another state or other country, then I have an obligation to know the local traffic regulations prior to traveling there. Thus, my lack of knowledge of these regulations would not be deemed to be a good excuse. However, also consider the case where there was no practical way for me to learn about these regulations; e. g., consider the case where a stranger to a town fails to stop at an intersection where a stop sign has been removed by vandals and where there is a subsequent accident. I take it that the stranger's ignorance of the regulation here, due to the fact that it was not promulgated to them, should at a minimum be construed as a mitigating circumstance and perhaps should be construed as a complete excuse. I will be further elaborating on some of these points, in the context of ignorance of legal statutes, in Chapter Seven.

I will now turn to my discussion of justificatory excuses. It can be recalled that these excuses were defined as involving situations where, even though an agent is cognizant of what a rule is, they still hold that they are ethically justified in breaking it. In particular, consider cases where the consequences of breaking either a moral rule or a legal statute are clearly both fair to all parties con-cerned and also better than the consequences of not breaking the rule or statute. An example for the legal statute case would be breaking a traffic rule in order to rush someone to a hospital in a life-threatening situation. An analogous example for the moral rule case would be telling a lie in order to save a life. An important caveat concerning these excuses comes from the fairness constraint, where a violation of the constraint might involve using another party just as a means. For example, there would be a violation of this constraint if another person's life were to be endangered in the case of rushing someone to a hospital or, in the case of lying to help someone out, if another person's reputation were to be slandered in the process.

Justificatory excuses can be supported under my system in the following circumstances. First, from the fairness constraint, the consequences of the course of action must be fair to all parties involved. Then, within the confines of this constraint, if the course of action clearly has better consequences than any other alternative potential course of action, the pursuit of the course of action can be legitimized. This is because the course of action is then the best fair potential one. It should again be emphasized that the rules (legal statutes or moral rules) being broken here are construed as just constituting strong general guidelines for determining best fair potential courses of action. Of course, the existence of these guidelines may be taken to create at least a strong presumption that they be followed. Still, it is held that they can be broken when the consequences of following the rule clearly result in circumstances that are significantly worse than the best fair potential ones.

I will postpone until Chapters Seven and Eight any more detailed discussion of justificatory excuses involving the breaking of legal statutes. Thus, I will now turn to my discussion of the connection between ascriptions of causal responsibility, as just analyzed, and liability. This will be followed by a discussion of the connection between ascriptions of causal responsibility and culpability both under the law and in ethics.

Section Three Causal Responsibility and Liability

In this section I will examine the issue of under what conditions the fact that an agent is causally responsible (in the sense just analyzed) for an untoward situation should make that agent liable for either remedying the situation (i. e., making restitution to the victim) or compensating for irreparable damage. It should be emphasized that since I am using a future-oriented approach here, no moral judgment is to be made against the causally responsible agent in this process; i. e., a judgment of moral responsibility. At the outset, I should take note of a paradox here which I will at least attempt to resolve. The paradox, as I also mentioned in Chapter Four, involves the fact that the very concept of 'restitution' is past-oriented, holding that we owe compensation to a victim in virtue of what we did to them in the past. It can also be observed that the present legal system also distinguishes between claims to restitution and claims about desert by handling torts (at least when issues of culpability do not arise) under the civil law rather than the criminal law. That is, it is held that even though a party may not be criminally at fault, they still are obligated to make compensation for the harm that they caused. Of course, the invocation of these two bodies of law need not be mutually exclusive, since a person may be subject to a civil suit (from a victim) for the same act that they are subject to criminal prosecution from the state.

I will now show how it is possible to use elements from the theory of distributive justice which I developed in Chapter Two so as to justify the foregoing practices. To begin my analysis, it can first be pointed out that ascriptions of causal responsibility do at least identify a temporally antecedent factor (of course, as noted there may be more than one factor here) the absence of which would result in either morally or legally proscribed types of situations not coming into existence. It can also be remarked that, inasmuch as another party has suffered damage which they did not cause, then presumably someone has to make good on the damage. The question can then be raised as to who would be a better candidate to do so then the person causing the damage.

I will now flesh out the preceding ideas by applying concepts from distributive justice. I should note that much of this discussion was influenced by Feinberg (1970). One key issue here concerns the partiality to either individual agents or groups of agents of any recommended distributions of indemnifications for losses. It can be recalled from Chapter Two that I analyzed the concept of 'partiality' in terms of the violation of the moral interests of an agent. It can also be recalled that moral interests were analyzed as needs and those objects of mere desire that do not violate either the needs of others or objects of desire of others justified on independent grounds, as in the case of property rights. Thus, in cases where one agent causes harm to others when they did not need to do so (it can be noted that in the case of needs the legal doctrine of necessity may be applicable) it follows that there will be no violation of the first agent's moral interests if they are prevented from acting on their desire. This is because the other agents have a moral interest (established either through a property right or such positive rights as those to the necessities of life) in not being harmed, and since for the first agent to act on their mere desires would thus involve a violation of the moral interests of others.

Next, I wish to take note of a utilitarian justification for the practice of holding agents liable for harms that they cause to others. The chief consideration here will be the deterrence power of the practice, since presumably agents will be less inclined to cause harm to others if they know that they will have to make good on the damage. While it is true that liability is imposed here in virtue of what an agent did in the past, a point can be made analogous to one which Rawls (1955) makes with respect to the institution of punishment. Rawls, arguing at the time as a rule utilitarian, attempts there to justify the whole institution of punishment in terms of its consequences, including its deterrence value on criminal activities. However, he also states that once we have decided to set up the institution of punishment on utilitarian grounds, then we have to live with the rules as we have set them up; e. g., enforcing the rules by punishing those found guilty of crimes. It can be noted in justification of the past-oriented element (i. e., the fact that penalties are imposed temporally subsequent to an action) of this practice, that an empty threat, at least if it is perceived to be empty, will not be effective. Thus, it is the practice of holding agents liable for their actions which is being defended on utilitarian grounds and not individual acts of imposing liability. This is because, in order for the practice to have an effective deterrent value, it has to be enforced; i. e., carried out on the basis of what an agent has actually done in the past.

An added benefit of the practice of holding agents liable for the consequences of their actions is that the victim is also being compensated. Thus, so to speak, two birds are being killed at one time. We are not wronging the agent with either practice here, since, as previously argued, we are not infringing on any of their moral interests. Still, what is going on here contrasts significantly with the retributive theory, since under that theory penalties and compensation are linked; i. e., by the claim that the wrongdoer actually owes compensation to their victim. I will be elaborating on these points, particularly concerning the deterrence rationale behind punishment, in more detail in Chapter Eight. I will also be dealing there with a number of caveats concerning the rationale of deterring others.

It can be noted that ascriptions of vicarious liability can be also be defended on consequentialist grounds which are analogous to those given in the foregoing discussion. In vicarious liability, liability is transferred from the causally responsible party to another party. There is a wide range of cases here, including parents being held vicariously liable for damage caused by their children or the case of insurance, where essentially risks are transferred to another party for a fee. This latter case can be justified in terms of constituting a type of promise, which, being freely entered into, is binding on the parties.

This completes my discussion of how the practice of instituting liability can be justified on consequentialist grounds. Thus, I will now turn to make some comparable points concerning the justifiability of culpability; i. e., where the state attempts to change an agent's motives or character based on what they did in the past.

Section Four Causal Responsibility and Culpability

I will now turn to the subject of how it is possible to link ascriptions of 'causal responsibility' with claims to, respectively, legal or moral culpability. It can be recalled that I am using 'culpability' to refer to that version of accountability, where it is held that an authority figure (e. g., the state in the case of legal culpability) is justified either in attempting to change an agent's motives or character in order to make sure that the agent does not repeat an untoward course of action, or in denying them the opportunity for doing so. As with my discussion of the connection between causal responsibility and liability, it should be emphasized that, since I have been disavowing any retributive connection to 'causal responsibility,' any link drawn between causal responsibility and 'culpability' (in either the legal or moral sense) cannot be justified in terms of any alleged 'desert' resulting from ascriptions of causal responsibility.

Assuming that we are justified in at least minimizing violations of both moral rules and legal statutes, it follows that a society would be justified in introducing additional causal factors into a situation so that the identified causally necessary factor for the coming into existence of a proscribed type of situation does not occur. Under a consequentialist rationale for imposing culpability these causal factors may include (1) deterrence, which it can be recalled was also a rationale for imposing liability, and which involves changing a motive to one of fear; (2) incarceration, which involves the denial of physical freedom to commit crimes; or (3) attempts to change a lawbreaker's character through such programs as those of rehabilitation, re-education, job training, or therapy. I will now take note of a few points of both comparison and contrast between the cases of imposing liability and imposing culpability.

One point in common between the impositions of liability and culpability is that both will be only invoked when an agent is causally responsible for an untoward situation when they do not have a good excuse. Also, as I just noted, at least a partial justification for both practices involves their deterrence value in changing future conduct. There are also several points of contrast between the practices. One point of contrast is that while liability is handled under the civil law, culpability is handled under the criminal law. Thus, culpability cannot simply be transferred to another party (e. g., with the case of an insurance company assuming a risk for a fee) in the way that liability can be. It can be pointed out though that a vicarious case may still arise when another party is at fault; e. g., when a parent is negligent in the manner in which they supervise their child and the child commits a crime. Also, as I just remarked, in contrast to the case of imposing liability, an attempt may be made when imposing culpability to actually change the character of the lawbreaker by such programs as those of rehabilitation, re-education, job training, or therapy.

As with the case of imposing liability, it is very important in the case of the imposition of culpability that the moral interests of all parties be protected. However, as I noted in the liability case, people do not have a moral interest in either causing harms to others or otherwise interfering with the rights of others. Thus, in an analogous manner to the situation with imposing liability, it would appear that there need be no infringement on a lawbreaker's rights when they are held personally culpable for their actions infringing on the rights of others.

The imposition of culpability can be justified now along much the same consequentialist lines that I used to justify the imposition of liability. In particular, I wish to appeal to the fairness (in the consequentialist sense of 'impartiality' which I developed in Chapter Two) of the resulting system when people are held personally culpable for their actions. It can be pointed out in this regard that if people could freely break legal or moral rules without any resultant culpability being incurred, the system would be unfair (again, in the consequentialist sense of 'impartiality') to the individual law-abiders. Thus, the state or another authority figure may be justified in introducing new causal factors that do not violate the rights of the lawbreaker; e. g., either deterring factors such as the threat of punishment or such programs for changing the lawbreaker's character as the just-mentioned ones of rehabilitation, re-education, job training, or therapy.

A careful weighing of both the good and bad consequences of imposing any sorts of penalties in response to lawbreaking is necessary here inasmuch as the mere possession of political freedom is a good, and since this freedom is inherently restricted by the imposition of any sort of penalty. Thus, even if at times the consequences of courses of action are not ideal in character, the imposition of any sort of a penalty may sufficiently detract from the good of political freedom so that the total situation is even worse. It should also be emphasized that the foregoing rationale for imposing culpability does not extend to the justification of imposing penalties to deter others, unless this occurs incidentally in the process of deterring the original wrongdoer. This is because, in view of Kant's Practical Imperative, only minimal causal interference was justified under the foregoing analysis of 'culpability.' While a greater penalty might be more effective in deterring others the person being held culpable would then be used just as a means. For example, invoking the death penalty for shoplifting might be an effective way to deter other potential shoplifters. However, since a lesser penalty (e. g., a fine) would probably have the effect of changing the future behavior of an individual shoplifter, it can be seen that invoking the greater penalty for its effects on others is unfair to the moral interests of the original wrongdoer. I might point out that I will be elaborating on some of these points in more detail in my discussion of the post-judicial system in Chapter Eight.

I would like to now close this chapter by addressing a criticism which is sometimes leveled against causal theories of responsibility, such as the foregoing one. This criticism is that these theories do not take sufficient cognizance of the fact that all people deserve to be treated with respect. In particular, it may be held that inasmuch as the theories are formulated in terms of 'fixing' what is wrong with an agent, they in effect treat the agent as a piece of machinery; i. e., a 'thing.' Thus, it may be claimed that there is an inherent violation of Kant's Practical

Imperative here in that the net result is that people are just used as a means (towards what is desired by other people in a society) and not also as ends in themselves. There are two points which I wish to make in reply to this criticism. The first point pertains to what is meant by 'respect,' and the second involves the role of human consciousness.

Regarding the issue of what is meant by 'respect,' it can first be noted that to respect an entity, whether it be an inanimate object (say, a work of art) or a person, is to treat that entity as an end and not just as a means. Thus, Kant's Practical Imperative can be reformulated in terms of the claim that we should always respect persons for their own sakes. But the question arises concerning exactly what is meant by claiming that people should always be treated as ends. Need this entail that we can never legitimately interfere with the internal decision-making processes, even when we think that they are out of order and the person is a threat either to themselves or others? I do not see why this need be the case, although due to my fairness constraint obviously many more safeguards need to be required for involuntary than for voluntary cases. In fact, for purposes of this book, I will leave it as an open ethical question as to whether the former case is ever ethically justified.

To respect a person is to understand them for what they are, and not to impose our conceptions of what they ought to be on them, at least when this is done from some ulterior motive besides the person's own benefit. But it does not follow from this that we are never justified in following through on our understanding of a person by introducing changes for that person's own benefit, so long as we are also being 'fair' to the person in the sense of neither being partial to either the interests of others or even the interests of the overall society.

Thus, it would seem that what is entailed by the Practical Imperative is the caveat on permissible interference on other people that any changes made here must be for that individual person's own benefit and not be at least solely for the benefit of others; which would be a case of treating the person solely as a means.

It is true that this caveat does raise the issue of whether or not there is any objective method for determining what the best fair decision-making state for a given individual is, and I do not wish to underestimate the difficulties inherent in such a determination. Nevertheless, it is not at all obvious that someone suffering from a mental illness, such as schizophrenia or paranoia, would not be objectively better off if they were cured of it.

I should note in this last context that both Barbara Wootton (1959) and Karl Menninger (1968) have made much of the claim that the function of a post-judicial system ought to be to treat law-breakers as patients so as to cure them of whatever causes them to break laws. While I will argue in Chapter Eight that there are other legitimate functions of such a system as well, I see no reason for thinking that this function necessitates not respecting the person per se, at least in the voluntary case.

A second point which I wish to make in reply to the criticism that insufficient respect is being given to an agent here is that it can be recalled that I have been arguing that it is the consciousness of an agent which gives the agent their intrinsic value rather than any facet of their personality traits per se. This is because the nature of these traits is governed by memory and cognitive capacities, both of which are grounded by the nature of the physical brain. Thus, it is possible to respect the fact that a person is conscious, yet hold that, because there is something wrong with their cognitive capacities, it is still justifiable to interfere with these capacities. This distinction is rarely drawn in this manner in the literature, although Jean Jacques Rousseau at least hints at it being relevant in the following passage where he defends animal rights:

> In fact, it seems that, if I am obliged not to injure any being like myself, it is not so much because he is a reasonable being, as because he is a sensible being; and this quality, by being common to men and beasts, ought to exempt the latter from any unnecessary injuries the former might be able to do them. (Rousseau (1754/1967), p. 172)

It is necessary to distinguish between two separate issues at this point; the issue of who is to be treated with respect by the law (i. e., to possess various civil rights) and who is to be held culpable for their actions. With respect to the first issue, it follows from the foregoing considerations that even if a person is not fully rational (which it can be recalled from my discussion in Chapter Four, I hold admits of degree), so long as they are at least potentially conscious (i. e., are not brain dead), then they still deserve to be treated with respect under the law. A few relevant cases here would include the very young, the severely mentally retarded, and elderly people suffering from senility. An extension could also be made to some animals; e. g., with laws against cruelty to animals, where it is claimed that even if animals do not have a legal right to life, they do have a legal right to humane treatment. As pointed out in Chapter One, this would involve an extension of the moral point of view. However, I will not attempt to address the issue as to whether humans possess some additional element besides consciousness (e. g., self-consciousness) which gives us more of a right to life than animals have.

The situation is a bit different with respect to the issue of being held culpable for actions. This is both because verbal arguments (and hence re-education programs) will not be effective in many of these cases, and also since even deterrence may not be effective in some cases. Since, under a consequentialist rationale, interference here is only justified to the extent that it is effective in changing future behavior, it follows that it should only be invoked in cases where it is effective. It might be observed in this last context though that something very much like deterrence occurs with animal training when penalties are used. In any event, I will be elaborating on these considerations in considerably more detail in Part Two of the book, to which I will now turn.

PART TWO
PRACTICAL APPLICATIONS IN THE JUDICIAL AND POST-JUDICIAL SYSTEMS

Chapter Seven
The Judicial System

In this chapter I will be concerned with stating the nature of an ideal judicial system using the principles developed in Part One. That is, I will attempt to ascertain what the best fair type of judicial system which is attainable is. I will begin the chapter by presenting a consequentialist critique of most western present-day judicial systems in light of my earlier conclusions concerning both the free will problem and my critiques of the retributive theory of punishment and our common sense concept of 'moral responsibility.' Thus, to the extent that our present systems of justice make use of these concepts, in particular by claiming that people are to be held either morally reprehensible or blameworthy because of their past courses of action, I will argue that the systems are unjustified. In spite of this critique though, it can be recalled that at the end of Chapter Five I showed that it is possible to reconstruct an alternative causal sense of 'responsibility' that is compatible with consequentialism. In this chapter I will show how it is possible to make use of this sense in constructing a non-retributive system of justice that is based on consequentialist lines. I will then go on to discuss the nature of one such possible system in some detail. To begin my critique of present-day judicial systems, I will now present a short analysis of the nature of 'justice.' I will then be using that analysis in both making my critiques of present-day judicial systems and in showing how alternative systems to these based on purely-consequentialist lines could be developed.

Section One An Analysis of Justice

In my analysis of 'justice' I will first trace the etymology of the term and then turn to an analysis of the modern usage. MacIntyre (1988), in his *Whose Justice? Which Rationality*, traces our modern western conception of 'justice' from the Greek '*dike*' as used to express the Homeric conception of justice. Under this conception, a course of action was spoken of as being '*dike*' when it was in accordance with a universal cosmic order. '*Arete*,' or 'virtue,' was used to refer to character traits used to preserve this order. With Plato's use of '*dikaiosame*' in the *Republic* (Book 4, p. 433) comes the conception of justice as each person playing his proper role in a society; "each in his own place." Thus, the concept here refers to the relative effectiveness of individual roles as judged by an overall societal perspective.

MacIntyre sees Aristotle as enlarging on Plato's conception whereby '*dike*' is characterized as a teleological conception which is presupposed by the other virtues. Also, it, like the other virtues, is epitomized as being a mean between extremes. This is comparable, for example, to the way that the virtue of bravery is characterized as being a mean between the extreme character traits of cowardice and foolhardiness. This sense is also relativized to a state or '*polis*,' the Greek city state, and thus represents a much narrower point of view than the moral point of view. Under this sense of 'justice' then, a citizen of the *polis* would be held to be acting justly if they were fulfilling their proper purpose with respect to the well-being of the *polis*.

The Stoics broadened the Aristotelian conception of 'justice' so as to be a universal notion again, and a theological basis was then given for it by Aquinas. MacIntyre traces the further history through the Scottish Enlightenment, where Francis Hutcheson tried to give an empirical basis to our concept of 'justice' (the basis stemming from an alleged 'moral sense') but where the results were seen to coincide with the tenets of a Calvinist theology. MacIntyre views the resulting system as being inherently unstable though, with Hume using Hutcheson's empiricist epistemology to argue for an essentially utilitarian system. There are obvious links between Hume's work and the subsequent English utilitarian movement as developed by Bentham and Mill. MacIntyre thus contends that Hume's role was essentially antithetical to all that was traditional in the Scot-tish tradition, in particular the Calvinist roots. I will now turn to my analysis of the modern conception of 'justice.'

The modern conception of 'justice' is used, even within legal contexts, in more than one sense; one key distinction being between retributive and distri-butive senses. The retributive sense of 'justice' (which I noted in Chapter Five is sometimes also known as 'commutative justice') is the older one, although it still survives to a remarkable extent in reasoning used by the judicial system. Under this sense of 'justice,' it is claimed that every time a crime has been committed an 'injustice' has been created. It is also claimed that this 'injustice' will not be removed unless and until the original act of wrongdoing has been 'repaid' by means of the extraction of an amount of suffering on the part of the wrongdoer which is comparable in scope to that which the wrongdoer inflicted on others. The roles of the judicial and post-judicial systems are then seen as bringing wrong-doers 'to justice,' in this retributive sense by means of seeing to it that they receive their 'deserved' punishment. Hence, the post-judicial system is seen as being exclusively penal in character. It can also be seen that the sense of 'justice' being invoked here is past-oriented rather than future-oriented (as are consequentialist senses) since that which is held to 'justify' the act of punishment is the wrong-doing which occurred in the past.

In contrast to the foregoing retributive sense of 'justice,' 'distributive justice' is consequence-oriented and refers to the claim that whenever either a set of goods or harms is distributed among the members of a population, the distri-bution ought to be done in a fair manner. That is, preference should be given here to taking care of 'basic' course of life needs (as these were analyzed in Chapter

Two) among members of the population. The distribution of goods and harms not involving these basic needs ought then to be conducted without showing favoritism to any particular group, at least outside of the merits (in the ability sense of 'fairness' previously analyzed) of the individuals involved. Notice here that, in contrast to the case of retributive justice, no act of wrongdoing need have been performed prior to instituting the just distribution. Still, it can be noted that one feature held in common between the two cases is that the notion of 'balancing' goods and harms is involved. In any event, I wish to now take note of a third sense of 'justice,' which is also consequence-oriented, by means of building on the analysis of the concept which Plato gave in his *Republic*. Unlike the sense of distributive justice, which at least primarily applies to issues of societal policies, this sense will apply to decisions by individual agents.

As I noted in my discussion of the etymology of 'justice,' in his *Republic*, Plato analyzed the nature of 'justice' in terms of "doing one's own business," in the sense of performing one's 'right' (in the sense of 'best' for Plato, and ‘best fair’ for my system) role in a given society. A potential course of action was then held to be unjust to the extent that it constituted a deviation away from this role. Of course the consequences of such a deviation will vary in different circumstances and will sometimes be very minor. For example, in a very competitive society where a large number of people are almost identically qualified for a given role, say that of being a janitor, it may not make much difference whether or not the truly best qualified person plays that role or not. On the other hand, if an airplane pilot is the only one qualified to fly a plane full of passengers when the plane is already in the air, or if a doctor is called on to care for a critically-ill patient and nobody else who is similarly qualified is around, the consequences of a deviation by an agent from their best fair role may be disastrous. Thus, it should be emphasized that only in certain situations will a particular agent actually have a moral duty to play their best fair role, even though the best fair criterion still applies for determining whether a choice is ethical in other situations as well.

Before using this analysis of 'justice' and 'injustice' for the purposes of giving a foundation for an ideal judicial system, it may be worthwhile to note that in Plato's *Protagoras*, Protagoras is portrayed as favoring a future-oriented philosophy of punishment as follows:

> In punishing wrongdoers, no one concentrates on the fact that a man has done wrong in the past, or punishes him on that account, unless taking blind vengeance like a beast. No, punishment is not inflicted by a rational man for the sake of the crime that has been committed—after all one cannot undo what is past—but for the sake of the future, to prevent either the same man or, by the spectacle of his punishment, someone else, from doing wrong again. (Plato, *Protagoras*, p. 324)

It would seem then that consequentialist theories of jurisprudence have been around (although often just in the background) for a long time. I will thus move on now to sketch how to use such a theory in an ideal judicial system. In Chapter Seven I will move on to discuss the use in the post-judicial system.

Section Two The Nature of Law

I will begin my discussion of the judicial system by means of analyzing the concept of a 'law.' I will then move on to investigate the subject of law enforcement and also the issue of what the best fair system of laws within a societal context would be. To begin, a 'law' can be at least partially defined as being a rule (at least usually in the sense of being an exceptionless principle) which either requires or prohibits the pursuit of various possible courses of action whenever these courses of action possess (or sometimes are just judged as being likely to possess) certain types of consequences. I believe that it is a mistake to put anything into the definition of a law about the origin of these rules (such as their having been duly enacted by a legislature, or having been determined by legal precedents through court decisions as with the common law) since some legal systems are simply imposed on a populace, as by a dictatorship, without their consent. Still, inasmuch as not all systems of rules (e. g., the rules of a club) constitute legal systems, something needs to be said both about who may enforce the law and what justified them in doing so. In particular, I take it that it is part of the definition of a law that it is enforceable by the state, at least at some level of jurisdiction.

Since the subjects of the origin of the law, what legitimates the law, and who may enforce the law, have been developed in detail by others (e. g., Hart, 1994, in *The Concept of Law*), I will not develop these issues in any more detail in this book. However, since it is relevant to my subsequent discussion, I do wish to next make a series of point to show the extent to which the law constitutes an external coercive force (i. e., it will be recalled from Chapter Four, a threat or a bribe originating from outside the agent) imposed by the state in such a manner as to affect the rationality of personal decision-making.

To lead into my discussion of the coercive aspect of the law, it can first be noted that most people are capable of breaking the law if they try to do so. Clearly this does not necessarily entail that all people will want to try to break the law, since they may be using the same broad point of view in making decisions which was used to motivate the enactment of the law to begin with. However, it can also be noted, as I emphasized in Chapter Four, that it is rational to use a narrow point of view (e. g., egoism or somewhat broader provincialist viewpoints such as just looking for the well-being of one's family, possibly a 'crime family,' or one's corporation), as well as to use a broad point of view (e. g., the moral point of view) in making personal decisions. Thus, since it is rational to be an egoist as well as to use a broad point of view, there will be people using these narrower points of view, and these people may need an added incentive in order to make it still rational (from the narrow point of view) to obey the law. Otherwise, from the perspective of the narrower point of view, there may be occasions where these people would come out further ahead personally by breaking the law.

This is where the coercive aspect of the law comes in. It typically involves negative coercion with the threat of punishment, but also sometimes involves positive coercion by rewarding law-abiding courses of action; e. g., by being taken off of probation or having points taken off a driver's license. Of course not everyone who breaks a law will be caught, and even if they are caught they may still escape punishment. Still, as Locke (1690/1960) points out in Section Twelve of his *Second Treatise of Government*, due to the risk of punishment, the external coercion from the state may cause it to be a 'bad bargain' (in the sense that the positive expected utility to be gained by breaking the law is more than compensated for by the negative expected utility associated with the risk of punishment) for the egotistical potential lawbreaker to actually break the law. Bentham (1781/1988, Ch. 14) makes a similar point stating "the value of the punishment must not be less in any case than what is sufficient to outweigh that of the profit of the offence." The net effect here is then, through its constituting an external coercive force imposed by the state, the law makes it still be in the rational self-interest of the person who is using a narrow point of view for them to obey the law.

Laws which require the pursuit of particular types of possible courses of action will constitute positive external coercive factors, and laws which prohibit the pursuit of particular types of possible courses of action will constitute negative external coercive factors. As I noted in my discussion of compulsions and coercions in Section One of Chapter Four the distinction between coercion towards and away from situations (i. e., being a requirement as opposed to a prohibition), while sometimes helpful in stating a law, ultimately breaks down. This is because, by the law of contraposition, the prohibition of a class of possible courses of action is logically equivalent to the requirement that actions be in conformance with the logical complement of that class. It is noteworthy that Bentham takes makes an analogous point with respect to positive and negative actions when he states:

> It is to be observed, that the nature of the act, whether positive or negative, is not to be determined immediately by the form of the discourse made to express it. An act which is positive in its nature may be characterized by a negative expression: thus not to be at rest, is as much as to say to move. (Bentham (1781/1988, p. 72)

Several distinctions among types of laws are often drawn. These include distinctions in terms of the nature of the parties involved (e. g., between the criminal law and the civil law); in terms of levels of jurisdiction (e. g., between federal, state, county, and municipal law); and in terms of the associated penalties; e. g., between felonies and misdemeanors. Distinctions are also often drawn in terms of the origins of laws, as with the distinctions among constitutional law, legal statutes enacted by legislatures, administrative regulations drawn up by government agencies, and the common law based on a series of historical court precedents. Inasmuch as it is both the case that these subjects are extensively covered elsewhere, and since for the most part the distinctions are not germane to the points which I wish to address in my analysis, I will not develop these distinctions further here. Instead, I will now move on to make a series of points both applying consequentialist considerations regarding justifications for the enactment and enforcement of laws, and analyzing the concept of 'lawbreaking.'

Even though, as I just noted, I believe that it is a mistake to put anything about its origins into the definition of the law, it would still seem that, in order to be fair to the moral interests of all citizens, it must both be the case that laws be duly enacted by some type of legitimate authority (e. g., an elected legislature), and it must also be the case that it be promulgated; i. e., be made known to the general populace. In fact, it might be questioned as to whether our system of common law can be justified under the consequentialist system which I have developed, just on the grounds that it has not been duly enacted by a body representing the general populace. Of course it must be admitted that in a sense judges are also chosen by the people, but not as a substitute for the legislative process. Indeed, I think that there is much to be said for specifying any desired limitations and qualifications to laws in the actual legal statutes themselves, rather than leaving these matters to be determined by judicial interpreters. Still, it is not at all clear that the issue of court interpretation can be completely avoided inasmuch as, practically speaking, it is not possible for legislators to anticipate all of the possible contingencies and complications which may arise subsequent to the time of enactment of a statute. Also, there may be dangers of inordinate clutter if this were to be attempted, making the resulting laws both harder to understand and to apply. I will now turn to a discussion of the requirement that a law be promulgated.

The requirement that the law be promulgated is the claim that the content of legislation be made generally known to the public (or at least that the public have ready access to learn it) prior to the legislation's enforcement. There is more than one type of case of lack of promulgation. One type of case involves enacted laws being kept secret from the general populace. Another type of case involves *ex post facto* legislation, where an agent is held liable for breaking a law even though their law-breaking act was performed temporally prior to the enactment of the law. I will now present both utilitarian considerations and considerations of lack of fairness against the justifiability of the enactment of unpromulgated legislation in both of these senses.

A utilitarian consideration against the enforcement of unpromulgated legislation, that has been pointed out by Rawls (1955), Hart (1958/1961), and D. H. Hodgson (1967, Ch. 4), involves the fact that there is positive utility in having the general populace have the expectation that they will not be punished so long as they abide by priorly-enacted laws which have been promulgated to them. Obviously, such expectations would be thwarted by the enforcement of legislation which has not been promulgated. Thus, even if at times it might seem on an individual level that utility is maximized by having an action type be declared to be illegal after the fact, this probably will not be the case due to the change in expectations. It can also be pointed out that these expectations are formed by looking backwards at causal links in the past between law-breaking actions and negative consequences (e. g. being punished).

The foregoing points also tie in nicely with what I have been saying about cooperative utilitarianism, inasmuch as there the courses of action of other agents (in particular courses of action involving the judicial and post-judicial systems) are determined by assigned roles. Thus, as just noted, the fact that these agents can be predicted to play these roles will allow potential lawbreakers to have at least relatively fixed expectations concerning the consequences of breaking a law and thus to make a rational decision as to whether it is in their self-interest to do so using the concepts developed in my section on rationality in Chapter Four.

I also wish to claim that the enforcement of unpromulgated legislation will be unfair to individuals charged under it. I am using the strong sense of 'fairness' here of being partial to the interests of a whole society over those of an individual. Thus, here the interests of the whole society in having the unpromulgated law be enforced would be given priority over the interests of the individuals charged under the law. In particular, it can be noted that if a potential lawbreaker desires to obey the law, then (assuming that the law is a moral law, in the sense of being compatible with moral rules) a potential lawbreaker's interest in obeying the law will constitute a 'moral interest,' as this term has been previously analyzed. However, it would seem that the potential lawbreaker's moral interest in obeying the law is not being given due consideration in the case of enforcing unpromulgated legislation. This is because the lawbreaker's liberty and even physical freedom (if incarceration is involved) are being restricted, while the lawbreaker was not given a reasonable opportunity to avoid breaking the law, since they were both ignorant of the law and also not given a reasonable opportunity to know its contents. This completes my discussion of the requirement that the law be promulgated, and I will now turn to my analysis of 'lawbreaking.'

'Lawbreaking' can now be analyzed in terms of the causal consequences of the courses of action of either individual agents or groups of agents. When a group of agents are cooperatively (as I previously analyzed the concept) involved, the lawbreaking is sometimes referred to as involving a 'conspiracy.' Thus, I wish to claim that in order to be an act of lawbreaking either the course of action of an individual or the courses of actions of several cooperating individuals must constitute a necessary part of a sufficient condition for either the creation of a type of situation which is proscribed by the law (in which case the law will constitute a negative coercive force), or for the failure to create a type of situation prescribed by the law; in which case the law will constitute a positive coercive force.

It can be seen that, as thus analyzed, the issue of whether a law is broken or not will be independent of the intentions of the lawbreaker. Thus it will be independent of whether or not the agent breaking the law realized that their course of action fell under the description proscribed by the law or failed to fall under the description prescribed by the law. In fact, in my sections on law enforcement and the court system I will also be arguing that it may even be justifiable at times to break a law, such as in the case of breaking a speeding law during a genuine emergency. Regardless of the issue of whether these or other mitigating circumstances arise though, the fact remains that the criterion for whether a law was broken or not is causal in character.

I should note that the foregoing analysis of 'lawbreaking' in terms of properties of actual courses of action is consistent with my conclusions in Part One that only actual courses of action, but not their causes, are right or wrong. The nature of the causes (e. g., motives and intentions) though will be relevant concerning the issue of how best fairly to deal with law violators once they have been brought before a judicial system. For example, either in cases where the consequences of an actual course of action are proscribed by the law or in cases of the failure to perform a possible course of action which has consequences prescribed by the law, the issue as to whether the act of lawbreaking was deliberate or not under the description respectively either proscribed or prescribed, or whether instead the course of action was the result of ignorance (either of a person's true situation or of the law) or coercion (either physical or psychological) may make a great deal of difference in deciding how best fairly to deal with a lawbreaker. The fact remains that the person is still a lawbreaker in spite of the existence of any of these mitigating (from the viewpoint of either the judicial or post-judicial systems) factors though.

I will now turn to the subject of choosing a system of laws (i. e., the legislative process) utilizing the principles of Part One. It should first be noted in this regard that since a cooperative approach was being espoused in Part One, it is necessary to see how the individual laws work together as a group in determining which ones ought to be picked. In particular, it is important in this regard that individual laws not work at cross purposes, such as with creating conflicting standards in such matters as weights and measures, or perhaps both allowing testimony to be used against a testifier and having a goal of determining the truth in a conspiracy. It can be noted next that due to my fairness constraint, the first criterion in choosing a system of laws is to make sure that each law in a proposed system of laws is fair to the moral interests of all of the affected parties. Then, the consequences of having such a system of fair laws and strictly enforcing each of the laws in the system should be compared with the consequences of strictly enforcing alternative systems of laws. The system of fair laws which has better overall consequences than any other fair system would then be the one which ought to be adopted.

Assuming that the resulting laws are fair to the moral interests of all affected parties, in general, presumably, these laws will be justified under negative utilitarian considerations in terms of the fact that they provide protection for others, as in the cases of laws against theft, rape, murder etc. The issue arises though concerning the justifiability of other laws, such as those which are paternalistic in character (i. e., in place for the protection of potential lawbreakers themselves), and so-called laws without victims. I will now make a few remarks on these cases separately, starting with the case of paternalistic laws.

Consider such paternalistic laws as anti-suicide laws, laws requiring the use of seatbelts, airbags, motorcycle helmets, and laws mandating the partial withholding of salaries for social security. Here the laws are presumably in place for the protection of the potential lawbreakers themselves. Since, as Mill (1859/1975, Ch. 5) points out, people are apt to believe that they themselves are the best judges of their own best interests, these laws tend to be more controversial than laws for the protection of others. Nevertheless, at least some of these laws can be defended on such utilitarian grounds as that people tend to be short-sighted, tend to undervalue remote risks, and possess such character traits as 'weakness of the will' where they are prone to act contrary to their own better judgment.

I will now discuss the merits of so-called crimes without victims. Here, unlike the case of paternalistic laws, it is not at all clear that even the lawbreakers themselves would be victims. Examples of these laws would include legal prohibitions on gambling (which may be a mixed case if gambling is seen as an addiction), prostitution, pornography, and certain sex crimes, such as sodomy and other so-called 'unnatural' sex acts. Often the sole motivation behind these prohibitions appears to be the fact that the prohibited acts give psychological offense (perhaps on religious grounds) to others from merely thinking about the acts, without there being any other clear-cut objective harms.

Since needs, with respect to either party, are not involved in these cases, under the consequentialist rationale being defended in this book, the issue is who would have the stronger claim between conflicting objects of desire; i. e., the desire to have 'perverted sex' or the desire not to be disturbed by mere thoughts of its occurrence. It can be noted that there is not even a causal link (as there would be with cases of public nudity or indecent exposure) between the actual sex acts and the psychological states of the offended parties in these cases. Given the capricious nature of any non-causal links here, together with a conflict with the *prima facie* right to privacy (which was discussed in Chapter Two) of the parties engaged in sex, it would appear that no adequate consequentialist justification is present to merit the enactment of this type of legislation. This completes my analysis of the nature of law, and thus I will now turn to my discussion of law enforcement.

Section Three Law Enforcement

The first issue which I wish to address on the subject of law enforcement is that of whether laws should be strictly enforced whenever it is realized that they have been broken, or whether instead this should be up to the discretion of the law enforcers, in particular when various ‘excusing conditions’ are present. In other words, do law enforcers have a duty or just a right to enforce laws when they have been observed to be broken? An obvious danger in the claim that discretion is to be allowed for here is that it may allow for the enforcement to be capricious, and thus to be unfair in the sense that it shows partiality to some citizens over others. There is also a danger that such capricious enforcement will be used as an 'excuse' to 'put someone away' when the real rationale involves an entirely different matter. There may be a trade-off though between these motivations for strict law enforcement and the issue of how complex a law should be allowed to become. Obviously with more complexity more special cases can be covered. However, this may also result in it being harder to determine whether the law actually applies, in the sense of accurately describing the situation, in a given situation.

However, even if the laws are not perfect with respect to taking into account all plausible excusing conditions, it can still be maintained that even a justified lawbreaker should be brought before the judicial system, even though no 'correction' or punishment would be called for in a case like this. In other words, the fact that an agent broke a law constitutes *prima facie* evidence that they should be corrected, and it should be up to a judicial system to determine when this is not the case. Thus, for the reasons just noted, it would seem that laws should at least in general be strictly enforced. I also take it that if a law is either systematically ignored or only enforced on certain occasions (e. g., laws against loitering, vagrancy or possibly jaywalking) then this is a sign that it was either poorly written or poorly conceived; i. e., that its strict enforcement would not really be in the best fair interest of a whole society.

My next series of points concern arrest procedures. In accordance with the best fair consequentialist system which I am defending, it is important that these procedures be effective, but also respect the rights of lawbreakers; i. e., be fair to their moral interests. Thus, in general, arrests of lawbreakers should involve a minimal use of force, since the point under a best fair consequentialist system is merely to effect custody and not to punish in a retributive sense.

An added point in the foregoing regard is that if there is a policy which only allows police to only shoot in self defense (as in certain jurisdictions in the United States), there is a real danger that the use of firearms in police work will often be either ineffective (as with a fleeing suspect who is not actually threatening the police officer) or will lead to abuses; as in calling cases self defense which really are not. A better fair alternative under a consequentialist system would be to use methods which are effective at incapacitating lawbreakers without endangering their lives, as in the use of tasers, of various sprays such as pepper spray or mace, or shooting rubber bullets. Another example, along somewhat the same lines, involves high-speed police chases of drivers who refuse to pull over. Here there are clear dangers not only to the officers and the drivers being pursued, but also to other drivers and pedestrians. Hence, again under consequentialist reasoning a better solution to effect an arrest would be to use technologies to cause the pursued car to stop, possibly by a special radio signal to make it stall.

It is not at all clear that any moral interests of suspects are infringed on in the just-given cases, since their lives are not endangered and they have the opportunity still to defend themselves later in a court of law. Also, additional safeguards could be mandated to make sure that abuses of the arrest policies not occur. For example, it could be made a legal offense for an arresting officer to use the techniques when they were not called for ; e. g., in cases when no law had been broken, or when a suspect had already surrendered.

I now wish to address several issues of contention with most present judicial systems. Under most present systems, a person's commission of a crime (carrying out a course of action which is not in accordance with some law) constitutes both a necessary and sufficient condition for bringing that person before the judicial system for purposes of instituting either punishment or 'correction' in the post-judicial system. However, I will argue against the commission of a crime being a sufficient condition for follow-through, in particular in the case where the lawbreaker has a 'good excuse.' It might also be thought that the commission of a crime should not be a necessary condition for follow-through under a consequentialist system, on possible grounds of crime prevention. However, I believe that a series of considerations can be raised to show that such a policy is not justified even under purely consequentialist grounds. I will first raise the issue of whether it is fair to the moral interests of a potential lawbreaker who has yet to break the law to bring them before the judicial system, and will then turn to a series of practical considerations against doing so.

With respect to the subject of fairness, I wish to argue that even if such practices as preventative detention could be justified on purely utilitarian grounds in terms of benefits for the overall population (e. g., in terms of future crime prevention), there would still be an inherent violation of the fairness constraint which I have been defending. It is true that the interest of a potential lawbreaker in breaking a law will at least typically be an immoral interest, since it presumably interferes with the moral interests of others. Nevertheless, it would appear to be very difficult here to avoid interfering with the moral interests of a potential lawbreaker as well. In order to establish this point it can first be noted that when a potential lawbreaker is dealt with in the post-judicial system there is an inherent interference with their physical freedom (as in the case of incarceration) or with their moral freedom, as with probation and the threat of punishment. It can be noted then that, to the extent that at least some of the desires that are thus interfered with do not involve conflicts with the moral interests of others, this constitutes interference with interests that are moral in character.

Admittedly, this last consideration does not distinguish between the cases of interfering before and after a crime has been committed. This is because there will be interference with the moral interests of lawbreakers by follow-through in the post-judicial system in this latter case as well. Also, the issue of deserving punishment only after a crime has been committed cannot be brought in here since I have been arguing that nobody actually deserves punishment. However, a series of practical considerations, which I will be developing next, concerning both the administration and the effectiveness of the resulting institution of punishment can still be raised in favor of only allowing punishment once a crime has been committed. It can then be noted that once these institutions have been set up along these lines, then it would be an exhibition of partiality towards lawbreakers and against law-followers (and hence be unfair to the moral interests of the latter) if some people were allowed to break the rules without being held 'accountable' for their actions, in the consequentialist sense developed in Chapter Six.

The first practical consideration that I wish to point out for having the commission of a crime be a necessary consideration for follow-through in the judicial system involves the issue of the justification of legal policies and practices; i. e., jurisprudence. It should be remembered here that laws are inherently rule- and not act-based. Hence, it is impossible to take account of all possible exigencies in the creation of the laws, at least if they are to be kept reasonably simple. The point here then is comparable to one which I made in comparing act and rule versions of utilitarianism; i. e., it is possible to make the two coincide but at the expense of building exceptions into the rules and thus making them be extremely complex in character. Thus, while it might be possible to construct a legal system where those only judged to be likely to commit a crime are brought before the judicial system, from a practical point of view this would appear to be very difficult to administer in an objective manner. It also might be easily subject to abuse; e. g., if a person was claimed to be a threat when they were either just not liked or were perceived to be a rival.

A second point to make in this context is that allowing preventative detention tends to undercut the force of the conditional statement behind the principle of deterrence; i. e., that if one commits a crime then one will be punished. This is because what is held to motivate obedience to the law under the deterrence rationale of punishment is fear of punishment. Thus, if that fear is present even if one has not committed a crime, but is merely judged to be likely to do so, then this lessens the incentive not to commit the crime. This may also lead to an anxiety among members of the general population that, even if they remain law-abiding, they may still be subject to arrest and prosecution. In view of these considerations I believe that deterrence may be best construed in terms of a biconditional statement asserting that one will be punished if and only if one commits a crime.

Still a third point to make in this regard is that there is a series of alternative measures which can be used to mitigate against the force of the purely-utilitarian argument favoring preventative detention. These measures involve achieving many of the same effects by making other activities illegal. Examples here include laws against conspiracy, threatening, stalking, and also restraining orders. What each of theses laws has in common is that, while they are designed to prevent a different future offense, when they are broken it is in terms of present activity. For example, instead of using preventative detention to prevent a case of domestic violence, a restraining order can be issued, where if the recipient of the order puts themselves in a position to be violent, they are *ipso facto* already breaking the restraining order. Thus, law-enforcement officials can then legally intervene before any violence actually occurs. In extreme cases (such as a serious threat to life) here surveillance techniques may also be used in conjunction with a restraining order to ensure an immediate apprehension if the order is violated.

This completes my discussion of why, despite initial appearances, I do not believe that under a consequentialist system such as the one which I have been advocating, the judicial system is justified in intervention prior to the commission of a crime. Thus, I still believe that the commission of a crime should be a necessary condition for intervention. I will now turn to my arguments as for why I do not believe that the commission of a crime should be sufficient grounds for intervention. I will leave it as an open question in this discussion whether all of the decisions about the relevance of various excusing conditions should be up to the courts, or whether sometimes this role should also be played by discretionary powers of law enforcers.

In general, the commission of a crime will constitute a sufficient condition under consequentialism for bringing someone before both the judicial and post-judicial systems since the fact that a person has committed a crime constitutes at least *prima facie* evidence that something is 'wrong' (at least from an overall societal viewpoint) with that person with regard to their social functioning. This is because it is the purpose of these systems to 'correct' these wrongs; i. e., to serve as adjudicating agents. However, according to act consequentialism, which I have been defending, there will also be exceptions here, namely when the consequences are better, and fair to all parties involved, when the law is broken. It can be noted that, in effect, I am advocating a comparable attitude towards laws to that which act utilitarians take towards moral rules. That is, rather than being taken as absolute strictures, the laws or rules are taken just to be valid for the most part, and whereby exceptions can be justified in special circumstances. Their status is thus taken to be that of guidelines, although possibly guidelines creating strong presumptions that a course of action was wrong. In other words, the fact that a law or a moral rule exists can be seen to shift the burden of proof to a law- or rule-breaker to show that their course of action was in fact justified.

This raises the subject matter of the status to be given to legal excuses in my system. The criteria for excuses which I developed in my section on excuses in Chapter Six can be applied here by confining the rules being discussed to just legal statutes and other types of law (as the concept was just analyzed), and not also to moral rules. As was discussed in that section, excuses can be classified in terms of those involving coercion, those involving ignorance, and justificatory excuses. Each of these can, in turn, be applied to legal situations, as I will now illustrate, although only sketchily so as to not inordinately duplicate my previous treatment.

As I noted in my section on excuses in Chapter Six, a good case can be made that ignorance of the law is not a sufficient excuse, assuming that the law has been promulgated. However, ignorance of fact may still be a sufficient excuse, in particular when an agent has not been remiss, such as by being negligent, in the determination of these facts. Also, in the case of coercion, as in the previously-mentioned case of negative external coercion of committing a crime at the point of a gun, the existence of the coercive factor can certainly be a mitigating if not always a completely-exonerating factor.

Justificatory excuses, in the legal context, could use more elaboration than the other types of legal excuses, since they tend to be more controversial. As an illustration of a justificatory legal excuse, consider the previously-mentioned case involving a person breaking a traffic regulation while rushing another, seriously-ill, person to a hospital, and where clearly they are not endangering anyone else in the process. Here, according to the best fair approach to consequentialism which I have been defending, the extenuating circumstances just mentioned would constitute a 'sufficient excuse' (as that concept was analyzed in Chapter Six) for breaking the law. This is because there are presumably better consequences with this choice than with alternative choices and, since no one else is endangered in the process, there is no violation of the fairness constraint. Hence, the person breaking the law should not be 'corrected' here, since there is nothing to correct.

It is true that cases, such as the preceding one, or killing in self defense, could be dealt with by means of having a more complex law, where in effect the exception is built into the law. However, as I previously noted, there would be a tradeoff concerning how easy it is to apply these complex laws and the complications of judicially determining the adequacy of excuses. Still, a society may often be better off by having the simpler, more easily-applicable, laws on the books and allowing overrides; i. e., justificatory legal excuses. A 'sufficient justificatory legal excuse' will exist then in those situations where the lawbreaking course of action has better overall consequences than any other alternative course of action, and where there is no infringement on the moral interests of any parties involved.

However, in cases where a lawbreaker is not prosecuted the burden of proof would be on the lawbreaker to show that their course of action was in fact justified. Presumably this would involve invoking the judicial system even if corrections were not called for. Otherwise, to the extent that obedience to the law is actually motivated by fear of punishment, people might break laws at will whenever they were confident that the judicial system would not be able to demonstrate that the course of action was not justified. Thus, the deterrent force of the whole institution of punishment would be undermined by such a policy.

It would seem then that, under the system of best fair act consequentialism which I have been defending, legal statutes, like moral rules, in effect constitute strong generalities concerning what should or should not be done for the most part, and that in extreme circumstances they will at least almost always possess justified exceptions. Also, according to this system of act consequentialism, the criteria for deciding whether or not making an exception to a law is justified (i. e., whether or not a sufficient justificatory excuse is present) on any particular occasion will involve appeals to what the lawbreaker's best fair potential course of action in fact was. That is, the best overall potential course of action should be chosen within the confines of the fairness constraint of not imposing on the moral interests of any of the parties involved. If someone in fact pursues their best fair potential course of action, as this concept was analyzed in Part One, and this course of action involves breaking a law, then that person is legally justified in doing so. Thus, assuming that they can establish that this is the case, they should not be 'corrected' for pursuing the course of action in question. This is because, since the course of action here was the best fair potential course of action for the agent to pursue, there is nothing to 'correct,' and hence no need to invoke the 'correctional' or post-judicial system.

Section Four The Court System

In this section, I will discuss the role of the court system based on the consequentialist lines developed in Part One. In particular, I will address how such a system should administer the law with respect to adjudicating disputes, determining the 'guilt' or 'innocence' of parties, and in determining proper 'sentences' (or other forms of 'correction') for those judged 'guilty.' The key point which I wish to make here is that judges should pick best fair (as I have previously analyzed those concepts) solutions for all concerned, and that this should be done on an individual basis. Thus, I am advocating that judicial decisions be made in terms of individual circumstances, and at least not exclusively in terms of applying rules. The attitude which I am thus advocating that judges should use towards legal statutes is that of strong policy guidelines. Here, even though as I previously noted the guidelines may constitute a strong presumption in favor of being followed, as I also noted, they will be allowed to have exceptions when these exceptions are clearly merited by the circumstances. It should also be noted that, inasmuch as I am advocating a consequentialist rationale here, what has occurred in the past concerning an agent will only be germane to the extent that it constitutes evidence concerning their probable future courses of action. I wish to show now that this last point contrasts with the way in which at least most present-day court systems are run.

As was shown in my discussion of law enforcement in general, at least most present-day judicial systems conflate two distinct issues; whether someone actually committed a course of action of a type prohibited by the law, and whether they ought to be either punished or corrected because of this commission. While breaking a law may constitute strong *prima facie* evidence for the need for correction, as I have shown, it does not entail it. This also shows what is going on with disputes over such pleas as those of being 'not guilty' by reason of insanity, or with problems concerning how to treat mercy killings. The agents are 'guilty' of the acts in the sense of having committed them, but still may not be 'guilty' in the sense of meriting correction. I see the present-day judicial system as conflating the two different senses of 'guilt.' Thus, in a judicial system set up on consequentialist lines it will be important to keep separate the two issues of whether a party performed a course of action of a particular type, and what ought to be done because of this.

The next issue which I will discuss here concerns the role of judges in determining facts in court cases. I believe that the present American system is too adversarial in character inasmuch as there is no strong incentive for either the defense or the prosecution to be objective in determining whether a party actually committed a crime or not. I also believe that there is too much emphasis on lawyers winning cases regardless of the actual merits of the cases. Thus, I hold that it is important that a neutral party—e. g., a judge or a jury (possibly a professsional one)—be given a stronger role in this determination. The institution of plea bargaining can also be criticized in this regard since the resulting plea may have very little to do with whatever crime was actually committed. There may even be cases where a genuinely innocent party pleads 'guilty' in such an arrangement so as to protect themselves from the risk of being found guilty of a more serious charge.

Another criticism against plea bargaining or granting immunity or reducing charges under coercive circumstances such as those just mentioned is that it violates Kant's Practical Imperative that people should never be used just as a means. That there is such a violation should be clear since a threat (of a harsher penalty if an alleged lawbreaker does not cooperate) is being used as a means to gain cooperation in these cases. It is true that an alleged lawbreaker may accept a deal, such as that of a reduced sentence, in a sense willingly since, from their own point of view, its acceptance may be construed as being the lesser of two evils. Nevertheless, inasmuch as the judicial system is deliberately not giving the alleged lawbreaker the most fitting (from the viewpoint of correcting what is wrong with the alleged lawbreaker) treatment, it is clearly not dealing with them for their own sake; i. e., as an end. This should be particularly clear if one considers cases where the genuinely innocent actually end up being punished more severely than the guilty because of either a refusal to enter into plea bargaining or a failure to exhibit remorse for their alleged crime.

A closely related issue to those just discussed concerns what sort of evidence should be admissible to a court, both in terms of what sort should be included and what sort should be excluded. A good example of courts excluding evidence in the United States is the exclusionary rule, which is the result of court interpretations of the clause "against unreasonable searches and seizures" in the Fourth Amendment of the U. S. constitution. The rule excludes the courtroom usage of evidence against defendants when the evidence has been illegally obtained; e. g., without probable cause. While, as I have previously argued, under the best fair version of consequentialism it is required that the moral interests of defendants be protected, I believe that other modes are available to insure this than to actually exclude evidence. For example, those who conduct an illegal search could be prosecuted for doing so.

A converse point to the foregoing one about excluding evidence is that too much questionable evidence is often allowed. Consider, in this regard, the testimony of witnesses who have something to gain in the process. Here, the motivation behind testifying may be just to evade or to lessen a sentence rather than to tell the truth. A good example here is the case of allowing inmate testimony against other inmates where rewards, such as reductions in sentences, are given for providing testimony. Other examples would include cases where, prior to conviction, alleged lawbreakers are either given immunity from prosecution or promised a reduced charge or sentence in exchange for testimony against others.

In summary, I do not see the present judicial system as necessarily oriented towards actually determining the truth behind a situation. This is particularly apparent both with cases of excluding evidence, as with the usage of the exclusionary rule, and also with allowing questionable evidence, as with plea bargains and with cases where agents are coerced into giving evidence against one another. In these sorts of cases, I see the present judicial system as giving positive incentives to overstate cases, leave out relevant evidence, distort facts, and even commit outright perjury. The net result of using the best fair consequentialist approach as an alternative would be for the court system to be objective in discovering the actual facts of cases while still protecting agents against truly unreasonable searches.

Since my next several points involve the alleged sharp distinction between the motives behind an act of lawbreaking and the issue of whether the act was intentional or not I wish to say something on the nature of the distinction. I might note that Sidgwick (1907/1981, p. 202) and Anscombe (1957/1963, Sec. 12) also question how sharp this distinction is, As I noted earlier, to intentionally break a law can be analyzed in terms of the issue of whether or not the act was performed while conceived under the same description which is proscribed by the law. In contrast, a motive is best seen as being a teleological concept which refers to the reason for having a particular intention. Thus, acting under the intention can be seen as a means to accomplish the end given by the motive. Also, motives tend to be stated in terms of referring to possible situations which an agent is trying to bring into existence (e. g., to attain greater personal wealth), while intentions usually are used to refer to either actual or possible courses of action; e. g., robbing a bank. However, I wish to question whether the distinction between motives and intentions is always a sharp one, in particular for cases where means and ends coincide. For example, my intention to eat an ice cream cone would seem to be very close in content to the motive of desiring ice cream.

It can now be noted that while our present judicial system does take the issue of intentionality into account with the concept of 'criminal intent,' or '*mens rea*' (e. g., in distinguishing between first degree murder and negligent homicide), it tends to claim that the motivation behind breaking the law is not a relevant consideration at least for the determination of whether a crime has been committed. While this can clearly be justified in cases where immoral means (e. g., the just cited case of bank robbery) are used for moral ends (e. g., giving the resulting money to a needy charity), I find other cases more dubious. For example, active euthanasia is often classified as murder since it involves the intentional killing of another human, even though the motivation may just involve love and not malice, in the sense of 'ill-will.' However, it could certainly be argued that such killing need not be immoral since the person whose life is being taken is presumably being treated as an end and not just a means. This is because it is being judged that they would be better off no longer living. It might also be noted with respect to this last example, that the legal system has taken motives out of its usage of 'malice' when it defines it as "the intentional doing of a wrongful act."

In contrast to the situation with our present judicial system, I wish to argue that the nature of the motives behind an action should be at least one of the prime relevant factors for determining appropriate follow-through in the post-judicial system. Admittedly, it may often be quite difficult to objectively determine motives and thus in many cases it just may not be practical to even attempt to do this. For example, just asking someone is not always trustworthy, although even here stories can be checked both for internal consistency and consistency with known facts. Nevertheless, in cases where a lot may ride on the subject, I believe that at least the issue should at least be raised as to whether a claimed motive is at all credible or not. For example, in the just-mentioned case of euthanasia, the fact that a close relative took the life of another family member suffering from a terminal illness should be solid evidence that the motive was probably love and not malice in the sense of ill-will. I also want to stress that there can be many different possible motives for people to commit essentially identical crimes. Thus, I will now review what I take to be some of the chief motives behind criminal behavior.

There are many distinct possible motivations for why people commit crimes, not all or which are mutually exclusive in character. First, there are cases where the commission of a crime is the result of acting under either coercion or compulsion. Here, as was seen in Chapter Four, distinctions can be drawn both between external and internal cases, and between positive and negative cases. Examples of internal coercive factors (and possibly sometimes compulsive factors) would include cases of agents stealing because they are kleptomaniacs or cases of theft to support a drug habit. Many of these cases involve what is sometimes known as 'weakness of the will,' since there a course of action is performed in spite of an individual's better judgment. However, there will also be cases where an agent is either coerced or compelled to break a law to take care of a necessity of life, such as in cases of agents stealing food because they are starving or stealing medicine to deal with a fatal illness.

Crimes of passion, including some acts of vengeance, can also be included under the category of acting under coercion or compulsion, assuming that the lawbreaker is not able to at least completely control their passion. Cases of acting out of revenge (a subject which I previously touched on in Chapter Five), where the acting out is dispassionate in character, need to be distinguished though, since here it is more the case that the lawbreaker is acting under what I have argued is a misguided theory. While still on this topic, cases can also be cited where a situation between two parties escalates, from perhaps a fairly trivial cause to begin with, until one party or the other does something criminal in character to the other. Clear-cut cases of external compulsion are somewhat harder to come by than those involving external coercion, but the case of an agent being bodily forced to commit an act of trespass would be an example.

The second type of motivation for crime which I wish to discuss involves cases where a law was not deliberately broken under the description of a situation which is proscribed by a law. Included here are cases of accidents and negligence, where a lawbreaker is ignorant of either their true external situation (their environment) or the true nature of their abilities. An example of a lawbreaker acting under ignorance of their abilities would be a case where one person strikes another person during an attack of epilepsy. Examples of acting under ignorance of a lawbreaker's true external situation would include the case of a hunter mistakenly shooting another person believing that that person is a deer, and a case of inadvertently shooting another person while playing with a gun, believing it to be unloaded.

A third possible motivation for crime (this is probably the most common motivation) involves cases where, instead of using the moral point of view in making their decisions, a lawbreaker uses a narrower viewpoint with respect to deciding what their best fair course of action is. Ideally, as I have shown, laws should be written from the standpoint of an extremely wide point of view, such as that of the well-being of a nation, or possibly the whole world. However, the self-interests of individual agents, or even somewhat larger collections of agents (e. g., crime families or types of organized crime), may not always coincide with what is both best and fair under the standpoint of this wider point of view. Hence, a conflict of interests may arise between the two. The lawbreaker then may be acting under the scope of their own narrowly-defined decision-making process and not under the wider viewpoint under which the laws were written. There are other possible motives besides plain greed here, including cases where laws are broken for the thrill of it or even out of boredom. There may also be cases where lawbreakers want to see if they can get away with the 'perfect' crime, or even cases where they take a perverse pleasure in breaking laws or causing harm for its own sake.

It can be noted that in each of the foregoing cases the lawbreaker is making a rational decision (albeit from a narrow or short-term point of view) whereby they weigh whatever is to be gained by breaking the law (e. g., stolen merchandise, a thrill, or even time as with a speeding infraction) against the downside risks if they are caught; e. g., spending jail time, paying a fine, or effects on the lawbreaker's personal reputation. Obviously, the actual rationality of these decisions depends both on the nature of opportunities to commit crimes, and also on the natures of the law enforcement, judicial, and post-judicial systems which a potential lawbreaker is likely to encounter. These latter institutions can be judged both in terms of their relative efficiency (i. e., the chances of being caught, the chances of being convicted if caught, and the chances of incurring various penalties even if both caught and convicted) and in terms of likely consequences if the systems in fact work as intended.

In different contexts, depending on a potential lawbreaker's stakes in different possible outcomes, it is rational for the potential lawbreaker to use different decision-making procedures with respect to the scenarios just alluded to. The points concerning when these different procedures are appropriate which I made in Chapters Two and Four can then be applied. For example, if a potential lawbreaker has a great deal at stake in what will happen if a law is not broken (e. g., in the cases of stealing food to prevent starving to death, or lying on one's tax returns so as to prevent getting caught up in a major scandal) it may even be rational to use the maximax strategy since the potential lawbreaker is not willing to live with the consequences if the law is not broken. In other contexts, where there is less at stake if a potential lawbreaker does not break a given law, it will be more rational to use the strategy of maximizing expected utility. For example, one can imagine a professional thief here carefully weighing the relative utilities of what is to be gained if a particular burglary is successful with the downside risks if they were to be caught. There may also be contexts where a potential law-breaker is not willing to live with the consequences of being caught breaking a law (as with the case of a politician), whereby it will be rational to use the maximin decision strategy. Here a potential lawbreaker will only break a law if they are completely confident that they will not be caught even though they know that they will probably be able to get away with it and will maximize expected utility by trying to do so.

Other possible motivations for breaking laws include cases whereby a law-breaker's decision-making process is flawed in its determination of what is best and/or fair for a whole society, either due to poor information concerning either the lawbreaker's actual situation or in predicting the way in which their different potential courses of action would affect future situations; e. g., cases of what Sellars (1963, p. 6) would call a "flawed manifest image." There may also be cases where a lawbreaker is unable to make a living in any other way besides committing crimes, such as in cases of lacking marketable job skills or severe physical or mental handicaps. Other possible motivations include peer pressure (as from the family or friends of the lawbreaker, as in the case of a gang); cases of ignorance of the law (which, unlike cases of ignorance of fact, under our system does not serve as an excuse, at least when the law has been promulgated); and finally cases where laws are genuinely perceived as being unjust; i. e., where it is claimed that obeying the laws will not actually lead to what is best and fair from the viewpoint of the larger societal reference frame. This completes my review of different possible motivations behind criminal behavior, and I will thus now make use of the diversity of this list in discussing the subject of judicial sentencing per se.

The first point which I wish to make concerning judicial sentencing under a best fair consequentialist rationale concerns the way in which it differs from sentencing under the retributive theory of punishment. It can be recalled from

Chapter Five that a basic tenet of the act-based purely-retributive theory of punishment was that the punishment ought to match the crime regardless of the motive behind the crime. In contrast, under a best fair consequentialist system, the sole determining factor for appropriate follow-through in the post-judicial system is the consequences that the follow-through will have both on the lawbreaker and on the overall society. Obviously considerations of motivation will be highly relevant here inasmuch as different follow-throughs will have very different effects on lawbreakers depending on what motivated them to commit a crime in the first place.

It follows from the foregoing considerations that under a best fair consequentialist judicial system a court must first at least attempt (to the extent that this can be objectively determined) to identify whatever caused a lawbreaker to break a law (i. e., determine what motivated their decision to act as they did), and then, in cases where there is in fact a 'problem,' determine a 'sentence' that will constitute the best possible fair 'correction' for the problem. Under some of the motivations for crime which were noted, such as in the case of external compulsion, since there is no 'problem' to 'correct,' clearly the lawbreaker can be exonerated. Presumably in these cases legal responsibility will then have to be shifted vicariously to the agents responsible for the compulsion, which would justify bringing them before the judicial system instead. Similarly, in the case of external coercion, at least a partial exoneration can typically take place inasmuch as if the coercive factor had not been present, then at least typically the crime would not have been committed. Thus, in these cases the fact that a crime was committed does not constitute evidence of how the coerced lawbreaker would act in non-coercive circumstances. It can be seen then that the fact that coercion was present when a crime was committed should typically constitute at least a partially mitigating circumstance in adjudicating a proper sentence. Also, as was the case with external compulsion, this may be a reason for a vicarious shift in ascriptions of legal responsibility.

In the case of lack of information about either the surroundings or the abilities of a lawbreaker, if this is the sole cause for the commission of a crime, presumably providing the relevant information would solve the problem. However, the nature of best fair remedies for other types of situations may not be nearly so clear-cut. In cases of internal compulsion and coercion, such as in cases of 'weakness of the will' and crimes of passion, where a lawbreaker could not help doing what they did (in either the strong compulsive sense of where they could not have done otherwise even if they tried to, or a weaker coercive sense where this turns out to be at least an extremely difficult thing to do), it would seem that the 'correction' might very well occur best in a hospital-like environment. Relevant cases here would include cases of drug addiction and such psychologically 'compulsive' behaviors as those involved with megalomania, kleptomania, or pyromania. Perhaps this would also be the best fair setting for treating either psychopathic or schizophrenic lawbreakers as well.

In cases where a law is broken because of lack of alternatives for making a living, such as in a case where a lawbreaker has few job skills, placement in a rehabilitative job-training program may be called for. Similarly, in cases where a law is broken either out of boredom or peer pressure, changes in the environment of the lawbreaker may be called for, such as by getting them connected with a new set of friends. In cases where a law is genuinely perceived as being unjust, the situation may vary. Sometimes the lawbreaker may, by being presented with relevant information, become convinced that the law is just after all, and sometimes it may even turn out that the law itself should be changed.

With respect to the group of cases which I identified where the problem was that a lawbreaker's decision-making viewpoint was too narrow, a variety of possible remedies may be tried. First, in a few cases it is possible that if the lawbreaker was to be educated about the merits of the moral point of view, this in itself would suffice to change their future behavior. For most cases though it will not be very easy to cause a lawbreaker to enlarge their point of view. In these sorts of cases the most effective means of changing future behavior of law-breakers will be to either give them, or at least threaten to give them, unpleasant experiences, such as prison terms. The rationale here is to make the situation such that it becomes irrational, even under an egotistical point of view, for a potential lawbreaker to break the law. As I previously noted both Locke (1690/1960) and Bentham (1789/1988) point out that this makes it become a poor bargain for the potential lawbreaker, even from the perspective of self interest. It should be emphasized that the justification for the 'punishment' or threat of 'punishment' here will be in terms of deterrence of individual potential lawbreakers themselves, but at least not necessarily other potential lawbreakers, such as if one person is made an 'example of' for others. There may also be some cases in which even this last treatment will be to no avail—e. g., in cases of 'incorrigibles'—in which case just keeping someone in prison to deny them the opportunity to commit future crimes may be called for.

In summary, under a best fair consequentialist rationale, such as the one that I have been defending in this book, a court system should first determine what the actual facts of a case are. It should then determine which potential course of action is appropriate for a particular criminal case on an individual basis. It should be emphasized again that this determination cannot be done solely in terms of the nature of the crime. Instead, once the facts of a case are known and the cause of the criminal behavior is also determined, then the best fair (as judged by its effectiveness in crime prevention) 'correction' should be accorded a law-breaker. It should also be emphasized again that I am not advocating the use of 'correction' as retribution here. Thus, even though the corrective experience may be unpleasant, it is being invoked for the lawbreaker's own benefit, and any interference here for other purposes will involve using the lawbreaker just as a means.

I will now examine each of the just-mentioned possible 'corrections' in more detail in my next chapter on the post-judicial system, inasmuch as that system is the one that actually carries out the 'corrections,' the nature of which are determined by the courts.

Chapter Eight
The Post-Judicial System

In this chapter I will be concerned with determining the nature of an ideal post-judicial system using both the consequentialist principles concerning the nature of a best fair system developed in Part One and the principles of justice developed in my last chapter. I should emphasize right at the beginning that I am using 'post-judicial system' here as a value-neutral term to refer to what is imposed by a judicial system on an agent either for purposes of punishment (where the motivation is that of retribution) or for 'correction'; where the motivation is to 'correct' for something wrong with the agent, as with the case of rehabilitation. I will refer to agents who are causally responsible for laws being broken as 'lawbreakers' and I will use 'potential lawbreakers' to refer to agents who are judged as being likely to break laws in at least certain circumstances. Again, it should be emphasized that I will be using both of these terms in a purely descriptive and hence value-neutral sense. I should also note that some of my discussion was influenced by Ronald Goldfarb and Linda Singer's (1973) *After Conviction*.

As in the case of my treatment of the judicial system in Chapter Seven, I will both present a critique of present-day post-judicial systems (which are at least largely, although obviously not completely, based on retributive conceptions of justice) and also suggest ways in which they could be replaced by a system that is consequence-based. It is noteworthy that the two approaches are not always even sharply distinguished by the system, and in fact ordinary language sometimes combines the two in such phrases as "you deserve to be taught a lesson you will never forget." In any event, I will examine the relative merits of five distinct possible consequence-based rationales here; namely those based on therapy for a lawbreaker, rehabilitation, denial of opportunity for a lawbreaker to commit a crime in the future, deterrence of lawbreakers themselves, and deterrence of other potential lawbreakers. I will only be defending the first four rationales though due to the conflict of the final one with principles of fairness.

I will begin my discussion of post-judicial systems by means of raising issues concerning both what types of rationale are actually given for them, and also which, if any, of these types are actually justified; i. e., what purposes the systems should be designed to serve. To begin this discussion, I take it that at least one of the fundamental rationales, although certainly not the only one, behind the practices of at least most current post-judicial systems is that of retribution. Thus, these post-judicial systems are primarily penal in character rather than correctional. That is, they are based on the position that, since lawbreakers (with the exception of the insane and the very young, because they are not fully rational, and those who were coerced into breaking the law) are 'morally responsible' for their courses of action, they 'deserve' punishment. Inasmuch as I gave a critique of the very coherency of the concept of 'retribution' in Part One, it would seem that, to the extent that present-day post-judicial systems are based on that notion, they would not be justified.

I would like to now turn to a discussion of what a consequentialist alternative to present retribution-based post-judicial systems would be like. In particular, I will now review four possible consequentialist rationales which have often been given as supplementing a retributive justification for a post-judicial system, although they do not necessarily involve a 'prison-like' environment. These include therapeutic rationales, reformative or rehabilitative rationales, preventative rationales, and deterrence rationales. As far as I can see, at least roughly, the preferential ranking in which these rationales ought to be invoked by the post-judicial system is that the system should first stress either rehabilitation or therapy if a lawbreaker is susceptible to being helped by going through these programs. If the lawbreaker cannot be helped by these programs, or if invoking them is deemed to be too expensive or too inefficient, the system should then be used to deter the lawbreaker from breaking laws in the future. Finally, if a law-breaker is not even susceptible of being deterred here (at least by reasonable means), then the preventative rationale would come into play, and the system should be used so as to deny them the opportunity to perform these types of courses of action. I shall now turn to a discussion of each of the foregoing rationales in some detail, beginning with the therapeutic rationale. I might also remark that in my discussion I will subdivide the deterrence rationale into two sub-categories; those of deterring lawbreakers themselves, and of deterring other potential lawbreakers by punishing a lawbreaker.

Section One Therapeutic Rationales

There is a certain class of lawbreakers whose members cannot be deterred by ordinary methods; e. g., by either rehabilitation programs or by deterrence. This class includes at least certain individuals from the following groups—drug addicts; alcoholics; schizophrenics; psychopaths; people possessing various psychological 'compulsions,' such as kleptomania, pyromania, megalomania, and such sexual 'compulsions' as pedophilia or necrophilia; and people possessing various phobias. A key distinction to make with respect to these cases involves the issue of whether or not the lawbreaker could have done otherwise if they so tried. If they could not, then using my terminology from Chapter Four, the action would be characterized as being 'internally compulsive,' and the person would not have been physically free to have done otherwise. The other category involves cases where, while the lawbreaker could have done otherwise if they had tried, there was a powerful internal inducement not to do so. I will characterize these sorts of cases as cases of acting under 'internal coercion,' which I am using in the very broad sense introduced in Chapter Four which includes both positive and negative inducements to act in certain ways, but where these inducements are not so powerful that they could not have been overcome if an agent had tried to do so.

It is obvious that in cases of internal compulsion a therapeutic (i. e., a curative approach) attitude on the part of the post-judicial system would be the only one which could be justifiable under a consequentialist rationale for correction. Certainly, giving a lawbreaker an unpleasant experience as a deterrent makes no sense in cases where deterrents are not effective (as, by definition, they are not in these sorts of cases) if the justification is completely consequentialist and not retributive in nature. In fact, many retributivists would go along with this to the extent that they only apply the retributive theory to fully-rational adults. It would also seem then that, with respect to cases of internal coercion, a therapeutic approach would be justifiable, at least to the extent that the lawbreaker's decisions are not completely their own; i. e., do not coincide with what they would have been if the internal coercive factors were missing. Thus, under the therapeutic rationale the post-judicial system will engage in activities designed to actually change the decision-making processes of lawbreakers rather than just to introduce new causal factors on existing decision-making systems as in the other consequentialist rationales. As I noted, such activity would seem to be justified in cases of internal coercive and compulsive factors, since, by definition, the other consequentialist rationales will be ineffective in these cases.

I might note that both Menninger (1968) and Wootton (1959) have advocated a therapeutic attitude towards lawbreakers in general. However, this would clearly seem to be too broad of an approach since, as I noted in Chapter Seven, there are many other motivations for breaking laws besides cases of compulsion and coercion. Still, such cases do constitute an important and sizeable class. Thus, it is important that these cases be accurately identified as such and dealt with appropriately.

Treatment for lawbreakers 'suffering' from either internal compulsive or internal coercive factors may, but need not, take place within the confines of an institution; i. e., it may either occur on an 'out patient' basis or be completely 'in house.' In fact, the issue as to whether a treatment ought to involve confinement to an institution cuts across the lines of its justification. For example, the institutions of probation and parole, at least a partial justification for which is deterrence, do not involve incarceration, but merely the threat of it. Similarly, as just noted, a therapeutic treatment program may or may not occur within a confinement setting. When there is an added societal need to protect people from a dangerous individual, there may be an added rationale for having it involve confinement though. It is also important to note that, unlike many current 'mental hospitals,' the places which I have in mind here would actually attempt to cure 'patients' instead of just serving as holding facilities.

One key difference between cases of internal coercion and cases of internal compulsion is that, unlike the internal compulsive case, in cases of internal coercion deterrence will sometimes work. That is, a threatened penalty will sometimes serve as a strong enough incentive that it will make an agent under coercion act otherwise than if the threat were not present. For example, a drug addict, kleptomaniac, or pyromaniac may not commit a crime in front of a police officer. Similarly, there are limits on what most psychopaths and schizophrenics will do when they are being watched by authority figures. However, as was noted, it would seem that a therapeutic attitude is also appropriate in cases of at least internal coercion. This is because there is still something wrong with the internal decision-making processes of the individual. Treatments here would largely parallel those discussed with respect to the compulsive cases, although unlike the case of compulsion a combination of a therapeutic and deterrence approach could be used as well.

The defense of being "not guilty by reason of insanity" is often given with respect to both cases of internal compulsion and internal coercion. However, I believe that this way of characterizing these situations is seriously misleading. Using my distinction from the last chapter between guilt and reprehensibility, it would seem that a more apt characterization would be as "guilty but not reprehensible" (at least in a morally judgmental sense), with the implication being that a therapeutic treatment would be more appropriate than one based on either retribution or deterrence. This completes my discussion of the therapeutic rationale, and I will now move on to my discussion of reformative rationales.

Section Two Reformative Rationales

The aim of reformative rationales for correction is to so change a lawbreaker's thought processes that they will no longer have propensities for committing crimes. Since the nature of the appropriate reformative program will depend on the nature of the cause for the lawbreaker's propensity for criminal behavior, it is obviously very important to correctly identify this cause in order for the reformative program to be effective. For example, assuming (which may sometimes be a big assumption) that the lawbreaker was ever habilitated or educated to begin with, programs called for here may include those of rehabilitation, such as a broadening of the lawbreaker's point of view with respect to their decision-making procedures so as to encompass the well-being of a much wider society; a general re-education; or help with specific job skills or with job placement. In the case of criminal motivations involving 'perverse' desires (e. g., sexual ones), the habilitation or rehabilitation may also involve finding a way either to 'suppress' these desires or to 'channel' the corresponding energy into something more 'constructive.'

Various behavioristic techniques either involving 'rewards' or 'penalties' (notice that a 'penalty' here is not construed as being a punishment, in the sense of being retributive in character, but rather as negative reinforcement) may also be involved here. The imposition of penalties is more controversial than the use of rewards, since it may be deemed that imposing at least some penalties involves an infringement on prisoner's rights. However, it can be recalled that in Chapter Five, in my treatment of the causal sense of 'responsibility,' I argued that we may be justified in interfering in cases like these because it would be unfair to the rest of the people in a society not to do so.

Some would also say that behavioristic techniques should only be used as a last resort since, in effect, they only treat symptoms and not root causes. However, in some cases it may be held that discovering and treating the root cause of criminal behavior may not be worth the effort; i. e., the cure may be worse than the disease. Also, it may be claimed that a certain lack of respect is being shown towards the lawbreaker here to the extent that they are not being reasoned with.

It is possible to perform many rehabilitative functions outside a prison setting, as with the institution of parole or half-way houses (for helping to ease a person back into society after they have been released from prison) or temporary releases from prison as with 'work release' and furloughs to help keep families functioning. Pardons and the expunging of criminal records should also be mentioned in this context, since by thus erasing the stigma of a conviction from an ex-prisoner's record, the ex-prisoner may be eligible for certain jobs that they would not otherwise be eligible for, and thus may not have the need to return to a criminal lifestyle in the future. I should emphasize in this last regard that I am not advocating that no parties whomsoever be allowed access to an ex-prisoner's past records in these sorts of cases (since clearly there may be cases where the information is genuinely germane; e. g., jobs requiring a security clearance), but it still would seem to be the case that many people who have gone through a rehabilitation program are capable of performing any number of jobs well. Thus, I am merely advocating that lawbreaker's past criminal records should not be held against them on this score.

The ease of performing any of the reformative tasks mentioned here should not be underestimated, and it is important that they be performed objectively. This completes my discussion of reformative rationales for correction, and thus I will now move on to discuss preventative rationales.

Section Three Preventative Rationales

In contrast to reformative rationales for correction, the aim of preventative rationales is not to change the character of lawbreakers, but instead to deny them any opportunities to commit future criminal courses of action. In particular, this rationale would come into play if lawbreakers, for any number of possible reasons, are judged not to be reformable, and thus to be dangerous to themselves or others if left alone outside of a controlled environment. Also, in some cases it may be deemed to be too 'expensive' (in either monetary or manpower terms) to rehabilitate certain lawbreakers. In these sorts of cases the claim is that the consequences of keeping lawbreakers under control—e. g., in prison, or possibly some analogue of a half-way house—will be better than those of allowing them to have uncontrolled freedom. This is because the lawbreaker will be prevented from committing other potential crimes, at least against people outside of the confines of the correctional institution.

There may still be a problem concerning crime prevention though if a lawbreaker constitutes a danger to other inmates within the correctional institution itself. In these cases still stronger measures than institutional confinement per se, such as solitary confinement, may even be called for. It should be emphasized though that there is no need for the confinement to be made unnecessarily unpleasant under the preventative rationale (remember that the rationale here is not that of retribution, to get back at the lawbreaker), and the rationale could also be used to justify making the prisoners be as productive as possible—such as by having them do useful work for the society. This last case might also have the side benefit of helping to make the post-judicial system to be more self-sufficient as far as costs of running the system go and thus maximizing overall utility within the fairness constraint.

I should consider two possible objections which have been historically raised against forcing prisoners to do useful work here: (1) it infringes on the rights of the prisoners and (2) it takes jobs away from others, who have broken no laws, and who could do the work instead. In reply to the first objection, I would note that the system is fair, inasmuch as it can be viewed as having the prisoners merely compensate the post-judicial system for its expenses and since relevantly similar cases are treated similarly. In reply to the second objection, so long as the jobs involved are the least-desirable ones to be done, and if no one else will do them at a reasonable cost, why not have the prisoners do them? After all, isn't it better that the work at least be done, and who would be a better candidate to perform the work than people, such as inmates, who otherwise have nothing better to do with their time?

I will now turn to my discussion of deterrence. There are two distinct subclasses under the consequentialist rationale of deterring lawbreakers from committing crimes—deterring lawbreakers themselves from committing future crimes, and deterring other potential lawbreakers from committing similar crimes. At the very outset of my discussion I should mention that I see a number of ethical problems concerning the justifiability of the second sort of rationale here, that of the deterrence of others, particularly when it is engaged for its own sake. In any event, I will discuss the rationale of deterring lawbreakers themselves first, and then will discuss the rationale of deterring others.

Section Four Deterring Lawbreakers Themselves

Under the rationale of deterring (i. e., in effect, scaring) lawbreakers themselves from committing future criminal courses of action, the aim is to either actually give, or just threaten to give, a lawbreaker a sufficiently unpleasant experience so that they will be afraid of committing similar courses of action in the future. As with the reformative rationale, this can be done outside of a prison setting, as with the institutions of probation and parole, where an unpleasant experience is threatened if a one-time lawbreaker repeats types of criminal courses of action. Thus, the rationale is to negatively coerce a one-time lawbreaker into not continuing to break laws in the future, not so much because they see that they should not break them (as would be the case if they were rehabilitated), but instead because they are afraid of the negative consequences to themselves personally of breaking them.

A complication here concerns the nature of the lessons that some lawbreakers may learn from the negative coercing situation. In effect, the lesson learned may just be the material conditional that if they continue to commit crimes then they should make sure that they are not caught; or equivalently, to either not continue committing crimes or to make sure that they are not caught after committing them. Since the motivation behind the deterrence rationale is to stop crime, it is important that the potential lawbreaker see the alternative of committing crimes and not being caught as being unlikely to occur. This may be accomplished by trying to make punishment seem a 'sure thing' if a crime is committed. Then, even under the point of view of narrow self interest, a rational potential lawbreaker will not break the law inasmuch as it is not even in their self interest to do so.

Another way to make the preceding point is that if the deterrence rationale is to be effective then a potential lawbreaker must be put in the position where they analyze their situation in terms of the material conditional that if they continue to break the law then they will suffer undesired consequences. The rationale will therefore only be effective to the extent that it is possible for a society to maintain the truth of the conditional, or at least make it be unlikely for it to fail. In the latter case the principle of expected utility (as defined in Section Three of Chapter Three) can be brought in here whereby a potential lawbreaker will weigh the consequences of being caught by its likelihood. When the maintenance of the conditional breaks down, as I take it that, with respect to at least certain laws, it has in many jurisdictions, the net effect is that the threat of punishment becomes an empty threat. For example, if a potential lawbreaker sees too many repeat offenders continue to be given probation even after they have been caught breaking it, they will have little or no incentive not to break the law, at least from the point of view of narrow self interest.

To summarize what can be learned from the preceding points, it would seem that, to the extent that the post-judicial system operates under the deterrence rationale, it both follows that laws ought to be strictly enforced and that there ought to be consistency in the administration of penalties. To the extent that this is not the case, any threatened penalties will be to that extent less effective. It may also be noted though that since the fixed sentences thus called for under the deterrence rationale do not take motives behind criminal behavior into account, the rationale may work at cross purposes with some of the other rationales which I have been discussing. In particular, it can be recalled that both the therapeutic rationale and the reformative rationale do take motives behind crime into account, and thus may work at cross purposes with deterrence.

It is important to emphasize that we are only justified in imposing the minimal penalty which will in fact serve as a deterrent under the rationale of deterring lawbreakers themselves. This is because the purpose here is not also to deter other potential lawbreakers, unless as a side benefit. Obviously, this need not result in the penalty matching the crime in scope, and thus the deterrence justification of punishment differs from the retributive theory on this score, as I noted in my criticism of retribution. However, it should also be noted, in fairness to advocates of the retributive approach, that this lack of matching between crime and punishment has sometimes been taken as constituting a criticism of the deterrence theory, since it is held that following the theory may lead to either over-punishing or under-punishing lawbreakers.

Many of the preceding points can also be made from within the context of behaviorism theory. From this standpoint, either the actual infliction of unpleasant experiences or the mere threat of doing so can be seen as constituting negative reinforcements against the performance of certain types of behaviors; or, in the language of this book, types of courses of action. Thus, it is held that a lawbreaker will be less inclined to pursue these sorts of behaviors in the future, having been 'conditioned' against their pursuit. Since behaviorism theory just deals with observables (e. g., either actual behaviors or probabilities of behaving in certain ways given various stimuli), references to 'internal' causes such as fears of consequences are not invoked by the theory. Nevertheless, the net effect of the theory when negative reinforcements are used is essentially identical with a deterrence rationale for correction. In this regard though it should be noted that most modern behaviorists stress positive reinforcement (rewards for proper behavior) rather than negative reinforcement of undesired behaviors. Thus, they may not go along with the usage of these negative methods, perhaps depending on the severity of the unpleasant experiences which are either threatened or actually invoked.

This form of the deterrence rationale for correction, where the motivation is merely to deter lawbreakers themselves and not necessarily others, can be justified under the consequentialist system which I have been espousing by taking note of a point which was developed by Herbert Morris (1976, p. 34) in the context of a retributive theory, and by Honderich (1988, Vol. 2, Ch. 4) in the context of consequentialism. Both Morris and Honderich claim that unpleasant experiences associated with correction can be justified due to the fact that they 'correct' for an unfair distribution of goods and harms caused by a lawbreaker. It can be pointed out that lawbreakers, in virtue of breaking laws, are acting unfairly (in the sense of 'unfairness' which I developed in Chapter Two of being partial to an agent's own interests over the moral interests of others) to other individuals in the society to the extent that the others are bound by the laws. Thus, it follows that in order to 'correct' for this unfairness there must be a countervailing force—i. e., a 'penalty' —to make the total situation be fair. That is, one may only break a law if one is also willing to pay the penalty for breaking it, since otherwise one would have an unfair advantage over those who abide by the laws. It can be pointed out though that if the resulting penalty is just seen as a 'cost of doing business,' still stronger penalties may also be called for under this rationale. Still, It should be emphasized that the role of the penalties per se here is just that of providing a deterrent for agents who would otherwise break laws, and hence the justification for the rationale.

I might mention again that Locke (1690/1960), in Section 12 of his *Second Treatise of Government*, argued that even under the Law of Nature (i. e., man's state before the formation of a social contract), a man has a right to punish a transgressor against his natural rights (for Locke, life, liberty, and property) to such a degree as to hinder the violation (i. e., to serve as a deterrent on that particular person); or, as I have previously noted Locke states, "to make it an ill bargain for the offender." It is true that Locke includes the deterrent value on others as a further justification for punishment here as well, but as I have just shown this rationale can be separated from the foregoing consideration. As I also pointed out, Bentham (1789/1988, p. 72) makes a similar argument.

Two caveats should be taken note of at this point concerning the foregoing justification of the rationale for correction of deterring lawbreakers themselves. The first caveat involves cases where lawbreakers believe so strongly that what they are either doing or planning to do is in fact justified, that practically no proposed penalty on their courses of action will in fact deter them. Two distinct types of cases need to be distinguished here. In the first type of case, the law-breaker does not actually constitute a threat to the moral interests of other people in a society. Examples here may include such cases as those of a reporter refusing to divulge who an information source for a story is, or of civil rights marchers refusing to obey a legal statute which they perceive to be unjust. It can be observed that the interests (as I analyzed that concept in Chapter Two) of individuals with respect to these sorts of cases will be moral to the extent that no individuals are actually hurt by the pursuit of the activities in question. Thus, under the analysis of 'fairness' made in Chapter Two, it would be unfair to inflict a penalty on such an individual since to do so would involve exhibiting partiality to the other individuals in the overall society (assuming that there is in fact an overall societal interest in the case) over the moral interests of the individuals in question. It can also be noted that if the lawbreaker cannot at least be easily deterred here, the essential justification of such a penalty as imprisonment, is denial of opportunity and not deterrence, and it would seem that in these sorts of cases such a penalty would be unfair for the reasons just cited.

I will now consider the second type of case where a lawbreaker actually does constitute a threat to the well-being of a society, such as in the case of a fanatic bomber. Inasmuch as the interests of these sorts of individuals are non-moral in character, it follows again, under my analysis of 'fairness' in Chapter Two, that follow-through in the post-judicial system is not inherently unfair here, and hence may be justified on utilitarian grounds. It should also be emphasized that the justification for intervention here comes under the preventative rationale rather than the deterrence rationale, since, as with the preceding case where moral interests were being interfered with, by hypothesis the individual is incapable of at least easily being deterred.

The second caveat involves reemphasizing a point which I made earlier, and in effect constitutes a limiting case of what is going on with the fanatic. This is that the deterrence rationale will be ineffective with respect to truly compulsive behaviors, such as extreme forms of kleptomania, since here the presence of a coercive force, by definition, will not make a difference. In cases like these, it would make more sense to view the lawbreaker as someone suffering from an illness and to do whatever is necessary to cure the illness. I might note in this regard that Wootton (1959) has argued that there is only a gradation, with no drastic difference in kind, between cases like this one and other, more mundane cases of lawbreaking; and that she thus concludes that if punishment as retribution or as a deterrent is illogical in the one case it should make no sense with respect to the others either. Wootton makes this argument as follows:

Anyone with practical experience of offenders will have known some among them who were apparently totally lacking in regard for other people, and at the same time totally unresponsive either to reformative treatment or to such punitive measures as nowadays thought proper to impose. Such people used to be thought extremely wicked; today they are classified as cases of mental disorder. Paradoxically, this has the effect that, if you are consistently (in old-fashioned language) wicked enough, you may hope to be excused from responsibility for your misdeeds; but if your wickedness is only moderate, or if you show occasional signs of repentance or reform, then you must accept to take the blame for what you do and perhaps also to be punished for it. So illogical a position can hardly, one would think, prove tenable for long. Hence the psychopath may well prove to be the thin end of the wedge which will ultimately shatter the whole idea of moral responsibility as a factor in the treatment of anti-social personalities. (Wootton (1959, pp 250, 251)

One point which can be made in reply to Wootton is to observe that a threat of punishment will be completely ineffectual in either preventing or curing an illness (at least in any traditional sense of the concept), whereas clearly it will serve as a deterrent against at least most anti-social behaviors. This is not to deny that deterrence serves as a cause, since, as I pointed out in chapter Four, Davidson and Dretske have shown that reasons can serve as causes. Still, it can still be pointed out that, at least in any traditional sense of 'illness,' giving reasons for change is not the sort of cause which is going to be effectual. Thus, even if it is granted to Wootton that our traditional concept of 'moral responsibility' needs refinement, as I have been previously arguing, it does not follow that the use of penalties (where the rationale is their use as deterrents) should play no role in a post-judicial system. However, the justification here would have to be completely consequentialist in nature, and I have been arguing that this is fair to individual lawbreakers when the rationale is that of deterring the lawbreakers themselves from breaking laws in the future. I would like to turn now to an examination of a rationale for the use of penalties which I find to be much more ethically dubious than the foregoing though, namely that of deterring others from breaking laws.

Section Five Deterring Others

Under the rationale of deterring others from breaking laws, one offender is severely treated (i. e., "made an example of") for the primary purpose of the effects of this treatment on other individuals. It should be emphasized that if this treatment is held to constitute any analogue to 'punishment' then the original lawbreaker must still be at least guilty of some misdeed. Some retributionists (e. g., C. S. Lewis, 1970) even take this deterrent effect on others to be a side-benefit to punishment, which is itself justified solely in terms of retribution.

I take it that the rationale of deterring others is the most ethically controversial of the various consequentialist rationales for correction. The ethical controversy arises because it may be deemed to be unfair to 'correct' a person primarily for its consequences on someone else. Thus, there is at least a *prima facie* conflict between this rationale and my claim that we should always be treated fairly. In particular, it can be noted that this rationale seems to inherently violate Kant's Practical Imperative that people should always be treated as ends in themselves, and never just as a means to some other end. Here, even though it is true that a lawbreaker broke a law, they are being 'punished' (notice that it does not make sense to substitute 'corrected' for 'punished' here) as a means, not of changing their own future courses of action, but instead those of other people. Hence, the conflict with Kant's principle.

This last point can also be used in a critique of the institution of capital punishment. Capital punishment obviously ends the life of a human organism rather than just changing thought processes (as with the case of rehabilitation), and thus it destroys, rather than repairs, what is wrong with a person. While it could be argued that capital punishment prevents lawbreakers from committing further crimes in the future, it can be noted that the same effect could also be achieved by milder means, such as life imprisonment with no chance for parole, and, if necessary, the use of solitary confinement. Since we have an obligation to mitigate the existence of harms under the consequentialist system being advocated in this book, it would seem that this rationale is not justifiable under this context. This leaves as the sole consequentialist rationale that is even relevant here as that of deterring others from similar crimes, and, as was just argued, this rationale is unfair to the person being put to death. In actuality, I think that the root reason why most people who favor capital punishment favor it is retributive in character (e. g., in the case of a murderer, it is held that since they have taken a life, in order to even things out, they deserve to die regardless of the consequences), and I gave my critique of retributive theories of punishment in Chapter Five.

BIBLIOGRAPHY

Anscombe, G. E. M., 1957/1963, *Intention* (Ithaca: Cornell University Press).

Anscombe, G. E. M., 1958, "Modern Moral Philosophy" in *Philosophy* 33, pp. 1-19.

Aristotle, 1941, *The Basic Works of Aristotle*, edited by Richard McKeon (New York: Random House).

Austin, J. L., 1961/1979, *Philosophical Papers,* Third Edition (Oxford: Oxford University Press).

Austin, J. L., 1962a, *How To Do Things with Words* (Cambridge, MA: Harvard University Press).

Austin, J. L., 1962b. *Sense and Sensibilia* (Oxford: Clarendon Press).

Ayer, A. J., 1946/1952, *Language, Truth and Logic*, Second Edition (New York: Dover Publications).

Baer, Kurt, 1965, *The Moral Point of View* (New York: Random House).

Beardsley, Elizabeth, 1960,"Determinism and Moral Perspectives," in *Philosophy and Phenomenological Research* 21, pp. 1-20.

Bennett, Jonathan, 1988, *Events and their Names* (Indianapolis: Hackett Publishing Co.).

Bentham, Jeremy, 1781/1988, *The Principles of Morals and Legislation* (Amherst, NY: Prometheus Books).

Black, Max, 1964, "The Gap between 'Is' and 'Should," in *Philosophical Review* 73, pp. 165-181.

Brandt, Richard, 1959, *Ethical Theory* (Englewood Cliffs, NJ: Prentice Hall).

Bratman, Michael, 1999, *Faces of Intention: Selected Essays on Intention and Agency* (Cambridge: Cambridge University Press).

Braybrooke, David, 1987, *Meeting Needs* (Princeton: Princeton University Press).

Butler, Joseph, 1726/1961, *The Analogy of Religion* (New York: F. Ungar).

Campbell, C. A., 1957, *On Selfhood and Godhood* (London: George Allen and Unwin).

Castaneda, Hector Neri, 1968, "A Problem for Utilitarianism," in *Analysis* 28, pp. 141-142.

Chisholm, Roderick, 1976, *Person and Object: A Metaphysical Study* (London: George Allen & Unwin).

Danto, Arthur, 1973, *Analytical Philosophy of Action* (Cambridge: Cambridge University Press).

Davidson, Donald, 1980, *Essays on Actions and Events* (Oxford: Oxford University Press).

Dennett, Daniel, 1984, *Elbow Room* (Cambridge, MA: Bradford Books).

Dennett, Daniel, 1987, *The Intentional Stance* (Cambridge, MA: Bradford Books).

Double, Richard, 1991, *Non-Reality of Free Will* (Oxford: Oxford University Press).
Dretske, Fred, 1988, *Explaining Behavior: Reasons in a World of Causes* (Cambridge, MA: M.I.T. Press).
Edwards, Jonathan, 1754/1957, *Freedom of the Will* (New Haven: Yale University Press).
Feinberg, Joel, 1970, *Doing and Deserving: Essays in the Theory of Responsibility* (Princeton: Princeton University Press).
Feldman, Fred, 1986, *Doing the Best We Can* (Dordrecht, Holland: D. Reidel).
Feldman, Fred, 1997, *Utilitarianism, Hedonism and Desert* (Cambridge: Cambridge University Press).
Frey, R. G., 1984, *Utility and Rights* (Minneapolis: University of Minnesota Press).
Frankfurt Harry, 1969, "Alternative Possibilities and Moral Responsibility" in Journal of Philosophy 65 pp. 829-833.
Gert, Bernard, 1998, *Morality: Its Nature and Justification* (Oxford: Oxford University Press).
Gert, Bernard and Duggan, Timothy, 1979, "Free Will as the Ability to Will," in *Nous* 13, pp. 197-217.
Gleick, James, 1987, *Chaos: Making a New Science* (New York: Viking).
Goldfarb, Ronald and Singer, Linda, 1973, *After Conviction* (New York: Simon and Schuster)
Goldman, Alvin, 1973, *A Theory of Human Action* (Englewood Cliffs, NJ: Prentice Hall).
Grice, H. P., 1957, "Meaning" in *Philosophical Review* 66, pp. 377-388.
Hare, Richard, 1952/1964, *The Language of Morals* (Oxford: Oxford University Press).
Hare, Richard, 1981, *Moral Thinking* (Oxford: Oxford University Press).
Harsanyi, John, 1976, *Essays on Ethics, Social Behavior, and Scientific Explanation* (Dordrecht, Holland: D. Reidel).
Hart, H. L. A., 1959/1990, *Causation in the Law*, Second Edition (Oxford: Clarendon Press).
Hart, H. L. A., 1961, *The Concept of Law* (Oxford: Oxford University Press).
Hart, H. L. A., 1958/1961 "Legal Responsibility and Excuses" in Hook, *Determinism and Freedom.*
Hart, H. L. A., 1968, *Punishment and Responsibility: Essays in the Philosophy of Law* (Oxford: Oxford University Press).
Hodgson, D. H., 1967, *Consequences of Utilitarianism* (Oxford: Oxford University Press).
Hofstadter, Douglas, 1979, *Gödel, Escher, Bach: An Eternal Golden Braid* (New York: Basic Books).
Honderich, Ted, 1988, *A Theory of Determinism: The Mind, Neuroscience, and Life-Hopes* (Oxford: Oxford University Press).
Hook, Sidney, 1958/1961, *Determinism and Freedom* (New York: MacMillan).

Hooker, Brad, 2000 *Ideal Code, Real World: a Rule-Consequentialist Theory of Morality* (Oxford: Oxford University Press).

Hume, David, 1739/1975, *A Treatise of Human Nature* (Oxford, Oxford University Press).

Hume, David, 1751/1948, "An Inquiry Concerning the Principles of Morals," in *Hume's Moral and Political Philosophy*, edited by Henry Aiken (New York: Hafner Publishing).

James, William, 1884, "The Dilemma of Determinism," in *Unitarian Review* 22, pp. 193-224.

Kane, Robert, 1985, *Free Will and Values* (Albany: State University of New York Press).

Kant, Immanuel, 1781/1929, *A Critique of Pure Reason*, translated by Norman Kemp Smith, (Toronto: Macmillan).

Kant, Immanuel, 1786/1959, *Foundations of the Metaphysics of Morals*, translated by Lewis White Beck (New York: Liberal Arts Press).

Kant, Immanuel, 1788/1956, *A Critique of Practical Reason*, translated by Lewis White Beck (Indianapolis: Bobbs Merrill).

Kaufmann, Walter, 1956, *Existentialism from Dostoevsky to Sartre* (New York: Meridian).

Kaufmann, Walter, 1973, *Without Guilt and Justice* (New York: Dell Publishing Co.).

Kenny, Anthony, 1975, *Will, Freedom, and Power* (Oxford: Oxford University Press).

Laplace, Pierre, 1825/1995 *Philosophical Essay on Probabilities*, translated by Andrew Dale (New York: Springer).

Lewis, C. I., 1969, *Values and Imperatives* (Palo Alto: Stanford University Press).

Lewis, C. S., 1970, *God in the Dock* (London: Curtis Brown).

Locke, John, 1690/1960, *Two Treatises of Government*, edited by Peter Laslett (Cambridge: Cambridge University Press).

Locke, John, 1690/1959, *An Essay Concerning Human Understanding* (New York: Dover Publishing).

Lucas, J. R., 1961, "Minds, Machines and Godel" in *Philosophy* 36, pp. 112-127.

MacIntyre, Alasdair, 1978, *Against the Self Images of the Age* (South Bend: University of Notre Dame Press).

MacIntyre, Alasdair, 1981, *After Virtue* (South Bend: University of Notre Dame Press).

MacIntyre, Alasdair, 1988, *Whose Justice? Which Rationality?* (South Bend: University of Notre Dame Press).

Mackie, John, 1974, *The Cement of the Universe: A Study of Causation* (Oxford: Oxford University Press).

Manser, Anthony, 1962, *It Serves You Right*, in *Philosophy* 37, pp. 293-306.

Marcuse, Herbert, 1964, *One-Dimensional Man* (Boston: Beacon Press).

Melden, A. I., 1961, *Free Action*, (London: Routledge and Kegan Paul).

Menninger, Karl, 1968, "The Crime of Punishment," in *Saturday Review*.

Mill, John Stuart, 1859/1975, *On Liberty*, edited by Elizabeth Rapaport (Indianapolis: Hackett Publishing).

Mill, John Stuart, 1861/1969, "Utilitarianism," in *Mill's Utilitarianism: Text and Criticism*, edited by James Smith and Ernest Sosa, (Belmont, CA: Wadsworth).

Moore, G. E., 1903/1971, *Principia Ethica* (Cambridge: Cambridge University Press).

Moore, G. E., 1912, *Ethics* (New York: H. Holt).

Moore, G. E., 1922, "The Conception of Intrinsic Value," in *Philosophical Studies* (London: Routledge and Kegan Paul), pp. 243-275.

More, Sir Thomas, 1516/1964, *Utopia*, edited by Edward Surtz (New Haven: Yale University Press).

Morris, Herbert, 1976, *On Guilt and Innocence: Essays in Legal Philosophy and Moral Psychology* (Berkeley: University of California Press).

Nozick, Robert, 1974, *Anarchy, State, and Utopia* (New York: Basic Books).

Parfit, Derek, 1984, *Reasons and Persons* (Oxford: Oxford University Press).

Perry, R. B., 1926, *General Theory of Value* (New York: Longmans, Green and Co.).

Plato, 1961, *Collected Dialogues*, edited by Edith Hamilton and Huntington Cairns (Princeton: Princeton University Press, 1961).

Popper, Karl, 1945/1950, *The Open Society and Its Enemies* (Princeton: Princeton University Press).

Prichard, H. A., 1949, *Moral Obligation: Essays and Lectures* (Oxford: Oxford University Press).

Quinton, Anthony, 1989, *Utilitarian Ethics* (La Salle: Open Court).

Rawls, John, 1971, *A Theory of Justice* (Cambridge, MA: Harvard University Press).

Rawls, John, 1955, "Two Concepts of Rules" in *Philosophical Review* 64, pp. 3-13.

Regan, Donald, 1989, *Utilitarianism and Cooperation* (Oxford: Oxford University Press).

Ross, W. D., 1930/1988, *The Right and the Good* (Indianapolis: Hackett).

Rousseau, Jean Jacques, 1762/1964, *The Social Contract* (New York: Simon and Schuster).

Sartre, Jean Paul, 1946/1956, "Existential is a Humanism," in Kaufmann, *Existentialism from Dostoevsky to Sartre*, pp. 287-311.

Scheffler, Samuel, 1994, *The Rejection of Consequentialism* (Oxford: Clarendon)

Schopenhauer, Arthur, 1841/1960, *Essay on the Freedom of the Will*, translated by Konstantine Kolenda (Indianapolis: Bobbs Merrill).

Searle, John, 1964, "How to Derive 'Ought' from 'Is," in *Philosophical Review* 73, pp. 165-181.

Searle, John, 1970, *Speech Acts* (Cambridge: Cambridge University Press).

Sellars, Wilfred, 1963, *Science, Perception, and Reality* (London: Routledge and Kegan Paul).

Sen, Armatya and Williams, Bernard, 1982, *Utilitarianism and Beyond* (Cambridge: Cambridge University Press).

Sidgwick, Henry, 1907/1981, *Methods of Ethics*, Seventh Edition (Indianapolis: Hackett Publishing Co.).

Singer, Marcus, 1961, *Generalization in Ethics* (New York: Alfred E. Knopf).

Smart, Ninian., 1958, "Negative Utilitarianism" in *Mind* 67, 542.

Smith, Adam, 1776/1952, *An Inquiry into the Nature and Causes of the Wealth of Nations* (Chicago: Great Books Encyclopedia Britannica).

Stace, Walter, 1952, "The Problem of Free Will," in *Religion and the Modern Mind* (New York, Harper and Row), pp. 248-258.

Stevenson, Charles, 1944, *Ethics and Language* (New Haven: Yale University Press).

Stich, Stephen, 1983, *From Folk Psychology to Cognitive Science: the Case against Belief* (Cambridge, MA: Bradford Books).

Taylor, Richard, 1966, *Action and Purpose* (Englewood Cliffs: Prentice Hall).

Thomson, Judith, 1990, *The Realm of Rights* (Cambridge, MA: Harvard University Press).

Urmson, J. O. , 1958, "Saints and Heroes" in *Essays in Moral Philosophy*, edited by A. I. Meldon (Seattle: University of Washington Press), pp. 198-216.

Van Inwagen, Peter, 1983, *An Essay on Free Will* (Oxford: Oxford University Press).

Von Neumann, John and Morgenstern, Oskar, 1944/2004, *Theory of Games and Economic Behavior* (Princeton: Princeton University Press).

Webb, Judson, Mechanism, 1980, *Mechnism, Mentalism and Metamathematics* (Dordrecht, Holland: D. Reidel).

Wittgenstein, Ludwig, 1953/1967, *Philosophical Investigations* (New York: Macmillan).

Wootton, Barbara, 1959, *Social Science and Social Pathology* (London: G. Allen and Unwin).

Ziff, Paul, 1967, "On H. P. Grice's Account of Meaning," in *Analysis* 28, pp. 1-8.

Index of Names

Robert French

Dr. Robert E. French received his Ph.D. in Philosophy from Boston University, Massachusetts. He has taught at a number of colleges in the Detroit, Michigan area, including Wayne State University, the University of Windsor, and Central Michigan University.